Books by C. Vann Woodward

TOM WATSON: AGRARIAN REBEL

THE BATTLE FOR LEYTE GULF

ORIGINS OF THE NEW SOUTH

THE STRANGE CAREER OF JIM CROW

THE BURDEN OF SOUTHERN HISTORY

REUNION AND REACTION

Editor

George Fitzhugh, CANNIBALS ALL

Lewis H. Blair, A SOUTHERN PROPHECY

Whitelaw Reid, AFTER THE WAR

Coauthor

THE NATIONAL EXPERIENCE

REUNION AND REACTION

Reunion and Reaction

The Compromise of 1877
and the End of Reconstruction

by

C. VANN WOODWARD

Little, Brown and Company · Boston

LIBRARY OF CONGRESS CATALOG CARD NO. 66-22490

A

PRINTED IN THE UNITED STATES OF AMERICA

FOR GLENN

Acknowledgments

The American community of scholars is justly noted for its generosity with time and learning. I have partaken freely of both at the hands of historians, colleagues, editors, and friends in the preparation of this book. My debt to them is a large one. I hope that my obligation to their published works is adequately acknowledged in footnotes. In looking back over the citations, however, I was struck by the omission of one name—that of the late Charles A. Beard. It was, perhaps, an unconscious tribute that it did not seem necessary to mention him as the originator of the concept of the Civil War and Reconstruction as a revolution—the Second American Revolution, as he and Mary R. Beard called it. Yet my book is built upon that conception. I merely attempt to add a description of the final phase of the revolution, the phase that the French speak of as *Thermidor* in writing of their great revolution. I wish to acknowledge this debt to Beard and at the same time to express the hope that American historians will never permit honest differences of opinion over foreign policy to withhold from the late dean of the craft the honor that is justly due him.

My research was greatly assisted by several librarians and their staffs. Among these are first of all Miss Margaret Lough and Miss Beatrice Blakslee of the Johns Hopkins University History Library. I am also greatly indebted to Mr. Watt P. Marchman of the Hayes Memorial Library, Fremont, Ohio, as well as to his predecessor in that office, Mr. Curtis P. Garrison. I wish also to thank for their many courtesies the staffs of the Library of Congress, particularly its Division of Manuscripts, the Enoch Pratt Free Library of Baltimore, the New York Public Library, the John Crerar Library and the Newberry Library of Chicago, the Libraries of the University of Chicago, the Library of the Bureau of Railway Economics in Washington, the Indiana Historical Society of Indianapolis, the Iowa State Archives of Des Moines, the Mississippi State Department of Archives and History at Jackson, and the University of North Carolina Library at Chapel Hill.

Without involving any of them in responsibility for my views or my errors, I wish to thank those who have been kind enough to read the entire manuscript and offer valuable suggestions. These are Professors Howard K. Beale of the University of Wisconsin, Charles A. Barker of the Johns Hopkins University, and Manning J. Dauer and William G. Carleton of the University of Florida.

—C. V. W.

Preface to the Present Edition

The present edition of this book is a revival of the original edition published in 1951. In 1956 a revised and slightly abridged version appeared which eliminated the footnotes and added an introduction and a final chapter entitled "The Continuous Past." I have two reasons for dropping the revisions and returning to the original text. In the first place, I think there is value in placing the full documentation, vital clues in an elaborate piece of detective work, before the reader. And secondly, the added materials in the introduction and final chapter now appear dated. These afterthoughts for the revised edition were written before it was clear that the Compromise of 1877 had really been breached. It was a time when the Southern resistance to the Second Reconstruction was firm and determined, sustained by an alliance between Northern and Southern conservatives of the sort who had written off the idealistic aims of the First Reconstruction, abandoned national responsibility for civil rights, and turned the control of the Negroes over to the South. My emphasis was therefore upon continuity—the continuous past—with a suggestion of danger that the past might be repeated. That continuity is now broken and the danger seems no longer a threat. In the decade since 1956 what remained of the Compromise of 1877 has gone completely to pieces under smashing blows of federal action. These blows included armed intervention under Presidential order, congressional enactments to protect civil and political rights, and judicial decisions upholding these actions. By 1965 nothing was left in word or spirit of the old sectional accommodation that had not been breached and broken. It had gone the way of the historic compromises that preceded it. It had, however, far outlasted them all. Anyone who seeks an understanding of the century of frustration for civil rights between the First Reconstruction and the Second will still have to understand the Compromise of 1877.

C.V.W.

Contents

Contents

REUNION AND REACTION

CHAPTER I

The Unknown Compromise

FIVE TIMES in the course of the nineteenth century there arose political crises of such gravity as to call forth all the celebrated American genius for compromise. Four of these crises involved the threat of disunion or violence, if not war. In only one of them did the customary way of compromise fail, the threats materialize, and the crisis end in tragedy. All the others were settled by compromises that form some of the most important chapters in American history.

Compromise became part and parcel of the basic pattern of American political life. The one great departure from the tradition occurred in 1861 and the sixteen years that followed. In the clash between "right" on the side of the North and "rights" on the side of the South the normal processes of compromise broke down. Americans resorted to armed force to settle their differences. After the trial by battle the victors dictated the peace and imposed terms by force. For this brief and entirely exceptional period principles held sway and differences were framed in terms of moral issues. So long as this was true there was no room for compromise, for compromise had to come at the expense of principle. Neither side to the dispute could be permitted a monopoly of rectitude, and concessions were required of both. Principles had to give way to expediency and force to persuasion.

The Compromise of 1877 marked the abandonment of principles and of force and a return to the traditional ways of expediency and concession. The compromise laid the political foundation for reunion. It established a new sectional truce that proved more enduring than any previous one and provided a settlement for an issue that had troubled American politics for more than a generation. It wrote an end to Reconstruction and recognized a new regime in the South. More profoundly than Constitutional amendments and wordy statutes it shaped the future of four million freedmen and their progeny for generations to come. It preserved one part of the fruits of the "Second American Revolution"—the pragmatic and economic part—at the expense of the other part—the idealistic and humanitarian part. The settlement was not ideal from any point of view, nor was it very logical either. But that is the way of compromises.

In spite of the fact that the Compromise of 1877 proved more enduring in its basic aspects than any of its predecessors there has been less known about it than about any of them. The terms of the historic Compromises of 1820, 1833, and 1850 were publicly debated, openly arrived at, and published that all might read. Those who attempted to frame a Compromise of 1861 proceeded in the same manner until overwhelmed with failure. In all of them both of the parties to the dispute were called upon to surrender cherished hopes and claims in exchange for the concession of half measures and a suitable *quid pro quo*. There was usually a great deal of haggling over terms in the august oratory of the age. In the end an inspired leader—Henry Clay in the first three instances—brought forward a solution that overcame remaining objections and the compromise was made.

Such was the nature of the Compromise of 1877, however, and so dangerous was believed the menace of war or anarchy, that negotiations for an agreement were conducted secretly or in an extremely guarded fashion. The fact that Southern Democrats were in effect going behind the backs of the Northern members of their own party to arrive at an understanding with the Republicans was not conducive to publicity. Nor was the fact that the Republican managers were abandoning the platform on which they were elected and forfeiting principles to which a powerful wing of their party still clung. The diplomacy of 1877 might be described as secret covenants privately arrived at. The terms were never officially published, for neither party to the contract could afford to endorse all of the agreements publicly. Nor did some of the more important articles materialize as events. In some cases they proved impossible of fulfillment, and in others promises were broken or forgotten.

Remarkably few leaders were fully informed of the compromise proceedings, and those who were kept their counsel in later years. In 1937, sixty years after the event, Abram S. Hewitt's "Secret History" of the crisis was published.[1] This valuable document revealed much that had not been known and settled several controversies. But Hewitt was spokesman of the wing of Democrats that was by-passed and, some charged, betrayed by the compromise. If he was ever fully informed of the negotiations his "Secret History" does not reveal the fact. Milton H. Northrup, secretary of one of the congressional committees that studied the problem, wrote an "Inner History" of the events, but he was not concerned with aspects that lay beneath the surface.[2]

During his lifetime Henry Watterson published what he called an "Inside History" of the crisis. The Kentuckian was one of those few who were close to the inner circle of compromisers. His account, however, is distinguished more for its ostentatious reticence than for its revelations. He had resolved "long ago," he wrote in 1913, "that certain matters should remain a sealed book in my memory. I make no issue of veracity with the living; the dead should be sacred." He then told the story of a gay dinner party in Washington during Cleveland's first administration. It was a small convivial affair attended by the President. Among the guests were "two leading Democrats and two leading Republicans," identified only as having important roles in the crisis of '77. Late in the evening the four politicians began vying with each other in revealing secrets of the disputed election. "The little audience was rapt," recalled Watterson. "Finally Mr. Cleveland raised both hands and exclaimed, 'What

[1] Allan Nevins (ed.), *Selected Writings of Abram S. Hewitt* (New York, 1937), 156–194.

[2] Milton H. Northrup, "A Grave Crisis in American History, The Inner History of the Origins and Formation of the Electoral Commission of 1877," *Century Magazine*, LXII (1901), 923–934.

would the people of this country think if the roof could be lifted from this house and they could hear these men.' " Whereupon one of the raconteurs, "noted for his wealth both of money and humor," declared, "If anyone repeats what I have said I will denounce him as a liar." Watterson himself was confident that "the whole truth underlying the determinate incidents which led to the rejection of Tilden and the seating of Hayes will never be known." [3]

Modern historians have risen to this challenge and made repeated efforts to penetrate the curtain of silence deliberately dropped upon the past. But the more candid of them have confessed dissatisfaction with their results and pointed out the need for more illumination or despaired of ever gaining it. Thus one historian, who has written extensively on the subject and on figures prominent in the period, echoes Watterson when he writes of certain crucial events in the story that "the full truth will never be known." [4]

The "whole truth," as any historian knows, is a necessary fiction of the courtroom and the witness stand. It is admittedly an unattainable goal in the reconstruction of the past. Large parts of the truth regarding the subject of the present work are available in many books, the work of numerous minds. It is remarkable, however, that so many of what Watterson called the "determinate incidents," the forces underlying events, have been neglected or overlooked for three quarters of a century.

"But isn't the 'Bargain of 1877' an old story?" it will be asked. "Was it not the result of something called the Wormley Conference in Washington?" It is true that this story has a place reserved in every history schoolbook and that it has been treated with more or less seriousness by the more detailed accounts of the crisis. It has been accepted as explaining why the Southern Democrats, convinced to a man that Samuel J. Tilden had been legally elected President and hating everything that Republicanism stood for, were persuaded to desert the Democratic cause and assist in the seating of

[3] Henry Watterson, "The Hayes-Tilden Contest for the Presidency, Inside History of a Great Political Crisis," *ibid.*, LXXXVI (1913), 3–4.

[4] Allan Nevins, *Abram S. Hewitt, With Some Account of Peter Cooper* (New York, 1935), 373.

Rutherford B. Hayes, even though they had within their power the means of preventing what they believed to be a gigantic fraud.

The circumstances of the "Bargain" will be readily recalled. It was the last week of Grant's second administration and no successor had been chosen. Democrats in the House of Representatives, where the party enjoyed a large majority, were threatening by dilatory and filibustering tactics to prevent the completion of the electoral count before March 4. Should they be successful many people expected fighting to break out — "more people," according to one historian, "than had anticipated a like outcome to the secession movement of 1860–61."[5] Describing "the excitement and the apprehension which prevailed throughout the country," Hewitt wrote: "Business was arrested, the wheels of industry ceased to move, and it seemed as if the terrors of civil war were again to be renewed." In fact, he added, "to this dread issue we were much nearer than was even at that time supposed." He knew of fifteen states in which Democratic forces composed largely of war veterans were organized and prepared to move on Washington to compel the inauguration of Tilden. The commander-in-chief had been selected, and "the governors of many states," Hewitt wrote without specifying, and with probable exaggeration, had declared their willingness to use military force if necessary.[6]

At the very climax of this crisis, so the story goes, on February 26 and 27 intimate friends of Governor Hayes came to an understanding with a group of Southern representatives in a series of conferences. The upshot of these conferences was that the Republicans agreed to abandon the two remaining Republican governments in the South, those of Louisiana and South Carolina, in favor of the Democratic claimants. On their part the Southerners promised to defeat their party's filibuster, assist in completing the count, and see that Hayes was peacefully inaugurated. In effect, the Southerners were abandoning the cause of Tilden in exchange for control over

[5] Paul L. Haworth, *The Hayes-Tilden Disputed Presidential Election of 1876* (Cleveland, 1906), 168.

[6] Nevins (ed.), *Selected Writings of Hewitt,* 177–178.

two states, and the Republicans were abandoning the cause of the Negro in exchange for the peaceful possession of the Presidency. As part of the arrangement, however, the Southern representatives promised that the rights of the Negro would be safeguarded and that there would be no bloody reprisals against political enemies, while the Republican spokesmen undertook to persuade President Grant to withdraw Federal troops from the South as soon as the electoral count was completed and promised that if they were not successful in this effort Hayes would withdraw the troops after his inauguration. Two days later, after an impassioned appeal in the House by a Louisianan, the Democratic filibuster collapsed, the count was completed, and Hayes was declared elected.

This in summary is the traditional account of the Bargain of 1877. To explain the inadequacy of this account and place on record the large aspects it omits will require the remaining pages of this book. In passing, however, it might be mentioned that at the time the Wormley Conference was held and the so-called Bargain struck the Southerners were already committed to the course they pursued and Hayes was already committed to a policy of conciliating the South. The question of the removal of the troops is of particular interest. Everyone assumed as a matter of course that the collapse of the Republican regimes and the succession of the Democrats — or "Redemption" and "Home-Rule," as Southerners described it — would follow as soon as the troops were withdrawn. This has been presented as the critical point of the Wormley Conference and the *quid pro quo* of the Bargain from the Southern point of view. But the fact was that a week before these negotiations opened a means had been devised to insure the removal of the troops in case Hayes forgot his promises or was unable to carry them out. At a Democratic caucus on February 19, 1877, a majority of the members voted for a resolution to write into the army appropriations bill, then still pending, a clause forbidding the use of troops to support the claims of any state government in the South until it should be recognized by Congress. A bill containing such a clause was passed by the House and a penalty of hard labor and imprisonment provided for anyone found guilty of violating the act. When the Republican Senate refused to accept the clause the House stood its ground and adjourned without making any appropriations for the army whatever.

After he became President, the only way Hayes could get provisions, pay, and transportation for the army after the end of the fiscal year was to call an extra session of Congress. Since the new House would also have a hostile majority, Hayes postponed the extra session for seven months. He was thus compelled to rely upon unpaid and unhappy officers and men to suppress the violent labor upheavals in several states in August 1877. The army remained unpaid and unhappy until November 30, after Congress finally relented.[7]

This was the situation to which Mrs. Hayes referred in August 1877 when, during a conversation with Thomas Donaldson regarding the President's abandonment of the Republican governors in the South, she exclaimed: "Why, what could Mr. Hayes do but what he did? He had no army."[8] The President himself, talking with Donaldson at the White House on the same subject in October, remarked: "In addition, the House was against me and I had no army, and public sentiment demanded a change of policy."[9] Senator Oliver P. Morton of Indiana, while deploring the policy, completely absolved Hayes from blame for deserting the Carpetbaggers and placed the responsibility upon the stubborn majority of the House.[10]

In saying that "public sentiment demanded a change of policy," Hayes was acknowledging the power of a force so strong that it had

[7] *Congressional Record,* 44 Cong., 2 Sess., pp. 1886, 2119, 2111–2121, 2088, 2092, 2156–2161, 2171, 2193, 2214, 2230, 2241–2252; 45 Cong., 1 Sess., pp. 549, 560. Republican congressmen pointed out that in the labor crisis of August the "executive officers of States that were democratic called as lustily for the strong arm of the Government" as had Republican governors. A motion to retain the objectionable clause restraining the President from use of the troops in states was defeated. *Ibid.,* 337.

[8] Entry of August 28, 1877, in "Memoirs of Thomas Donaldson," MS. in Indiana State Historical Society, Indianapolis. Copy in Hayes Memorial Library, Fremont, Ohio.

[9] Entry of October 17, 1877, in *ibid.*

[10] Galveston *News,* May 27, 1877.

compelled President Grant to give up his own policy of intervening with force in the South to uphold Republican governments. During the last three months of his administration he maintained a benevolent neutrality that enabled the "Redeemers" of Louisiana and South Carolina to establish *de facto* control over those states and left the Carpetbaggers with a mere shadow of authority. On February 26 Grant publicly admitted that the people of the country were "clearly opposed to the further use of troops in upholding a state government." He also promised the Southerners to recall the troops as soon as the electoral count was completed, and that he did not succeed in fulfilling that promise does not appear to have been his fault.[11] Grant deserves much of the credit or blame that has been assigned to Hayes for initiating the new Southern policy.

In effect, Hayes's friends at the Wormley Conference were giving up something they no longer really possessed in exchange for something that had already been secured by other means. While on the other hand the Southerners were solemnly accepting something that had been secured by other means in exchange for adherence to a course to which, by that time, they were already committed. It was, on the whole, one of the strangest bargains in the annals of horse swapping.

The Bargain nevertheless had its practical uses and consequences — though not those popularly presumed. Shortly after the inauguration of Hayes certain Southern participants in the Bargain turned over some of the documents involved to the press and gave copious interviews in which they revealed the details of the negotiations.[12] By their own admission these men had been under severe criticism from their constituents for some time prior to the Bargain because of their co-operation with the Republicans, a course they had been pursuing for several weeks. Their press interviews, widely quoted and commented upon, did not underestimate the contribution these

[11] *House Miscellaneous Documents,* 45 Cong., 3 Sess., Doc. No. 31, vol. III, pp. 618, 625–630.

[12] For example, New York *Sun,* March 26, 27, 29, 1877; New York *Tribune,* March 30, 1877; Raleigh *Observer,* March 31, 1877; Louisville *Courier-Journal,* March 29, 1877.

gentlemen had made to statesmanship, nor the dramatic circumstances of their effort. Their stories of the Bargain served as a plausible justification of a course that had been the subject of angry criticism at home. They also served to magnify the role that certain politicians played in Redemption and to enhance their reputation as Redeemers. And finally, although Hayes had been previously committed to conciliatory Southern policy, and his hand had been forced by withholding of the army appropriation, the Bargain pledges of his friends may have assisted in smoothing the path for an early fulfillment of his policy.

Although the much-publicized Bargain story falls far short of being adequate, it has nevertheless been taken seriously by historians from the time of its origin. The continued stress, and even a renewed emphasis upon the story, is reflected by the most recent biographer of President Hayes. "The bargain with Hayes," he writes, "was one of the most important events in American history. It ended the Reconstruction and started the South on the road to prosperity and power."[13]

An event of anything like the importance attributed to this deserves a much more searching analysis than it has ever had. In the first place the Compromise of 1877 was not arrived at in two days of last-minute haggling. Instead, the negotiations stretched over a period of several months. They were not confined to a settlement of the domestic affairs of two states. For in the expanse of territory and the variety of interests embraced, the Compromise of 1877 is readily comparable with the classical compromises that preceded it. These interests ranged from the Eastern seaboard to the Pacific coast. The negotiators concerned themselves not merely with the political problems of two Southern states but with the economic, social, and political problems of the whole South. They sought the fulfillment of Southern hopes and aspirations that were older than the Civil War, as well as relief from grievances arising out of Reconstruction. They enlisted in their efforts the aid of the most power-

[13] H. J. Eckenrode, *Rutherford B. Hayes, Statesman of Reunion* (New York, 1930), 227.

ful capitalists in the country and bestirred the civic ambitions of points as remote as San Diego and Philadelphia, New Orleans and Chicago. They planned a reorientation of Southern politics along the old Democratic-Whig lines and a breaking up of the incipient white solidarity of the region by converting conservative whites to Republicanism.

Much more was at stake in the winter of 1876–1877 than the Presidency, the question of whether Samuel J. Tilden or Rutherford B. Hayes would occupy the White House. To many people in the North it appeared that all the hard-won fruits of the Civil War were in danger of being lost or placed in serious jeopardy. On one plane there were the more idealistic aims of the North's Civil War and Reconstruction policies, the aims centered around the freeing and protection of the Negro and reflected in the Thirteenth, Fourteenth, and Fifteenth Amendments to the Constitution. On a different plane there were the less idealistic, less publicized aims of Northern policy during the war and the period following. These aims centered in the protection of a sectional economy and numerous privileged interests, and were reflected in new statutes regarding taxes, money, tariffs, banks, land, railroads, subsidies, all placed upon the law books while the South was out of the Union. Should it come to a choice of saving the fruits of Northern policy on one plane at the cost of sacrificing those on the other, Northern sentiment would be confronted with a serious dilemma.

It was a depression year, the worst year of the severest depression yet experienced. In the East labor and the unemployed were in a bitter and violent temper that foreshadowed the unprecedented upheaval of the summer. Out West a tide of agrarian radicalism was rising in the shape of Granger, Greenbacker, and Silverite heresies. From both East and West there came threats against the elaborate structure of protective tariffs, national banks, railroad subsidies, and monetary arrangements upon which the new economic order was founded.

And now the South, the eleven former Confederate states under control of new leaders, presented a third threat to the new order.

Traditionally hostile to the new capitalistic arrangements, kept at bay for sixteen years, believed to be nursing bitter grievances, and suspected of harboring all manner of mischief, the South was at last returning in full force, united as never before, to upset the sectional balance of power. So long as Republican rule lasted in the South the region had proved a bulwark to the new economic order, for however radical the party had been in realizing its more idealistic aims of equality and freedom within the South, the congressmen it sent to Washington had voted solidly with Northern Republicans in support of the more pragmatic aims of economic privilege. But how would the South, under guidance of the Redeemers, cast her weight in the impending struggle over national issues? Would she make common cause with other rebellious elements? Would she join hands with restless labor in the East as she had in Jackson's time? Or would she, as many feared and predicted, rush into the arms of her ante-bellum ally, the agrarian West, break up the East-West alliance that won the war, and throw the East back into the position of an isolated minority section? Or, finally, could the South be induced to combine with the Northern conservatives and become a prop instead of a menace to the new capitalist order? If so, what inducements would be found necessary? These questions figured in the deliberations of those who sought a practical solution to the electoral crisis and played their part in the Compromise of 1877.

There was something else at stake, and it was probably of more consequence in the long run than any of the previous considerations. This was the question of whether the country could regain the ability to settle Presidential elections without the resort to force. The South had seceded in 1860 rather than accept the peacefully and regularly elected President. In 1864, 1868, and 1872 the election had turned in the last analysis on the employment of military force, or the threat of it. And again in 1876 the election hung upon returns from state governments that were maintained in power only by the employment of Federal troops for their protection. This time, however, there were large elements of the disappointed party who threatened to answer force with force rather than accept defeat as a result of the returns from the garrisoned Southern states. In the phraseology of the seventies, the question was, had American politics become permanently "Mexicanized" since 1860?

A candid survey of recent history did not provide a reassuring answer to the question.[14] Reliance upon force as a means of solving political problems had become almost a habit. Not only did North and South employ force without stint against each other during four years of war, but each side resorted to force to repress criticism and dissent within its own borders. For a brief interlude after the war Lincoln and later Johnson sought to return to the old way of persuasion in dealing with the South. Their program was restoration instead of reconstruction, and their method was conciliation instead of coercion. Electorates based largely on ante-bellum qualifications, and therefore excluding the Negroes, chose delegates who revised the old state constitutions, and voters elected new legislatures, state officials, and congressmen. In August 1866 President Johnson announced hopefully that "peace, order, tranquility, and civil authority now exist in and throughout the whole of the United States."

The announcement was premature. Johnson had evaded the question of Negro suffrage and civil rights, avoided revolutionary social changes, and tolerated the election of old leaders to office. The program of moderation proved vulnerable to attack by radicals who sought deeper changes in Southern society. Shrewdly enlisting the support of humanitarians who were concerned purely with protecting the Negro, and combining them with economic interests that feared the return of Southern Democratic congressmen as a menace to newly won privileges, the Radical Republican faction captured control of Congress in the elections of 1866.

Again coercion and force became the order of the day. Declaring

[14] Full and elaborate accounts are available in numerous places. The brief summary that follows contains nothing new, and those who are reasonably well posted on their American history may safely skip to Chapter II.

the state governments created under Johnson nonexistent, the Radicals divided ten Southern states into five military districts and put them under the rule of major generals and an army of occupation. Frankly revolutionary in mood, Thaddeus Stevens and his followers overrode constitutional restraints right and left. They created a new electorate of more than 700,000 Negroes and pared down the white voters by disfranchisement to a total of some 627,000. The Radicals displaced six governors and supplanted thousands of lesser officials with their own men; they purged three legislatures of conservative members, threw out laws that displeased them, suppressed or ignored civil courts, denied the right to trial by jury, and violated freedom of press and speech.

All this was done, of course, in the name of democracy. And in truth history does not record a more drastic application of the democratic dogma. In addition to the sudden creation of the new Negro electorate, the Radicals set up new state constitutions that were several leaps ahead of the old ones in a progressive direction. They reformed judicial procedure, court organization, and county organization, and established, on paper at least, a broad conception of the government's responsibility for the people's welfare that was new to the South.

Reconstruction was, nevertheless, an unfair test of the democratic faith as well as an unfair test of the Negro's capacity for self-government. Historically, revolutions of this magnitude have merely registered gains in economic power and social position that the emergent class had made prior to the revolution. This was not true of the freedmen. They had accumulated no such social and economic resources. They were not in command of their own revolution, nor did they "dominate" the whites. They were controlled, sometimes by sincere idealists, but too often by men who brought discredit upon the new governments.

Radical state governments began to topple early, partly from internal weaknesses and partly from determined attacks of the Southern white opposition. The strategy of the opposition was to meet force with force, and the response of the Federal government was more force. Repeated intervention with troops kept states of the Lower South in Radical hands for a time, but by the end of 1874 all but four states had slipped in large measure out of their grasp. That year the Republicans lost control of the lower House of the national government. Their prospects for the next election were not encouraging.

The Presidential election of 1876 stirred the country more deeply than any since 1860. It was the first election in two decades in which the major parties were of something like equal strength. An advantage of the Democrats lay in the series of congressional investigations of the Grant administration that had spread before the public a record of shameless graft and corruption permeating nearly all departments. So thoroughly had the reformers done their work of exposing the scandals of "Grantism" that Grant's own party could only appeal to the voters in the centennial election on the ground that the next Republican administration would be completely unlike the previous one. Partisan passions on both sides, however, exaggerated the sharpness of the issues of the election. In Tilden, governor of New York, and Hayes, governor of Ohio, each party had nominated a reform candidate. And each of them had written a reformer's platform. The issue of reform, therefore, seemed to have been largely settled before the election.

The Carpetbagger governments in the South shared the evil reputation earned among the reformers, independents, and Liberal Republicans by Grant's administration in Washington. The reformers, offended by the Carpetbaggers' record of corruption, did not stop to ask who bribed the Carpetbaggers, nor did they stop to reflect that the New York legislature, which had no Negro and Carpetbagger members, had probably been during the Reconstruction period as corrupt as any state legislature in the South. Nor were the reformers fair in blaming all Northern politicians operating in the South for the grave offenses undoubtedly committed by some of them. In this the influence of Redemption propaganda may be detected. If Reconstruction was a mixture of altruistic and selfish social motives, however, the Carpetbaggers reflected the same ambivalence. There were idealists as well as adventurers among them. But by 1876 the latter were the more conspicuous both on the local and on the national scene, and they contributed to the heavy burden of defense the Republican party had to bear in the Presidential election of that year.[15]

All over the country the first available election returns spread the conviction that Tilden was the President-elect. The returns had already settled virtually all the points on which the race was generally expected to hang. The Democrats had easily carried New York and by smaller margins the doubtful states of New Jersey, Connecticut, and Indiana. The Southern states were expected by all save the more hopeful Republicans to line up solidly behind Tilden. All except three of them, Florida, South Carolina, and Louisiana, were reported to have piled up safe Democratic majorities, and the Republican chairmen in Louisiana and Florida were rumored to have conceded those states to their opponents. Even without any votes from the three Southern states, Tilden had 184 electoral votes in the bag, only one short of the 185 required to elect. Hayes was trailing with only 166 electoral votes conceded. In popular votes Tilden, according to official returns later, led his opponent by more than a quarter of a million. In the face of these facts Zachariah Chandler, national Republican chairman, had closed up his New York headquarters and gone home under the belief that his party had gone down in defeat. Morning newspapers across the land, leading Republican journals among them, were rolling off the presses with the story of Tilden's victory.

Then in the early hours of the next morning William E. Chandler of New Hampshire and John C. Reid, managing editor of the Republican New York *Times,* awakened Zach Chandler at his hotel and got his permission to wire Republican officials in Florida, Louisiana, and South Carolina, asking if they could hold on to their states for Hayes. The scheme rested upon Republican control of

[15] In spite of unfairness to those who did not deserve the derogatory implications of the term "Carpetbagger," the use of the word seems unavoidable — so much so that the Carpetbaggers used it themselves.

the three state returning boards. If these partisan boards could "canvass" the returns and convert every one of the nineteen electoral votes of the three states into a Hayes vote, the Republican candidate would have exactly 185 votes, a majority of one. Later that day Zach Chandler boldly announced his claim that "Hayes has 185 electoral votes and is elected."

The audacity of the scheme made success appear improbable at first. But Hewitt, Chandler's opposite number, took immediate steps to checkmate Republican moves. First he caused committees of prominent Democrats to proceed immediately to the Southern state capitals to watch over party interests in the canvassing of returns. His second move was a flanking maneuver. Although Oregon was clearly a Republican state, one of the party's electors was a postmaster and therefore as a Federal officeholder disqualified under the Constitution from serving in the electoral college. The Democratic governor of the state promptly appointed an elector of his own party, having the next highest number of votes, to fill the vacancy. Hewitt intended by supporting this move to compel the Republicans in Congress to go behind official state returns in Oregon. In so doing they would pave the way for the Democrats to go behind the manipulations of the returning boards of Florida, South Carolina, and Louisiana, and undo their work.

In the meanwhile Grant had sent Republican delegations to follow the Democratic observers to the three contested Southern states, and national attention became focused on the deep South. While the situation was different in each state, there were elements common to all of them. First there was the returning board, solidly Republican in each state save Florida, where there was one Democrat to two Republicans. Evidence of the dishonesty and corruptibility of members of these boards, especially that of Louisiana, is still pungent in the musty records of the seventies. Likewise there is ample evidence of irregularities, fraud, intimidation, and violence on the part of both Republicans and Democrats in the elections that the returning boards were to canvass. In some cases there was little to choose between the methods used by the two parties. Meeting in secret sessions and using illegal procedures, the Louisiana returning board threw out some 13,000 Democratic votes and 2000 Republican votes and thereby converted a substantial Tilden majority into a substantial Hayes majority. Three of the five members of the South Carolina board were candidates for office in the election on which they passed judgment. Their canvass gave the state's Presidential electors to Hayes but the legislature and governorship to Wade Hampton and the Democrats. Flagrantly partisan and arbitrary decisions of the Florida board converted an apparent Tilden majority into Hayes votes.

Speculation on the possible results of a perfectly fair election and a fair canvass of returns in the three states are inconclusive and highly hypothetical. Negro majorities in the population of South Carolina and Louisiana gave the Republicans their strongest claim to those states, though evidence points to a revolt against Carpetbagger control among some Negroes. A white majority and a rift in Republican ranks in Florida are prima facie evidence of the same kind for a Democratic claim to that state. The consensus of recent historical scholarship is that Hayes was probably entitled to the electoral votes of South Carolina and Louisiana, that Tilden was entitled to the four votes of Florida, and that Tilden was therefore elected by a vote of 188 to 181. There has been no tendency to defend the members of the electoral boards or the methods used to influence them.[16]

On the appointed day, December 6, the Republican electors of the three states met in their capitals and cast their votes for Hayes and Wheeler, while at the same time electors with certificates from rival Democratic state authorities met and delivered their ballots solidly for Tilden and Hendricks. On the face of state returns, which included one vote of Oregon for Tilden and the nineteen votes of the

[16] Among historians holding that Tilden carried Florida are Nevins, *Abram S. Hewitt,* 329, 388; Eckenrode, *Rutherford B. Hayes,* 192–193; Alexander C. Flick, *Samuel J. Tilden, A Study in Political Sagacity* (New York, 1939), 415–416; and Leon B. Richardson, *William E. Chandler, Republican* (New York, 1940), 193. The older historians, Schouler, Dunning, and Rhodes, also put Louisiana in Tilden's column.

three contested Southern states for Hayes, the results stood Tilden 185 votes and Hayes 184.

In partisan bitterness and suspicion Congress convened on December 4 and immediately reflected the dangerous cleavage of sentiment in the country. To Democratic shouts of "fraud" and "Tilden-or-fight," the Republicans retorted that they had been robbed of their Negro support by Democratic fraud in all Southern states and would yield no further. While the Democratic opinion among leaders, newspapers, and rank and file appeared to be completely solid in the conviction that the Republicans were out to steal the election and that Tilden's claim was unassailable, there was less solidarity among Republicans. Such outstanding leaders as President Grant and Senator Roscoe Conkling of New York expressed their belief privately that Tilden was the victor, and several party journals were wavering or openly doubtful. The great majority of the party, however, was as convinced of Hayes's claims as the Democrats were of Tilden's.

The first act of the Democratic majority in the House of Representatives, after organizing and learning the results of the electoral count of December 6, was to appoint committees of investigation and dispatch them to the contested Southern states. The Senate, with a large Republican majority, followed suit by sending its committees southward. This was admittedly temporizing on both sides, for no solution could be expected by this means.

The fact was nobody could suggest an acceptable solution to the problem that was now the critical one — the question of how to count the electoral votes. Neither the Constitution, nor the law and rules, nor precedent and custom offered an acceptable solution. The Twelfth Amendment to the Constitution declared that "the President of the Senate shall, in the presence of the Senate and House of Representatives, open all the certificates and the votes shall then be counted." But it did not say who should do the counting. If it would be done by the temporary president of the Senate, Thomas W. Ferry, as the Republicans contended, the result would obviously be a Hayes victory. If by the two houses acting jointly the count would go in favor of Tilden. Since neither candidate had a clear majority, Democrats demanded that the election be thrown into the House, as provided in another clause of the Twelfth Amendment. Republicans refused to consider this solution because of the Democratic control of the House. There were other disturbing questions to which the law gave no clear and unequivocal answer. Could Congress go behind the official state returns and inquire into fraud? Or must these returns be accepted on their face? Reversing positions in the old state-rights dialogue, the Republicans solemnly demanded respect for state authority and the Democrats brushed it aside. Again, if no President were elected by March 4, who would succeed to power? And back of these questions the darker one — if it came to an appeal to force, where did the advantage lie? The Republicans had the regular army, but it was small and widely dispersed. On the other side were the Democratic governors in command of the National Guard.

The year drew toward its close with no prospect of a break in the deadlock between the two Houses and the two parties. On December 13 both Hewitt and Chandler announced equally firm claims to the Presidency for their candidates. Debates became angrier on Capitol Hill and members began to arm themselves. Scenes on the floors of the two Houses reminded old-timers of the days of 1860–1861. It had been less than twelve years since the country was at war and memories of those days were always present in this crisis.

CHAPTER II

The Rejuvenation of Whiggery

ON DECEMBER 12 Congressman James A. Garfield of Ohio gave Governor Hayes his estimate of the situation as it appeared in Washington and suggested a course of action. After describing the "ugly" conduct of "the more violent Democratic leaders" who were "trying to create as much sensation and popular clamor as possible," he pointed out some hopeful signs. "In the meantime two forces are at work," he wrote. "The Democratic business men of the country are more anxious for quiet than for Tilden; and the leading southern Democrats in Congress, especially those who were old Whigs, are saying that they have seen war enough, and don't care to follow the lead of their northern associates who, as Ben Hill says, were 'invincible in peace and invisible in war.'" Several Republican leaders had approached him with the idea of making inroads in the Democratic camp to split off the Southerners. Garfield told Hayes this might be done "if in some discreet way, these southern men, who are dissatisfied with Tilden and his violent followers, could know that the South is going to be treated with kind consideration by you. Several southern men have said within a week, that in the matter of internal improvements they had been much better treated by Republicans than they were likely to be by the Democrats — and they talk a good deal about the old Whigs having been forced, unwillingly, into the Democratic party." Garfield had no doubt that an understanding could be reached and urged Hayes to move swiftly.[1]

[1] James A. Garfield to Rutherford B. Hayes, December 12, 1876, Hayes Papers, Hayes Memorial Library, Fremont, Ohio.

Garfield was only one of several Republican chiefs, among them former Governor William Dennison of Ohio and William D. Kelley, the "pig-iron" congressman from Pennsylvania, who wrote Hayes in a similar vein.[2] Their suggestions met with a sympathetic, even a cordial reception. Replying to Garfield's letter, the governor wrote, "Your views are so nearly the same as mine that I need not say a word."[3]

The Republican campaign of 1876 was not an auspicious background for the proposed rapprochement between Hayes and the South. That campaign had been fought on a national platform defending and reasserting the Republican record of Reconstruction. Campaign oratory differed in no essential from that of 1868 and 1872. It rang all the changes on Southern atrocities, Southern disloyalty, treason, and wickedness. "The bloody shirt, as it is termed, was freely waved," as William E. Chandler said, "and Governor Hayes himself urged public men to put forward, as our best argument, the dangers of 'rebel rule and a solid South.'"[4] During the campagin Hayes had written James G. Blaine, leading bloody-shirt waver, "Our strong ground is a dread of a solid South, rebel rule, etc., etc. . . . It leads people away from 'hard times' which is our deadliest foe."[5] The candidate's letter of acceptance contained the vague assurance that he would "wipe out the distinction between North and South," of which much was made later on. But the same letter followed the platform in declaring that the government "shall protect all classes of citizens in their political and private rights," and that "all parts of the Constitution are sacred and must be sacredly obeyed—the parts that are new no less than the parts that are old." That was orthodox Radical doctrine.

Hayes had maintained an almost complete silence during the campaign, but on the day after the election, when he believed himself

[2] William Dennison to Hayes, December 13, 1876; William D. Kelley to Hayes, December 17, 1876, *ibid.*

[3] Hayes to Garfield, December 16, 1876. Garfield Papers, Library of Congress.

[4] Quoted in Richardson, *William E. Chandler*, 212.

[5] Quoted in James F. Rhodes, *History of the United States* (New York, 1906), VII, 220.

defeated, he said: "I don't care for myself; and the party, yes, and the country, too, can stand it; but I do care for the poor colored men of the South. . . . The result will be that the Southern people will practically treat the constitutional amendments as nullities, and then the colored man's fate will be worse than when he was in slavery."[6] A meeting of minds between Hayes and the South strongly implied a rapid change of mind on the part of Hayes — not to say a repudiation of the party platform and the campaign by which he claimed election.

On the other hand, Hayes's private letters reveal a long-standing sympathy for white Southerners of the ruling class and their problems. A correspondence of many years with Guy M. Bryan, a college classmate from Texas, shows an appreciation of many Southern points of view and suggests that Hayes was privately at odds with his party's Reconstruction policy. "As to Southern affairs, 'the let alone policy' seems now to be the true course," he wrote Bryan in 1875, and declared that he entertained "nothing but good will" toward the South.[7] Northerner and Southerner saw eye to eye on mutual labor problems. The Ohio governor complained to Bryan of striking local miners in his state who "make war on property"; and the Texan complained to Hayes of "similar troubles in the South ever since the war from a discontented and ignorant class" who also made "war on property."[8] An old Whig, like many Southern leaders who now called themselves Democrats or Conservatives, Hayes dreamed of breaking down the sectional barrier between men of property and reviving the ante-bellum political alliance between conservatives of North and South.

As a matter of fact, some two weeks before he received the suggestion from Garfield, Hayes took steps in the direction later proposed by the congressman. With the governor's consent his friend Murat Halstead of Cincinnati invited L. Q. C. Lamar of Mississippi

[6] Quoted in Charles R. Williams, *The Life of Rutherford Birchard Hayes, Nineteenth President of the United States,* 2 vols. (Boston, 1914), I, 493–494.

[7] Hayes to Guy M. Bryan, July 27, 1875, in E. W. Winkler (ed.), "The Hayes-Bryan Correspondence," *Southwestern Historical Quarterly,* XXVI (1922–1923), 159.

[8] Hayes to Bryan, May 6, 1876; Bryan to Hayes, June 8, 1876, in *ibid.,* 283–285.

to come by Columbus on his way to Washington for a conference with Hayes. Lamar stopped at Cincinnati for a talk with Halstead, but shied off with a courteous note from the visit to Hayes. Halstead then arranged for Hayes to see Lamar's friend, Colonel W. H. Roberts, managing editor of the New Orleans *Times,* who professed familiarity with the views of Lamar and General E. C. Walthall of Mississippi, Hampton of South Carolina, and Senator John B. Gordon of Georgia.[9] In a three-hour conference on December 1 the governor told the New Orleans editor that on Southern affairs "he desired to consult with such men as Mr. Lamar and General Hampton; that he thought Hampton had acted a noble part in recent events in South Carolina, for which the country owed him thanks." Hayes also believed "that carpet bag governments had not been successful; that the complaints of the southern people were just in this matter; that he should require absolute justice and fair play to the Negro, but that he was convinced this could be got best and most surely by trusting the honorable and influential southern whites."[10] Roberts thought that such a policy would attract Southern support to Hayes. "You will be President," said the editor, according to Hayes's diary. "We will not make trouble. We want peace."[11] The conference was by no means conclusive, however, for Roberts said that he "had no authority from General Hampton or Mr. Lamar to make any proposition looking to a compromise, nor," he emphasized, "did I state that I had any authority."[12]

While the Hayes-Roberts conference appeared to be a promising start toward a compromise, Halstead was at a loss for further suggestions. "I confess," he wrote Hayes, "I do not know what you can do now, any more than what Lincoln could have done in 1861."[13]

[9] Murat Halstead to Hayes, November 30, 1876, Hayes Papers.

[10] This story was first broken in the Cincinnati *Enquirer,* December 2, 1876; but because of alleged errors it contained, "a true account" was given by "a source thoroughly informed" in the New York *Herald,* December 4, 1876. The latter account is the one quoted.

[11] Hayes Diary, December 1, 1876, in Charles R. Williams (ed.), *Diary and Letters of Rutherford Birchard Hayes* (Columbus, 1922–1926), III, 382–383.

[12] Roberts quoted in New York *Herald,* December 4, 1876.

[13] Halstead to Hayes, December 10, 1876, in Hayes Papers.

Hayes's remarks to Roberts on Grant's Southern policy had leaked to the press and caused embarrassing comment. "He discredits and condemns the men who have been and are still most strenuously working to secure his inauguration," observed the New York *Herald* on the governor's "startling pronouncements" upon the Carpetbaggers.[14] Clearly Hayes himself could not go much further in his overtures than he had already gone. The politicians in the Washington limelight were suspicious of each other and wary of being accused of bargaining and party disloyalty. What was needed was some less conspicuous place of foregathering and negotiators who were accustomed to more intimate and confidential relations than existed at the moment between Northern Republican and Southern Democratic politicians.

The officials and agents who ran the Western Associated Press constituted just such an intersectional association of nonpolitical or quasi-political men as Halstead and Hayes needed in their quandary. Halstead, proprietor of the Cincinnati *Commercial,* was president of the Association, and William Henry Smith of Chicago, Hayes's closest personal friend, was general agent. On the board of directors sat Joseph Medill of the Chicago *Tribune,* Andrew J. Kellar, editor of the Memphis *Avalanche,* Richard Smith of the Cincinnati *Gazette,* and W. N. Haldeman, publisher of Watterson's Louisville *Courier-Journal.* The W.A.P. letterhead claimed as members "the leading journals of the Ohio and Mississippi Valleys and of the lakes." With a great wire-news service west of the Appalachians, the W.A.P. had since the end of the Civil War built up a membership stretching from New Orleans to Chicago. While officially out of politics, the officers of the association were actually in the very thick of it, in closer touch with day-by-day developments and behind-the-scenes maneuvers than the public figures in Washington. The national network of W.A.P. news gatherers was a vast intelligence organization that hourly pooled reports on public opinion in the hinterland, North and South. No group of men in the country was so strategically placed and so well informed for the delicate task of negotiating

[14] New York *Herald,* December 4, 1876.

an intersectional, interparty compromise in the midst of a national crisis as the Northern and Southern officials of the W.A.P.

The most active figure in the affairs of the press association was its general agent William Henry Smith, and it was also he who took the initiative and retained the leadership in the crucial part the association officials played in the political crisis of 1877. After serving two terms as secretary of state in Ohio, Smith had moved to Chicago to take up the Associated Press work but had kept a hand in politics. He was credited with having done "more than any one else, outside of Ohio, to prepare the way for Mr. Hayes' nomination for the Presidency."[15] Hayes placed Smith in 1877 "at the top of the list of most valued friends,"[16] and the President's official biographer called him "Mr. Hayes' most intimate and personal friend."[17] The relationship dated back many years and endured throughout the men's lives. Shortly after Hayes retired from the White House he wrote Smith, "You were at the cradle, and you have followed the hearse 'of this ambitious life.' I know that to you it has not brought the reward of the satisfaction which you deserve to have. No man ever had a more sincere, a more judicious, and a more unselfish friend than in this matter I have found in you."[18]

Since the time of the election Smith had been corresponding with Andrew J. Kellar of Memphis "to find a path of safety out of our great troubles." Kellar had visited in Smith's home in Chicago and had great confidence in him. On December 10 he wrote that he was coming up for a conference with Smith on the crisis.[19] The two men met and together they proceeded to Cincinnati on December 14 to include Richard Smith of the *Gazette* and probably Halstead in their

[15] Charles R. Williams, *The Life of Rutherford Birchard Hayes, Nineteenth President of the United States,* 2 vols. (Boston, 1914), II, 425–426.

[16] Hayes to William Henry Smith, June 24, 1877, in Williams (ed.), *Diary and Letters of Hayes,* III, 439.

[17] Williams, *Life of Hayes,* II, 424.

[18] Hayes to Smith, March 29, 1881, quoted in *ibid.,* 425.

[19] Andrew J. Kellar to Smith, November 14 and December 10, 1876, in William Henry Smith Papers, William Henry Smith Memorial Library of the Indiana Historical Society, Indianapolis, Indiana. Copies in Hayes Memorial Library.

deliberations. Richard Smith showed them three letters from the Washington representative of the *Gazette,* Henry Van Ness Boynton, two of which Hayes had already seen. Boynton had arrived independently at Garfield's idea of splitting off the Southern wing of the Democrats. He thought that prompt action was essential but needed the assistance of someone who had the complete confidence of the Southerners. It was decided that Colonel Kellar was the man for the job. William Henry Smith, who had kept Hayes informed, wrote him that the Cincinnati conference had "arranged a programme." "Col. Kellar leaves for Washington in a few hours," he reported, "and will enter zealously on the great work. He is an admirable man for it, discreet and wise and fully sympathizes with us." The colonel would co-operate with Boynton. "And now the work goes bravely on."[20]

In Kellar the conspirators had secured an invaluable assistant, who was to play a leading role in the compromise. A Douglas Democrat and a Union man at the outbreak of the war, Kellar had "gone with his state" into the Confederate Army. There he rose in rank, rendered distinguished service, and led a regiment at the battle of Nashville. After Appomattox he entered newspaper work in Memphis and became editor of the *Daily Avalanche.* In politics he was aligned with the Whig-industrialist wing of the Democratic party led by Colonel Arthur S. Colyar of Nashville and opposed to the state rights-planter wing led by Isham G. Harris, unreconstructed Confederate. "He has been fighting the Bourbon Democrats," reported Smith to Hayes, "& two years ago [1874] ran as an independent for Congress defeating a bad Confederate & letting in a Republican. We have often discussed the unhappy situation in the South, & it is his earnest desire to aid in building up a conservative Republican party in the South, that shall effectively destroy the color line & save the poor colored people. In my judgment much can be done with the help of such men, between now and February 10, to secure a good understanding with the better class of white Southerners."[21] In the opinion of

[20] William Henry Smith to Hayes, December 14, 1876, Hayes Papers.
[21] William Henry Smith to Hayes, December 7, 1876, *ibid.*

Richard Smith the colonel was "a splendid fellow, true as steel and brave as a lion."[22]

General Henry Van Ness Boynton, with whom Kellar was to cooperate, won his military title on the other side of the line. Born in Massachusetts, the son of a Congregational minister of abolitionist sentiments, Boynton grew up in Cincinnati, where he was teaching in a military institute when war came. He was severely wounded at Missionary Ridge and retired from service after promotion to the rank of brigadier general for gallantry. He became one of the best known newspapermen in Washington, representing the Cincinnati *Gazette* beginning in 1865 and later the Chicago *Tribune* and other W.A.P. papers. The author of books on military history, he was a bitter critic of General William T. Sherman and a eulogist of General George H. Thomas. During Grant's administration he became feared as a reformer, muckraker, and exposer of scandal. He assisted in exposing railroad deals of James G. Blaine and effectively publicized Secretary Benjamin H. Bristow's war on the whiskey ring and other government racketeers. As a reformer he was the ablest and most ardent manager of Bristow's unsuccessful campaign for the Republican nomination in 1876.[23] "He enjoyed confidential relations with Presidents, cabinet members, senators, representatives, and other officials," said the New York *Tribune* at his death, "and had much to do with many important public matters."[24] One of those Important Public Matters was the Compromise of 1877.

Union general and Confederate colonel hit it off wonderfully in Washington from the start. "He is everything you made me believe, & much more," wrote Kellar of Boynton, whom he pronounced "modest as he is brave and clear-headed."[25] Boynton re-

[22] Richard Smith to Hayes, February 21, 1877, *ibid.*

[23] E. Bruce Thompson, "The Bristow Presidential Boom of 1876," in *Mississippi Valley Historical Review,* XXXII (1945), 5.

[24] New York *Tribune,* June 4, 1905. Among Boynton's writings were "The Whiskey Ring," *North American Review,* CXXIII (1876), 280 ff.; *Sherman's Historical Raid* (Cincinnati, 1875); and with Donn Piatt, *The Life of General George H. Thomas* (Cincinnati, 1891). He published book reviews in the *American Historical Review,* VII (1901–1902), 580, 786.

[25] Kellar to William Henry Smith, December 21, 1876, Smith Papers.

ported that "the arrival of Colonel Kellar was timely and has given a decided impetus to the movement which we have in mind."[26]

In the meantime Garfield was keeping an ear to the ground in Washington. He had heard that Democratic Congressman Casey Young from Memphis believed that "fifty Democratic congressmen would stand by Hayes" if proper assurances were forthcoming. Garfield thought that number of converts improbable but believed that a third of the number might be decisive in the crisis. On the evening of December 17 he was kept up long past his bedtime by General Boynton and Congressman Charles Foster of Ohio who discussed the Southern situation, and on the following evening Boynton brought Colonel Kellar by and introduced him. Garfield watched with fascination while Kellar unfolded a new picture of the "Solid South." It was a South whose white rulers were not so solid as they appeared. The lines of cleavage followed roughly the old seams in the web where the Whigs and Union men of the South had been forcibly joined with the Democrats and Secessionists. This unstable union between traditional opponents was a relatively recent contrivance, dating in some cases only from the final struggle for Redemption. It was achieved under pressure of white supremacy propaganda. A conservative Republican president would have it in his power to diminish the appeal of that propaganda. If Hayes could break the political web along the old seams he would not only secure Southern support for his inauguration in the present crisis but "build up a sound Republican party there" in the future by winning the old Whigs away from the Democrats. Garfield pledged his best efforts in the movement. "I told the Col.," said his diary, "to leave the names of such men with Gen. B. as he wished me to see, & have them call on me."[27]

Colonel Kellar plunged into the work at hand with zeal. Back and forth from Senate to House, in and out of the old Ebbitt, the Willard, and Wormley's hotels, and from one red brick home to another in

[26] Boynton to Smith, December 18, 1876, *ibid.*

[27] Garfield Diary, December 7, 11, 17, 18, 1876, Garfield Papers.

the northwest section he moved on his mission. General Boynton reported enthusiastically to William Henry Smith that the colonel was "able to do that part of the work which was most difficult for us, namely sounding certain Southern men. He has their confidence & he easily got near them."[28] Kellar saw to it that the right people on both sides got together and was helpful in knowing who could be trusted as "discreet." On the whole he was pleased with the way the work started, "but," he warned Smith, "the work must be one of patience, fortitude, justice, & discretion tempered with that tact which is the offspring of a constant daily dealing with public opinion."[29]

It would undoubtedly be a mistake to attribute the numerous signs of change in Southern opinion to Kellar and his W.A.P. associates merely because those signs appeared simultaneously with their efforts. Kellar only acted as a messenger between lines, a diplomat who took advantage of a situation and a sentiment that he did not create. For the sentiment was already there. The press wires carried samples of it from dozens of towns and villages over the South — Norfolk, Raleigh, Columbus, Macon, La Grange, Memphis — some of which had scarcely dug their way from the ashes of the last war. A large number of Southern conservatives were alarmed by the violent talk of Northern Democrats. They wanted no part of this war talk. War was "a very practical reality" with them. They also recalled too well how their Northern Democratic friends had encouraged a resort to arms in 1861 and then deserted them. This was an old grudge still much alive. "People talk of war," said a little Holly Springs, Mississippi, paper. "The South is neither desirous nor prepared for such a calamity. The siren song of Northern Democrats may sound very sweet in Washington. . . . The South has heard it in Washington before." North Carolinians, reported a Raleigh paper, "feel keenly the outrage which threatens to rob the country of the results of its victory. But they have felt keenly before." It was not worth a war, at any rate. "One more fight," declared the Macon

[28] Boynton to Smith, December 18, 1876, Smith Papers.
[29] Kellar to Smith, December 21, 1876, *ibid.*

Telegraph, "and liberty and honesty would be indefinitely postponed on this continent." [30] The Southern press, with a few bellicose exceptions, was clearly not spoiling for a fight.

In Washington also it was the Southerners, despite their reputation for hot-blooded, hair-trigger temperament, who were throwing a wet blanket on incendiary talk of Tilden's Northern supporters. At a Democratic caucus in mid-December Congressman Fernando Wood, the wartime mayor of New York who threatened to take the city out of the Union, made one of the several fiery speeches of the occasion. As he finished, Benjamin H. Hill of Georgia arose and drawled, "Perhaps the gentleman is not aware of the conservative influence of a fifteen-inch shell with the fuse in process of combustion." [31] In the Senate David M. Key of Tennessee, at the suggestion of his friend Colonel Kellar, led off in the role of "pacificator" by a speech on December 18. Standing "on the brink of danger" he urged his colleagues to "be calm, considerate, and, as far as possible, dispassionate, in all that we shall say and do in regard to this important matter." He was for all legitimate means of seating Tilden, who had been fairly and plainly elected, but he would have nothing to do with "violent measures." [32] Colonel Casey Young of Memphis, another of Kellar's political associates, addressed the House in a similar vein. It was Kellar's conviction, he wrote William Henry Smith, that "Tennessee must take the leadership in the good work." [33]

Arkansas was another fertile field for "the good work" and the colonel had excellent connections there. Augustus H. Garland, Redeemer governor of Arkansas, wrote Kellar after conferring with his successor and other prominent Democrats, "We all conclude we want no war, no trouble and deprecate every appearance of placing

[30] Memphis *Appeal,* December 22, 1876; Holly Springs (Miss.) *Reporter* quoted in Memphis *Avalanche,* December 16, 1876; Columbus (Ga.) *Times* and La Grange (Tenn.) *Monitor* quoted in *ibid.,* December 13, 1876; Memphis *Ledger,* Macon *Telegraph and Messenger,* and Raleigh *Sentinel* quoted in *ibid.,* December 21, 1876; Norfolk *Landmark* in *ibid.,* December 23, 1876.

[31] Cincinnati *Daily Gazette,* December 14, 1876.

[32] *Congressional Record,* 44 Cong., 2 Sess. (December 18, 1876), 262.

[33] Kellar to Smith, December 21, 1876, Smith Papers.

the South in any hostile attitude toward the federal government."[34] His letter was forwarded to Governor Hayes. Governor Wade Hampton, Redeemer of South Carolina, wrote Hayes directly giving assurance of his "firm and deliberate purpose to condemn any solution of existing political problems that involves exhibition of armed force."[35] Governor Zebulon B. Vance of North Carolina took the same position in his inaugural address at Raleigh. And harmonizing with this chorus of peace from Southern politicians, like a deep bass off stage, was the voice of national business interests. "The business community," wrote a St. Louis businessman to Hayes, "is almost unanimous against trouble & I think the Southern men generally are so inclined."[36]

Southern opposition to revolutionary and warlike methods did not, of course, mean Southern acquiescence in the inauguration of Hayes and connivance with Republican schemes to seize the Presidency. The Southerners in their private and public expressions continued to maintain as firmly as the Northern Democrats that Tilden was rightfully elected. The cleavage within the party at this stage was confined to the matter of violence. But the division did provide an opening for Kellar and Hayes's W.A.P. friends and their plans for splitting off the Southern wing.

Washington was full of rumors by the middle of December concerning Southern overtures to Hayes and Republican deals with the South. The New York *Sun,* a strong Tilden paper, called these reports "the most often repeated and widely circulated political sensation" in the Capital.[37] Republican papers applauded and Democratic editors deplored rumors of a defection among Southerners. "The apprehension is becoming deeper every day that they are willing to temporize with Governor Hayes," said the Democratic Cincinnati *Enquirer.*[38] A. M. Gibson, an extraordinarily well-informed Wash-

[34] Augustus H. Garland to Andrew J. Kellar, January 1, 1877, Hayes Papers.

[35] Wade Hampton to Hayes, December 23, 1876, *ibid.*

[36] George H. Shields to Hayes, December 28, 1876, *ibid.*

[37] New York *Sun,* December 19, 1876.

[38] Cincinnati *Enquirer,* December 15, 1876; also Washington *Evening Star,* December 15, 1876; New York *Daily Graphic,* December 12, 1876; Cincinnati *Daily Gazette,* December 16, 22, 1876.

ington newspaperman who had been employed by Hewitt to write the Democratic campaign book of 1876, told Charles A. Dana of the *Sun* privately that "there is undoubtedly danger of defection among Southern Democrats. The friends of Hayes are certainly bidding high in that direction, and I *know* that their propositions are being entertained — listened to, considered." He believed that there were powerful railroad lobbyists involved and that Tilden's Washington managers "don't get below the surface of things." He implored the editor to "give Tilden a hint."[39] Dana forwarded the letter to Tilden on December 15, and the latter evidently moved promptly, for on the following day Hewitt sprang into action. "The war-like Hewitt," reported Murat Halstead's paper, "heard so much about the defection of Southern Democrats that he called a caucus of Southern members at his house on the night of the 16th." The results of the caucus were reported to be inconclusive, however, and the Southerners continued to exert "not an irritating but a soothing influence. They should have full credit for that," said Halstead.[40]

During the closing months of Grant's unhappy second administration Republican strategists conducted a searching analysis of the Southern mind — more accurately the mind of the Redeemers, the new rulers who had overthrown the Republican Radicals and were on the point of consolidating their control of the entire region. The Republicans were beginning to see these men and the Southern problem with new eyes, for it was a time of self-analysis and soul searching for themselves as well. Their Southern policy began to appear more and more like an anachronism. It dated from the piping, revolutionary days of '66 and '68 when grim old Thad Stevens was at the helm, Charles Sumner was in full voice, and the Radical-Abolitionist coalition was in control of the party. The Radicals' Southern policy was on the one hand disfranchisement and confiscation for conservatives and on the other hand votes, offices, civil rights, and maybe forty acres apiece for the Negroes, and control for

[39] A. M. Gibson to Charles A. Dana, December 13, 1876, enclosed in Dana to Samuel J. Tilden, December 15, 1876, in John Bigelow (ed.), *Letters and Literary Memorials of Samuel J. Tilden,* 2 vols. (New York and London, 1908), II, 505–506.

[40] Cincinnati *Commercial,* December 20, 1876.

Carpetbaggers. Since those days things had changed, North and South. Despite its professed radicalism, the Republican party had obviously become the conservative party, spokesman of vested interests and big business, defender of an elaborate system of tariffs, subsidies, currency laws, privileged banks, railroads, and corporations, a system entrenched in the law by Republicans while the voters were diverted by oratory about Reconstruction, civil rights, and Southern atrocities. The old Whig element of the North that had combined with the Free-Soil Democrats and Abolitionists in the fifties to form the Republican party was on top in 1876 and had written its antebellum economic program into law. It had nominated as party leader a conservative former Whig in Rutherford B. Hayes, a man of staunch Whig economic principles, wholly out of sympathy with the equalitarian Abolitionist Carpetbaggery in the South.

Stoutly conservative in its national character, the Republican party nevertheless clung nominally to the old Radical Southern policy, which was quite out of line with its true nature. The party of wealth and property and privilege in the North, it appealed in the South to a propertyless, oppressed Negro laboring class. "We have tried for eight years to uphold Negro rule in the South officered by carpet baggers," observed Joseph Medill to Richard Smith, "but without exception it has resulted in failure." [41] One by one the Southern states had been torn from Republican control by the Redeemers. These Redeemers seemed to be for the most part conservative, and conservative not merely on race policy but on economic questions as well, for they appeared to think like good Republicans in these matters. Now in the midst of a depression, under attack from radical agrarians in the West and radical labor in the East, the Republicans found themselves estranged from their natural allies in the South.

In the old days it had been different—in the days when a Federalist party or a Whig party had cut across sectional lines and united conservatives of both North and South in a common cause. That was the "normal" organization of American politics, believed the new Republican strategists, and it had been disrupted by an

[41] Joseph Medill to Richard Smith, February 17, 1877, Hayes Papers.

"abnormal" organization that aligned both conservatives and radicals artificially along sectional lines instead of class lines. A return to "normal" politics meant a change of Republican policy, but it was admittedly an outmoded policy of which Grant already despaired and with which Hayes had no sympathy. "It is evident that the Republican Party can no longer be maintained on past issues," wrote John Tyler, Jr., Republican son of the former Whig President from Virginia, to Hayes, "and that a new line of policy must be adopted." [42] With that sentiment the new leaders of the Republican party were in complete agreement.

Heirs to the Hamiltonian tradition of Federalism, the Whigs were the "broadcloth party" of the South in ante-bellum days. They opposed Jacksonian principles and measures as the Federalists had once fought Jeffersonian principles and measures. The Whigs constituted themselves the protectors of property rights and champions of financial, commercial, and industrial interests. They were the party of the big planter and the businessman. Henry Clay, their most brilliant leader, advanced a program he called the "American System," which combined internal improvements with protective tariff, favored the Bank of the United States, and denied cheap land to Western settlers. Like all major parties in American political tradition, the Whigs embraced diverse and sometimes contradictory elements. There were state-rights Whigs who opposed the protective tariff and subsidies to business. On the other hand, by holding out promise of Federal aid for transportation improvements to landlocked areas, and by outdoing the Jacksonians in demagogic methods, the Whigs attracted a considerable following among the humble folk, particularly in the mountainous areas. In this respect the Whigs were not unlike the post-bellum Republicans, who also attracted much support from the plain people for a program essentially devoted to the interests of property and wealth. Strongly Unionist in sympathies, opposing secession, and deploring all agitation of the slavery issue, the Whigs were always earnest advocates of sectional compromise. Clay was the architect of three great historical com-

[42] John Tyler, Jr., to Hayes, February 17, 1877, *ibid.*

promises, and his successor, Senator J. J. Crittenden of Kentucky, was sponsor of the compromise that failed in 1861.

American political history suddenly became a subject of absorbing interest among practical politicians, and the chief preoccupation was the forgotten history of Southern Whiggery. "The whole subject is a constant theme of earnest talk in Washington," reported the New York *Times,* "and will continue to be until there is a marked change of some kind in political prospects."[43] Medill's Chicago *Tribune* speculated that "of the total number who voted for Tilden and Hendricks [in the South], fully one-half belong to the old Whig or Douglas element."[44] And Richard Smith's paper observed that "the old Whig element is there, just as strong in proportion as it ever was. It has never been perfectly at home in the Democratic party."[45] Congressman "Pig-Iron" Kelley told Hayes: "The old Whig or Union party of the South should have been reinvigorated as it could have been, & it and the colored people would have given us clear majorities composed almost exclusively of Southern people in the States south of Kentucky and Virginia."[46]

The most elaborate analysis was made by a Republican writer in the New York *Times.* Examining state by state the former strength of the Whigs in the South and later of the Douglas Democrats and the Constitutional Unionists, he concluded that "the old Whig vote is then a basis of Democratic division in the South," the element that must be attracted to Hayes's cause. It was this element that had resisted secession in the Unionist party of 1860 and voted for Bell. Their votes in 1860 combined with those polled by Douglas, also anti-secessionist, totaled 626,885 in the twelve Southern states. This was a larger vote by more than 100,000 than the secessionist Democrat Breckinridge carried. Men who voted first in that election were only thirty-seven or thirty-eight years old in 1876, and the Southern conservative Unionists who had resisted secession in '61 would be the natural opponents of violence and revolution in '77. They had

[43] New York *Times,* January 11, 1877.
[44] Chicago *Tribune,* January 3, 1877.
[45] Cincinnati *Daily Gazette,* December 19, 1876.
[46] William D. Kelley to Hayes, December 17, 1876, Hayes Papers.

the power "by giving a hearty support to the Administration of President Hayes, and thus forming a coalition with the colored vote — to gain political control of their states against the more dangerous element of the whites." Acting with the Negroes, whom Hayes would remove from Carpetbagger control and turn over to their guidance, the conservatives could "control the governments of several States — certainly Louisiana, Mississippi, Alabama, North Carolina, South Carolina, Florida," and possibly others. "I but echo the sentiments of the great majority of Republican leaders," said the writer, "in saying that there has been since the war no such promising situation. . . . A disruption of the white Democratic voters of the South," he continued, "would be everywhere regarded as the greatest political event in this country since the organization of the Republican party. The prospect of such a division has already been sufficiently strong to exercise a very powerful influence on contemplated actions and to become an important factor of the political problems that are upon us."[47]

The more closely the Republicans scrutinized the new Southern Democracy, the less it resembled the old party of Jefferson or Jackson, or even Jefferson Davis, and the more it resembled the party of Henry Clay. The impression was brought home first of all by the Southerners with whom they were dealing in the crisis, the rulers of the New Order in the South, the "Redeemers." Zeb Vance, Democratic Redemption governor of North Carolina, was an old Whig, and so were Augustus H. Garland, Redemption governor of Arkansas, and George F. Drew, Redemption governor of Florida. The first ex-Confederate governor elected by Tennessee was John C. Brown, an ex-Whig and brother of an ante-bellum Whig governor of the state. Brown's successor, James D. Porter, was another old-line Whig. Hampton and Lamar, though not of Whig antecedents, descended from the conservative brand of the Democratic family, not the Andrew Johnson side. There certainly were Southern Democrats from the other branch, especially Texans, but their radical proclivities did not appear until later. Congressmen Ben Hill and

[47] New York *Times,* January 11, 1877.

Alexander H. Stephens of Georgia were only two of a large delegation of ex-Whigs who now sat on the Democratic side of the House. After counting noses in Congress one of Hayes's advisors in Washington wrote him: "There are twenty-six Southern members who before Secession were Whigs who are now secretly pledged, as I am informed, to resist all extreme measures, and who are at least desirous that you may be inaugurated." [48]

Could it be that the old Whig element had taken control of the Southern Democrats at the same time that the Whig philosophy was capturing the Northern Republicans? The Southern Whigs had been forced into the Democratic party and the Northern Whigs into the Republican party, but the Southern conservatives found their new surroundings much less congenial than their Northern brethren found the Republican party. Democrats and Whigs had long been traditional enemies in the South. "I despise the very name of Democrat," wrote a Southern Democrat of Whig antecedents. In fact most Southern Democrats did not use the name, but preferred to call themselves "Conservatives" or "Conservative Democrats." One of them, with a candor many must have admired, closed a letter to the New York *Tribune* with the words:

> I have the honor to subscribe myself an ex-Confederate officer — in principle an Old Line Whig, but, under existing circumstances, in practice and from necessity,
>
> A SOUTHERN DEMOCRAT
>
> *Washington, D.C., February 17, 1877*

In 1876–1877 there was some agitation for reorganizing the antebellum party. "It is quite the fashion," remarked the Raleigh *Observer,* "to talk about reviving the old Whig party, and to make appeals to the old Henry Clay Whigs once more to come to the front." [49] John Tyler, Jr., was one of those favoring this movement. But as the *Observer* pointed out, the local Whigs had pretty much taken charge of the Democratic party anyway, and there existed no real need for the new party.

[48] A. H. Markland to Hayes, January 5, 1877, Hayes Papers.
[49] Raleigh *Observer,* April 4, 1877.

Another thing that the Republicans could not help observing about the Redeemers — and this was probably more important than Whig antecedents — was that whether they were old Whigs or not, they were as a rule not the ante-bellum planter Whigs and conservatives. They spoke for much the same type of economic interests as the Republicans — railroads, industries, business enterprise of one kind or another. Ex-Governor Brown of Tennessee was vice president of the Texas & Pacific Railroad and a lobbyist for its interests. Ex-Governor James W. Throckmorton of Texas was an official and congressional friend of the same company. Colonel Arthur S. Colyar, boss of the Whig wing of Tennessee Democrats, was general counsel for the Tennessee Coal and Iron Company. Temporarily a Republican and now a Democrat again, ex-Governor Joseph E. Brown of Georgia was one of the leading Southern industrialists in iron, coal, and railroad operations. Senator John B. Gordon of the same state was friendly to the lobby of Collis P. Huntington, California railroad baron,[50] and Gordon's colleague Thomas M. Norwood, who lost his Senate seat to Ben Hill in January, was quickly employed by Huntington.[51] General Richard C. Taylor of Louisiana, only son of Zachary Taylor, the ante-bellum Whig president, was a house guest of Hewitt during the Presidential election crisis and a liaison officer between the Northern Democratic manager and the Southerners. Taylor was seeking employment with Huntington, who thought the Louisianan could "do us much good in the South." [52] Here were men who took a "practical" view of things and frequented the circles in which Republican politicians of the Gilded Age moved.

Old Southern commonwealths that had once been the bailiwicks of planter statesmen, with a peculiar institution to serve, were now found to be organized in the service of a new set of interests.

[50] Collis P. Huntington to David D. Colton, March 14, 1877, in Chicago *Tribune,* December 27, 1883.

[51] *United States Pacific Railway Commission Investigation,* in *Senate Executive Documents,* 50 Cong., 1 Sess., No. 51, pp. 3893–3894.

[52] Collis P. Huntington to David D. Colton, May 15, 1877, in Chicago *Tribune,* December 28, 1893; also Nevins, *Abram S. Hewitt,* 381.

Virginia had been redeemed by a combination of old-line Whigs, conservative Republicans, and Confederate Democrats who took the official name of Conservative party. The Redeemer governor was Gilbert C. Walker, an ex-Republican and banker from Norfolk, and all leading officials of the party were city men with business rather than agricultural affiliations. Two acts of the Conservative legislature anchored the new order in true Hamiltonian fashion to powerful capitalistic interests. These were the Funding Act, which dedicated almost the entire revenue of the state to the claims of bondholders, and the railroad act, which turned over to private interests valuable state-owned railroads with their special privileges and exemptions. Conservative rule in Virginia became the rule of bondholders, bankers, and railroads.[53] Similarly Governor George S. Houston and the Redeemers of Alabama were linked in their political and economic fortunes with the Louisville and Nashville Railroad and its numerous affiliated interests in the state. Engaged in a struggle with rival railroad combinations that were linked with the Republican party for control over the treasures of the north Alabama mineral region, the L & N Railroad enjoyed a victory that was simultaneous with the triumph of Redemption and White Supremacy.[54]

If the old-line Whigs of the South had achieved prominence in the leadership of the Democratic party, they had played an even more conspicuous role in the Republican party of certain Southern states. Indeed they were often attracted to the Republican alternative first, and only later as a last resort, after the White Supremacy crusade had drawn the color line in politics, had many reluctantly swung over to the party of their traditional enemies, the Democrats.

In Mississippi, where the Whigs had been strong enough as late as 1863 to gain control of the legislature and elect the governor and a Confederate senator, the old party of conservatism spurned the advances of the Democrats after the Civil War and moved over almost

[53] Charles S. Pearson, *The Readjuster Movement in Virginia* (New Haven, 1917), 22–23, 28–31.

[54] Horace M. Bond, *Negro Education in Alabama: A Study in Cotton and Steel* (Washington, 1939), 42–50, 54–62.

as a body into the Republican party. According to the best available estimate "from twenty-five to thirty per cent of the Mississippi white voters had by 1863 joined the Republican party, and nearly all of these were former Whigs." During the five years of Republican rule in the state, 1870–1875, "one-third of the congressmen, one of the governors, two of the three supreme court justices, and about one-third of both houses of the state legislature were southern-born white Republicans," and practically all of these officeholders had once been Whigs. Men of wealth, with property and business interests to defend, the Whigs were naturally attracted to the national party that spoke primarily for business interests.[55]

The traditional caricature of the Scalawag as the scum of the Southern white population is in some respects an invention of Democratic White Supremacy propagandists. James L. Alcorn, the first Republican governor of Mississippi and later Republican United States senator from that state, was quite as much of a planter aristocrat as Jefferson Davis. One of the wealthiest planters of the Mississippi delta and a large slaveholder, Alcorn had opposed secession as a Unionist and a Whig and only reluctantly "gone with his state" into the Confederacy. As Republican governor he held out to the Negro a program of civil rights, legal equality, and public education, and to his own class he promised state subsidies for rebuilding the levees and constructing railroads, reduction of land taxes, and the leasing of state convicts for labor. Where the ante-bellum delta planters had marshaled the power given them by the "Federal Ratio" to count three fifths of their slaves, the Republican planters under Alcorn's leadership proposed to improve the old arrangement by controlling five fifths of the Negroes for support of the old Whig class legislation in a new guise.[56]

Alcorn was succeeded as governor by another Whig-Republican of the same Hamiltonian sentiments and took his seat in the United States Senate in 1871. The Whig domination of the Republican party

[55] David H. Donald, "The Scalawag in Mississippi Reconstruction," *Journal of Southern History,* X (1944), 447–450.

[56] Vernon L. Wharton, *The Negro in Mississippi, 1865–1890* (Chapel Hill, 1947), 173–175.

was broken in 1873, however, by a strange alliance of Carpetbaggers and Democrats, both of whom were jealous of the planter-conservative control of the Negro voter. The Carpetbagger element with the aid of the Grant administration and the connivance of the Democrats elected Adelbert Ames, a son-in-law of Ben Butler, governor of the state. The Democrats then launched a campaign of fanatical race propaganda designed to drive the Negro completely out of politics and unite all white men in their own party. Between the two extremes of race equality and Negro rights preached by the Carpetbaggers and race hatred and strict drawing of the color line preached by the Democrats, there was no room left for the Whig program of moderation and compromise. Slowly and reluctantly the Conservatives were forced over into the party of their former Democratic antagonists. For the success of the Mississippi Plan, much imitated by the Redeemers of other states, was due more to the consolidation of the Whig Scalawags with the Democrats than to the intimidation of the Negroes.[57]

Pig-Iron Kelley pointed out to Hayes that "in almost every Southern State you can find men like Alcorn in Mississippi, Settle in North Carolina, and Hunt, the recent candidate for Attorney General in Louisiana." Native Southerners of the upper class and usually a Whig background, they had been undermined in their co-operation with the Republicans by Grant's support of their rivals, the Carpetbaggers, as well as by Democratic propaganda of racism. In Kelley's opinion, "the determination of the national administration to supplant Alcorn by Ames in Mississippi was perhaps its most fatal blunder." He urged that the Carpetbaggers be repudiated and the Whig element "reinvigorated." Alcorn was still in the Senate during the electoral crisis and might, thought Kelley, be used as a rallying point for Southerners of like mind.[58]

Evidence of the discontent of the old Whigs in the Democratic party poured in upon Governor Hayes and his advisors. A letter from ex-Senator John Pool of North Carolina is typical. Formerly a

[57] Donald, "Scalawag in Mississippi Reconstruction," *loc. cit.*, 451–460.
[58] William D. Kelley to Hayes, December 17, 1876, Hayes Papers.

Whig and a Unionist during the war, Pool served as a Republican senator from 1868 to 1873, but did not stand for re-election. He was believed to have "the confidence of that element of the new Democratic party who were originally Whigs."[59] After talking with several Southern congressmen he wrote: "I find that I was right in calculating upon these old union Whigs who pursued the same course that I did during the war, but went over to the Democracy upon the questions involved in reconstruction or because of occurrences since. I have known for the last three years that they were dissatisfied with their party affiliations and were held to them only because they could see no satisfactory place to go to. They talk most favorably and resolutely about the present emergency, and see in it an opportunity of uniting the anti-secession and union element in the South against the extremists of the secession school. They have evidently neither forgotten nor forgiven the manner in which unionists in the South were treated by those with whom they are now affiliated." As for the movement to throw the election into the House and prevent the seating of Hayes, proposed by Northern Democrats and supported by some Southerners, he wrote, "I am quite sure I can name twenty odd members on the Democratic side who will make a determined stand against it—and I believe the number may be considerably increased before the time comes."[60]

John Tyler, Jr., complained to Hayes of being repeatedly frustrated by Carpetbaggers and Democrats working together to prevent his efforts to capture the Southern Whigs for the Republicans. Jealous of the influence of the native Whigs in the Republican party councils, as well as their influence over the Negro, the Carpetbaggers made common cause with the Democrats in blocking Republican overtures to Southern Whigs. "Twice in Florida—and so has it been in Virginia—" he wrote, "I have had the old line Whig element of the Democratic Party—one half of the whole throughout the South—in the very act of breaking loose from their present Democratic allies and arraying themselves publicly under our Na-

[59] A. H. Markland to Hayes, January 5, 1877, *ibid.*
[60] John Pool to A. H. Markland, January 4, 1877, *ibid.*

tional banner, when the miserable carpetbaggers in the U.S. Senate, and holding the gubernatorial office, would commence counter games for Democratic support, and take them up the back stairs of the Republican Official House, and instantly break up the whole movement. This has been the way in which the Southern States have become lost to the Republican Party."[61] Tyler's proposals for a new Republican policy toward the South were completely in line with Hayes's ideas: "Avoid the carpetbaggers—draw a true Southern man into your cabinet—a Conservative man who has been opposed to Democratic frauds and Ku-Klux atrocities—some such man as Robert Tyler of Alabama—and address yourself to the material and industrial interests of the South and the entire South will rally to the support of your administration."[62]

For several reasons, not all of them their fault, the Carpetbaggers had become a political liability to the Republican party. The most important of these reasons was their inability to meet the elemental requirement of retaining power, and this in spite of repeated intervention of Federal troops in their support and the backing of Federal patronage. By becoming involved in factional disputes with the Negro or the native white wing of the party, the Carpetbaggers had assisted in dividing Republican ranks in the South and permitting the Redeemers to seize control of state after state. For another thing, the Carpetbaggers had given offense to two elements whose support the Republicans desired. One of these was the old Whigs of the South, and the other was the businessmen, North and South, who blamed the Carpetbagger for the economic and political instability of the region. It is true that the votes of both Carpetbagger and Negro in Congress had proved a prop to the new economic order, but there were those who believed that in this respect the Redeemers would prove quite useful if sufficiently encouraged.

On Southern affairs Charles Nordhoff in the New York *Herald,* a reformer who admitted voting for Tilden, could qualify as something of an expert in view of his well-informed book on the subject

[61] John Tyler, Jr., to Hayes, January 8, 1877, *ibid.*
[62] Tyler to Hayes, February 17, 1877, *ibid.*

published in 1876.[63] He told Charles Foster that if Hayes co-operated with the Whigs and repudiated the Carpetbaggers he would "find it very easy to form a real honest Republican party in the South." Nordhoff believed there should be two Southern men in the new cabinet and that "they should both be *Whigs*." He enumerated as "Whig states" Virginia, North Carolina, South Carolina, Louisiana, Florida, and Arkansas, and declared that in all of them Hayes could "make a respectable party — but only on condition that the carpetbag leaders are dropped entirely."[64] Similar advice came from Oliver H. Dockery, a North Carolina Unionist who had served two terms in Congress as a Republican. "You need live men *of Southern birth — of means — of honesty of purpose* and *integrity of action*," he wrote Hayes. "The old Whig element in the South must and will coalesce and you can help us materially in your selections." Hayes's appointees should be "natives and 'to the manner born' — representative men of their selection of Henry Clay Unionism."[65]

From within the ranks of the Southern Democrats came mutterings of a threatened mutiny against the Northern wing of the party, and these whispers became louder and louder as the electoral crisis drew toward its climax. The prominent railroad lawyer Blanton Duncan, a Democrat from Louisville, wrote Hayes that there were "plenty of conservative men, Whigs and others" in the South who were ready to go over to the Republicans. "Senator Alcorn has had more sense than all the other leaders in Mississippi," he thought.[66] Congressman Casey Young from Memphis publicly expressed his admiration for Alcorn and said that his relations with the senator were "of a most intimate and friendly character." A personal letter to L. Q. C. Lamar from Henry S. Foote, ante-bellum governor and United States senator from Mississippi, found its way into Republican hands and was published in the Washington *National Re-*

[63] *The Cotton States in the Spring and Summer of 1875* (New York, 1876). For Nordhoff's emphasis on Whig survival power in the South, see pp. 15, 37, 92.

[64] Charles Nordhoff to Charles Foster, February 15, 1877, Hayes Papers.

[65] O. H. Dockery, Mangum, N.C., to Hayes, February 19, 1877, *ibid.*

[66] Blanton Duncan to Hayes, December 25, 1876, *ibid.*

publican. An outstanding champion of the Compromise of 1850 against Southern fire-eaters and an opponent of secession in 1860, Senator Foote was again, in 1876, begging conservatives of both sections to join hands against extremists. "I do verily believe," he told Lamar, "that at this moment a bright and golden opportunity is offered to the people of our much-loved section by the election of Mr. Hayes to the Presidency." [67]

The Republican hopes of capturing the Southern Democracy appear less fantastic in the light of earlier than of later events. It had been only four years since, in 1872, the Democrats had virtually disbanded their organization to support Horace Greeley, the Liberal Republican nominee for the Presidency. And it had been the Southern Democrats, Gordon, Watterson, and John H. Reagan, who were foremost in promoting the "New Departure." If the South had been able to swallow Greeley, with all his brands of reformism, socialism, spiritualism, and radicalism and his long record of South-baiting, it was easier to imagine her embracing the conservative and friendly Hayes.

Assisting the work of Kellar, Boynton, and the Republican strategists was a growing breach between Northern and Southern Democrats. "There is a general and open sneering in the South as to the purposes of the Northern Democrats," observed a Republican paper.[68] And it was very true. In large part the bitterness was the result of repeated failures of the Northern wing of the party to lend cordial support to appropriation bills and internal improvement measures of Southern origin — a subject that will be more fully treated in chapters that follow. Another source of bad feeling was the resentment of the politicians against alleged indifference, neglect, or discrimination by Northern Democratic leaders. Though Southern Democrats furnished the great bulk of the party's voting strength and of Tilden's electoral votes, they complained that they were not aided in their campaigns, that their methods of "redeem-

[67] Henry S. Foote to L. Q. C. Lamar, December 31, 1876, in Washington *National Republican,* January 2, 1877.

[68] Editorial in *ibid.,* January 9, 1877.

ing" their states were criticized, and that their support was taken for granted while their wishes and interests were not consulted. Charging that "millions of Democrats in the North" were guilty of "sacrificing us on the ignominious altar of their own ease and comfort and money bags," a Columbus, Georgia, editor raised a question many Southerners were asking "whether prudence and self-interest will not require us to form new alliances — whether we cannot find in another party a conservative element with which to combine." [69]

Friction between state and national Democratic leaders was the cause of trouble in South Carolina. Upon hearing that his candidacy would be embarrassing to Tilden, Wade Hampton wrote the New Yorker offering to withdraw from the race. Receiving no reply, he accepted the nomination but during the campaign wrote Tilden's friend Manton Marble proposing the withdrawal of the Democratic Presidential electors from the race. The electors were not withdrawn, but relations between New York and Columbia continued to be strained, and appeals for campaign funds from the national committee treasury were unsuccessful. Hampton accepted the support of two Republican judges, Thomas J. Mackey and Thompson H. Cooke, who campaigned with him in favor of a Democratic governor and a Republican president, for Hampton and Hayes. Courting the support of Negro voters, Hampton boasted that he was the first white man in the South to advocate Negro suffrage and promised to defend their right against all comers. He preferred to call himself a "Conservative" rather than a "Democrat," to stress the state rather than the national election, and to remain cool regarding Tilden's cause. The outcome of the race was that the Democratic Presidential electors fell behind the state ticket and Hayes and Hampton were the victors. Although the Republican state supreme court recognized Hampton's claim to office, a rival government led by the Carpetbagger Daniel H. Chamberlain retained possession of the state house under protection of Federal troops. Both Republicans and Democrats, of course, claimed the electoral votes for President. The deadlock was to continue throughout the period of crisis. Toward the

[69] Columbus *Times* quoted in Memphis *Avalanche,* December 13, 1876.

end of December Judge Mackey, Hampton's Republican supporter from South Carolina, visited Hayes and presented a letter from Hampton. The conference gave rise to much speculation, but nothing is actually known of its nature except that Hayes was pleased with the results.[70]

Kellar, Boynton, and the W.A.P. group were agreed upon the strategic importance of Tennessee in their scheme. "Tennessee is the most hopeful Southern State," said Joseph Medill. "Her influence if she was with us would be powerful on Arkansas, Georgia, Louisiana, North Carolina, and Kentucky." [71] Tennessee was selected as the first practical proving ground for combining Union Democrats, Whigs, and Republicans in the South. The test was to be made first in the race of Senator David M. Key, whose term expired March 4, to win one of his state's seats in the Senate. Colonel Kellar dropped his important work in Washington before the Christmas holidays and hurried home to take charge of Senator Key's campaign.

Kellar presented Key in his Memphis paper as "the choice of Conservative elements in Tennessee, as represented by the old Douglas Democrats and Bell and Everett Whigs, not only in East Tennessee, but throughout the State." [72] Key's recent speeches in the Senate advocating moderation and a peaceful solution of the electoral crisis had dissociated him from the more ardent Tildenites, and his contest would to some degree test the popularity of his position. He was opposed by the unreconstructed planter-state rights wing of the West Tennessee, cotton-country Democrats led by the secessionist Isham G. Harris, who was seeking election for a full term in the Senate, and James E. Bailey, who was standing for the same seat that Key sought. Colonel Arthur S. Colyar, spokesman of powerful business, railroad, and mining interests of Nashville and East Tennessee and chief of the Whig-industrialist wing of the Democrats, sup-

[70] Hayes Diary, December 30, 1876, in Williams (ed.), *Diary and Letters of Hayes*, III, 396; William A. Sheppard, *Red Shirts Remembered* (Atlanta, 1940), 140–143, 162, 183, 187–197; Hampton M. Jarrell, *Wade Hampton and the Negro, The Road Not Taken* (Columbia, S.C., 1949), 114–120.

[71] Joseph Medill to Richard Smith, February 17, 1877, Hayes Papers.

[72] Memphis *Avalanche*, January 7, 1877.

ported Key's cause before the legislature. Key made an impressive race, winning the entire Democratic and Republican vote of East Tennessee and the solid support of all Republican members. The Whig-Republican combination had proved workable, but it was not quite strong enough to win the race for Key. Kellar and his Republican friends were nevertheless pleased by the showing Key had made and began grooming him for Hayes's cabinet.[73]

In the meantime news from other Southern states had brightened the prospects of Hayes's strategy and strengthened the Senate delegation of ex-Whigs from the South by three new members. Ben Hill, the former Whig who had taken the same position on the Hayes-Tilden contest that Key had announced, was elected to the Senate from Georgia. Garland, the Whig-Democrat governor of Arkansas with whom Kellar was in close touch, won election to the Senate from his state, and the old-line Democrat Lamar was promoted to the Senate from Mississippi. The title of General Matthew C. Butler to his place in the next Senate would depend upon the success of Hampton's government in South Carolina. His prospects looked good. All things considered, the rejuvenation of Whiggery was proceeding at an encouraging pace.

[73] *Ibid.*, January 21, 1877; New York *Times*, January 11, 15, 1877; Louisville *Courier-Journal*, January 19, 1877; Cincinnati *Commercial*, January 20, 1877.

CHAPTER III

The *Quid Pro Quo*

WHAT did the South want? Or rather, what did the men who presumed to speak for the South want? That was the question uppermost in the minds of Colonel Kellar, General Boynton, and Congressman Garfield as they undertook their exploration of the mind of the Redeemers in the winter of 1876–1877. It was plain enough what Hayes and his friends wanted of the South, and it was becoming apparent that the old Whig connection was predisposed to co-operate. But practical politics are not based entirely on appeals to sentiment and tradition, and Hayes and his able advisors were perfectly aware of that fact.

Everyone knew that the Southern Redeemers wanted to rid themselves of the last vestiges of political Carpetbaggery. They had already displayed impressive ingenuity in this endeavor unaided, however, and the political Carpetbagger's days were clearly numbered. Tilden or any other Democratic President could surely be counted upon in this respect. It was absurd to suppose that Hayes could outbid his New York rival on the issue of "home rule." Having promised that much as a minimum he would have to go further in some important respect than did Tilden.

"Just what sort of assurances the South wants," wrote Garfield to Hayes, "is not quite so clear, for they are a little vague in their expressions." He did note that several Southerners had remarked that "in the matters of internal improvements they had been better treated by Republicans than they were likely to be by Democrats."[1] It did not take very long after Kellar arrived on the scene and he

[1] James A. Garfield to R. B. Hayes, December 12, 1876, Hayes Papers.

and Boynton went to work, to clear up the "vagueness" of expression concerning what the Southerners wanted. The answer in brief was, they wanted plenty.

No other ruling class in our history ever found itself in such a plight as that in which the Southerners were sunk in the middle seventies. The inherited wealth that normally sustains an economic elite had been virtually wiped out by the Civil War and its aftermath. The confiscation of more than a billion dollars' worth of slave property without compensation, the repudiation of all Confederate bonds and paper, the denial of war claims for destruction and pillage inflicted by invaders, and the confiscatory taxes levied by the national and state governments in hostile hands had just about completed the work of destroying the old planter aristocracy. Involved in their downfall was the greater part of the financial, commercial, and industrial families of the region. While some of the more energetic of these people were struggling to their feet, the panic of 1873 flattened them out again and the long depression that reached its depths in 1877 kept them hammered down to the margin of desperation.

Writing on "The South, Her Condition and Needs" during the election crisis, J. L. M. Curry noted "a prevailing impression of gloom and grief," and "a hopelessness as to the future" among people of his class and region. "Some have sunk into despair," he wrote, "while others, with more of unsubdued energy, are willing for almost anything to turn up which gives promise or possibility of change."[2] In the hard-bitten struggle to recoup their losses a considerable Southern element, as Curry suggested, seemed desperate in pursuit of the main chance, "willing for almost anything to turn up."

Numbers of prominent Southerners attached themselves to the fortunes of Yankee capitalist adventurers, lending the fame of military reputations as vice presidents, directors, or retainers to Northern corporations that came south in search of profits. Northern railroad

[2] J. L. M. Curry, "The South, Her Condition and Needs," *Galaxy,* XXIII (1877), 544, 548.

and land companies, with the assistance of their Southern retainers, secured handsome subsidies and doles in the shape of bond issues and loans of credit from the Carpetbagger state governments. Charles Nordhoff, who was highly critical of the Carpetbaggers, observed in 1875 that "where conspicuous financial jobbery took place Democrats have, oftener than not, been parties in interest."[3] He was referring especially to the railroad bond issues, which were the main cause of scandal and corruption in the Radical regimes.

There was no plainer indication of the Redeemers' eagerness to co-operate with *economic* Carpetbaggers, Northerners who came South with money to invest, than their drive to repeal the Southern Homestead Act of 1866. That act had changed the Southern land system drastically by reserving all Federal lands for homesteaders only and by putting a stop to cash sales and pre-emption entries. A great blow at speculators and monopolists, the act applied to an empire of 47,700,000 acres, nearly one third of the area of the five public-land states in the South — Alabama, Arkansas, Florida, Louisiana, and Mississippi. With that curious combination of advanced social reform and vindictive persecution, typical of so many Reconstruction acts, the Southern Homestead Act excluded ex-Confederates from homestead privileges for a year at the same time it shut the door on speculators and opened the way for the landless freedman to acquire his elusive forty acres. The act applied exclusively to the South. While it lasted, from 1866 to 1876, there was more homesteading in the region in proportion to the amount of land available than anywhere else in the public-land states. The act did not prove a panacea for the landless freedmen, for few of them benefited from it, but it did stop the speculator — and there was the rub.[4]

As soon as the Redeemers gained places in Congress they began an aggressive movement to repeal the discriminatory land act. Picturing it as an obstacle to the recovery of the South, they maintained that the restricted lands were not suitable for agriculture. The real effect

[3] Nordhoff, *The Southern Cotton States in 1875,* 89.

[4] Paul W. Gates, "Federal Land Policy in the South, 1866–1888," *Journal of Southern History,* VI (1940), 303–310.

of the restriction, they insisted, was to keep out capitalist groups that would otherwise come south and develop the region's rich resources in coal, iron, and timber and incidentally restore the stricken economy to prosperity. A Louisiana Democrat told the House in January 1876 that "in the last four years petition after petition" had come from the South demanding repeal of the land restriction, and an Alabama congressman declared that the people of his state were "almost unanimously in favor of the passage of this bill" repealing the land act.[5]

The opposition to the Southerners' movement for repeal was led by a Northern member of their own party, William S. Holman, a Democrat from Indiana. An old champion of the homestead principle, Holman denounced repeal as a scheme of speculators and land grabbers. He believed it would "enable capitalists to monopolize large portions of the public domain at a price greatly disproportionate to its value," and would end "in the impoverishment and wretchedness of the multitudes."[6] He wished "to extend these laws to all the States and Territories, instead of repealing them as far as they go."[7]

After a long fight the South won enough Northern support to repeal the Southern Homestead Act in July 1876. Southern congressmen were almost a unit for repeal. Only one senator and eight representatives from the South voted against it. All restrictions removed, speculators and timbermen, mainly nonresidents, moved in and bought up great tracts of the best timberlands in the South during the next decade. Their purpose was not to develop these lands but to withhold them from development and await profits or to keep them out of competition with their Northern lands and mills. But this did not become apparent until later.[8]

In the meantime it became more and more difficult after the panic of 1873 to attract Northern capital to the South, or to persuade the

[5] *Congressional Record,* 44 Cong., 1 Sess. (January 14, 1876), 417–418.
[6] *Ibid.* (April 19, 1876), 2603–2604.
[7] *Ibid.* (January 14, 1876), 417.
[8] Gates, "Federal Land Policy in the South," *loc. cit.,* 313–330.

economic Carpetbaggers to carry forward and complete the large operations, schemes, and developments they had launched in better times before the panic. By the winter of 1876–1877 the Yankee capitalists had for the most part suspended or abandoned their Southern operations and fallen back on their home bases to salvage what they could from the ruins of the depression. Carpetbagger state bond issues had been squandered, stolen, or repudiated, and the state governments, now in the hands of the Redeemers, were impoverished or bankrupt.

Carpetbagger capitalists and state treasuries having failed them or proved inadequate to their needs, Southerners were turning to the only remaining hope—the Federal Treasury. By means of appropriations, subsidies, grants, and bonds such as Congress had so lavishly showered upon capitalist enterprise in the North, the South might yet mend its fortunes—or at any rate the fortunes of a privileged elite.

Although the drive for Federal subsidies to improve Southern railroads, harbors, levees, and canals was inspired by enterprisers who sought their own gain, the improvements they demanded often attracted wide support among the mass of people. So it had been in the West in the 1850's and 1860's, when the radical Free-Soil farmers enthusiastically endorsed the demand of the capitalists for Federal subsidies to build the Western railroads and other improvements. No one was more eager for the railroads than the farmers. It was only after they got the railroads and the railroads began to overcharge and mistreat them that the farmers became Grangers and antimonopolists and fought the railroads. In this respect popular sentiment on subsidies in the South of the mid-seventies had arrived at approximately the stage attained in the West two decades earlier. Thus at the very time one finds the West aflame with antimonopoly sentiment and Granger laws aimed at railroad abuses, one finds state granges in the South petitioning Congress in behalf of the subsidy bills of the railroad capitalists. This indulgent spirit among Southern agrarians was not to last long. In fact it changed very quickly after Redemption. But while it lasted the subsidy seekers among the Redeemers and their Northern friends could command an impressive amount of popular support in the South. The Southern white masses had already been persuaded to submerge their differences with the upper class temporarily and follow its leadership in the struggle for Redemption. Along with White Supremacy the Redeemers held up Internal Improvements as part of their bid for the continued allegiance of the poorer class of whites.

Southern spokesmen could point out no end of opportunities for Federal aid and "internal improvements" — projects of such size and scope as to require the resources of the national government. Some of the schemes were of truly national importance and therefore a national responsibility. The fine harbors of Savannah and Mobile, for example, remained choked by wartime obstructions that the government had neglected to remove. The mouths of the Mississippi River, entrance to the nation's greatest internal navigation system, were stopped by mud bars that kept ships of all but shallow draft out of New Orleans Harbor. Whether the discrimination was for that purpose or not, it had the effect of blighting the Southern ports, throwing Southern shipping into Northern hands, increasing Southern freight rates, and forestalling general economic recovery. Even tropical imports that normally would have entered the country through Gulf ports now entered through New York, Boston, or Philadelphia. And bounties for the Northeastern shippers further blocked the opportunities of their Southern competitors.[9]

Flood control in the lower Mississippi was another gigantic task that required the strength of a Federal Paul Bunyan. Wartime neglect or military destruction of the levee system had left millions of acres defenseless against the spring floods that rolled down upon them from the North. Levee construction by individual planters or state commissions, the ante-bellum answer to the problem, was never adequate, and now the problem had got out of hand. More than 28,000,000 acres in Louisiana alone, including the richest planta-

[9] E. Merton Coulter, *The South During Reconstruction, 1865–1877* (Baton Rouge, 1947), 247–251.

tions in the state, were subject to floods. A disastrous flood in 1874 had made thousands homeless in that state and spread destruction through the lowlands of Mississippi, Arkansas, and Tennessee. Great tracts of potentially valuable delta lands remained to be recovered from flood and swamp. The flood-control problem created a great community of interest in Federal aid among the Southwestern states.

Hundreds of smaller operations started in more hopeful days and blighted by depression saw in Federal largess the only hope of fulfillment. Among them were choked canals, fallen bridges, rivers in need of dredging, and, most of all, railroads the South over. The Southern railroad system was embryonic when the war started, and when the war was over the greater part of the existing system was depleted or in ruins. Railroad building during Reconstruction years, characterized by chicanery and waste, had only accomplished a small part of what was desired. Between New Orleans and the immense undeveloped Texas empire, for example, there was as yet no complete railroad connection.

It was more than a coincidence that Mark Twain selected the Southwest as the habitat of his Beriah Sellers, hero of *The Gilded Age,* the novel that gave the period its name. Beriah Sellerses thrived there by the thousand in the seventies and their prayers ascended to Washington in the form of petitions, claims, and appropriation bills. Each of these bills and petitions embodied dreams of recouping lost fortunes, restoring the prestige of fallen family names, and sometimes the prosperity of whole states and regions.

It remained for John Tyler, Jr., the son of a Whig President, to reduce Beriah Sellers's daydreams to a political philosophy and offer it to the nation as a panacea for the depression. Picturing Napoleon III as "the wisest and greatest civil ruler of modern times," he called on American statesmen to "learn from this chapter in the history of France a lesson in the solution of the problem of our financial depression and industrial prostration." He outlined a scheme of South-wide projects. "Let the Government of the United States extend its beneficent arm in behalf of the people in aid of the leveeing of the Mississippi completely throughout its length . . . and in aid of a Southern railroad connection between the waters of the Mississippi River and those of the Pacific Ocean, together with other great enterprises of national import and undoubted national fruition." Among the latter were the Tennessee, Georgia, and Alabama canal transit, "the Inland Coast Canal, sweeping around from Texas to Florida and across, connecting the waters of the Gulf with those of the Atlantic." He was sure that such enterprises "would subordinate all the strife of politics, liberate the hoarded capital of the country, and reanimate the industries of the people, gladdening the national heart." Tyler enclosed a copy of his message in a letter to Hayes, making it clear that he expected the governor to play the part of Napoleon III.[10]

Traditional Jeffersonian and Jacksonian principles against Federal subsidy of internal improvement, one of the main points of difference between ante-bellum Democrats and Whigs, were brushed aside impatiently by Democrats of the postwar Redeemer type. "It is also time," said the Montgomery *News* in 1874, "that the Southern States should become practical in the changed condition of affairs, and no longer hesitate to unite with one voice in asking for the definite and ample assistance of the Federal Government towards their grand work of internal improvement, and especially towards the Southern Pacific Railroad, the most leading of these."[11]

A favorite and telling argument of Southern advocates of the Whiggish program of internal improvements was a comparison of Federal expenditures for public works and improvements in the North and West with those in the South. Official figures from the Treasury Department provided impressive evidence to support the argument that the South had a legitimate grievance over the distribution of these funds. Of the $103,294,501 spent on public works from 1865 to 1873, the South (the eleven ex-Confederate states plus Kentucky) received only $9,469,363. The share of New York State

[10] John Tyler, Jr., to Editor, January 21, 1877, in New York *Tribune,* February 17, 1877; Tyler to Hayes, February 17, 1877, Hayes Papers.

[11] Montgomery *News,* November 29, 1874.

alone was $15,688,222, and that of Massachusetts was $6,071,197. The appropriations were unequally distributed among Northern states also, but that did not make Kentucky happier about her $24,417 as compared with her neighbor Ohio's $1,080,975. Mississippi could not understand why she should receive $136,505 when Maine received $3,030,500, and Arkansas with $49,103 could compare her appropriation with New Hampshire's $1,285,212.[12]

These sectional inequalities, according to the argument, were not confined to the period of Reconstruction, but ran back to the beginning of the government. The total of Federal expenditures in aid of railroads, canals, and wagon roads from 1789 to 1873 was $104,705,173. Of that amount only $4,430,192 had been spent in the Southern states. As a matter of fact, however, $83,354,543 of the whole amount had gone into the Union Pacific and Central Pacific companies to build the transcontinental line through the Western states and territories.[13] The reply of the Southern subsidy seekers was that this huge appropriation, along with lavish donations of public lands, was made while the South was out of the Union to serve Northern and Western interests in which the South did not share. If the Federal Treasury could spare eighty-three millions to lay rails through the uninhabited Western plains, why had the South received less than four and a half millions since the time of President Washington for roads, railroads, and canals, and Texas nothing at all? One important meaning of Redemption, ran the argument, was that the South should at last step in and get her share.

"Would any sane man believe, if that part of the Mississippi River which is able to overflow its banks, ran through northern territory, that the Government would not long ago have taken upon itself the care of building the levees?" asked the New Orleans *Times*.[14] Observing that for fifty of the eighty-four years of national history the South had been the dominant voice in the gov-

[12] Treasury Report on "Public Works in States and Territories," in *Senate Executive Documents,* 43 Cong., 1 Sess., No. 12, p. 59.

[13] *Ibid.,* 18–19, 59.

[14] New Orleans *Times,* January 31, 1877.

ernment of the country, the Nashville *Banner* asked, "What have we to show for this power? A great deal of glory and mighty little plunder. A few tumble down buildings and a gigantic poverty tell the tale of the shirt which was all ruffle." And yet, said the editor, "The village of Kickapoo, in Wisconsin, got an appropriation of two hundred thousand dollars five years after its original settlement." There was food for thought here. "Our statesmen were after glory, those from the north were after something more substantial." The *Banner* was for seeking first the "substantial" things.[15] "Shall we have a share of the crumbs which inevitably fall from the rich man's table?" inquired the Vicksburg *Herald*. "The shower of subsidies to railroads has been something more than a slight mist, and we propose that the South shall hold her dish out to catch whatever may fall her way. We advise governmental aid to the Texas Pacific Railroad, and ask Congress to emulate the example of the late lamented Oakes Ames, and put the money of the people 'where it will do the most good.'"[16]

The trouble was that the South arrived tardily at "the Great Barbecue." She arrived hungry and perhaps a bit greedy and not a little angry at being uninvited—only to find the victuals just about cleaned up. The feasting had been rich and bounteous while it lasted, from about 1865 to 1873, but the South was unfortunately absent during that period. The depression had inaugurated an era of reform, remorse, and morality—moods characteristically reserved by Americans for hard times. The South, a belated reveler, arrived in a mood for tippling while the rest of the country was nursing a hangover. The "late lamented Oakes Ames" whom the Vicksburg *Herald* called upon Congress to emulate was no longer a pleasant memory upon Capitol Hill. Instead, he was the misleader and briber of virtuous congressmen, the symbol of Crédit Mobilier, the most notorious congressional scandal of the Gilded Age. Senators paled

[15] Nashville *Banner* quoted in *The Press and the People. On the Importance of a Southern Line Railway to the Pacific and in Favor of Government Aid to the Texas and Pacific Railway Co.* (Philadelphia, 1875), 46.

[16] Vicksburg *Herald* quoted in *ibid.*, 34.

at the mention of the name of Oakes Ames, and Mr. Garfield did not care to discuss the subject. It was rarely mentioned in polite circles.

Among the reformers who proclaimed that the Great Barbecue was over the Northern Democrats were the most virtuous and abstemious of the lot. They were frankly shocked by the appetites of their returning brethren from the South and inclined to read them lectures on public morality. "Retrenchment and Reform" were the watchwords of the economy-preaching Northern Democrats. Retrenchment meant paring down every appropriation bill, slashing expenses, stopping raids on the treasury, saving every penny possible. Especially it meant voting down railroad subsidies and appropriations for internal improvements. While Republicans were in control of the South the Northern Democrats had voted against appropriations for Southern postoffices, customhouses, river and harbor improvements — even those badly needed — on the theory that the money would fall into the pockets of the Carpetbaggers. But now that the Democratic Redeemers had largely replaced the Carpetbaggers the Northern economizers remained about as tightfisted with their friends as they had been with their enemies.[17]

Samuel J. Randall of Pennsylvania and William S. Holman of Indiana, successive Democratic chairmen of the House Committee on Appropriations, sat athwart the Treasury door and growled at every passer-by. Randall was supposed to have carried his retrenchment doctrine into the speakership, and Holman, who succeeded him as chairman of the appropriations committee, made the doctrine the Democratic party line. "Objector" Holman was an institution in the House, an antimonopolist from way back who fought every railroad land grant, salary grab, and subsidy that came along. His reply to critics of his "two-cent economy" was that it had cut government expenses $25,000,000 during the fiscal year preceding the election of 1876. "No scheme of public plunder has been successful," boasted Holman at the end of the same Congress. "No 'rebel claim'

[17] Albert V. House, Jr., "Northern Congressional Democrats as Defenders of the South During Reconstruction," *Journal of Southern History,* VI (1940), 59, 66–67.

has reached the Treasury, no new offices have been created, but a multitude have been abolished; no salaries have been increased, but a large number have been diminished; no new scheme of public expenditure has been inaugurated, while many have been discontinued."[18]

It was Holman who led the fight against the Southern movement to repeal the Southern Homestead Act, and he was also in the vanguard of the opposition to a renewal of the demand for subsidies and grants to corporations in the name of "internal improvements." Here he clashed head-on again with the Southern wing of his own party. In December 1875, Holman proposed a resolution that henceforth "no subsidies in money, bonds, public lands, indorsements, or by pledge of the public credit, should be granted by Congress to associations or corporations engaged or proposing to engage in public or private enterprise." Coming as it did on the eve of a Presidential election year, when the public was aroused over subsidy scandals of Grant's administration, the Holman resolution passed by an overwhelming vote of 223 to 33. Only two Northern Democrats and a handful of Republicans voted against it. Of the 33 votes against the resolution all but 7 were cast by Southerners, including L. Q. C. Lamar and other leading Redeemers.[19] The last foothold of the political philosophy of the Great Barbecue was the Redeemed South.

Such a chilly reception on the part of their pretended friends, the Northern Democrats, after a painful absence of many years, struck the Southern Redeemers as lacking in the elements of cordiality and good fellowship. They were plainly miffed and showed it. In the estimation of Colonel Andrew J. Kellar of Memphis the Holman antisubsidy resolution "was not only an injustice but an insult to the South, and it was leveled at the Texas and Pacific railroad project," a project in which the colonel was personally interested. "When a practical question like paying a Southern claim, or assisting an internal improvement such as the Texas and Pacific Railroad or the

[18] Israel G. Blake, *The Holmans of Veraestau* (Oxford, Ohio, 1943), 169–171.
[19] *Congressional Record,* 44 Cong., 1 Sess. (December 15, 1875), 227.

Mississippi levees came up," the colonel observed that Holman, like many Northern Democrats, "could be relied on to take the extreme Northern ground of opposition." [20] Other Southerners felt the same way. "It is not to be gainsaid that the Northern Democrats have not acted with fairness and full justice towards the South," remarked the New Orleans *Times*. "They have not done, when they had the opportunity, what they might have done." The editor of the *Times*, incidentally, was Colonel W. H. Roberts, the gentleman who visited Governor Hayes on December 1 and received the reassuring message for Hampton, Lamar, and Gordon. "The very Democrats of the North," said the colonel's editorial, "who aided and acquiesced in voting away hundreds of millions to build Northern railroads, canals, lighthouses, navy yards, docks, workshops, arsenals, forts, and fisheries . . . were suddenly seized with the conviction that they had done wrong the very moment the South asked for a little help, and refused to vote a dollar for Southern levees, railroads and other needs." It was strange indeed that "an excessive fit of economy should have seized the country when the North was gorged and the hungry South was begging a modicum of the same fostering generosity." And the perfidious Democrats of the North were the worst offenders of all, for "a specious 'economy and retrenchment' became the watchwords of the party." [21]

On the other hand the conduct of the Republicans on the question of Southern improvement bills was a subject that interested all but the most blindly partisan. Southern Democrats repeatedly found cordial support for their bills in the Republican Senate or among the Republican minority of the House, only to have the Democratic House Committee on Appropriations turn them down. With more than a suggestion of threat, the New Orleans *Times* declared that "these repeated rejections of similar bills for Southern aid or relief, on the part of a strongly Democratic House may prove at last too much for patient endurance." [22]

[20] Memphis *Avalanche*, January 11, 1877.
[21] New Orleans *Times*, February 24, 1877.
[22] Quoted in Memphis *Avalanche*, March 1, 1877.

The Southern congressmen who set forth in December 1876 to attend the last session of the Forty-fourth Congress left home in a determined frame of mind. "The Southern members of Congress are very wide awake this session," observed a Washington dispatch. "They have concluded not to wait any longer for outside help, but help themselves in the matter of internal improvements. I am able to say, upon the very best authority, that the South in Congress is a unit upon two questions: The first is that they mean to have some system of protection against overflows for the alluvial lands of the states on the Mississippi River, and the second is that they mean, and if constant exertion will do it they intend, to have a Southern railroad across the continent. . . . They mean to have these things."[23]

General Boynton and Colonel Kellar did not have far to seek for the answer to their question, What did the South want? Kellar knew it already, and Boynton could have found out in one evening around the bar of the Ebbitt. Of political Carpetbaggers the Redeemers had had more than their fill and were determined to rid themselves of the remaining ones. Redemption propaganda lumped the idealists with the corrupt adventures as equally obnoxious. But economic Carpetbaggers were a different kettle of fish. The Northern capitalists, who were interested in profits rather than politics, were welcomed cordially, especially the bigger ones, and the more the Redeemers could attract the better. They needed all the capital such men could supply, and when it proved insufficient they wanted the Federal government to make up the deficiency. If state rights and *laissez faire* meant an end to force bills, removal of Federal troops from Southern state capitals, and abandonment of intervention in local politics and race discriminations, the South was for them strong. On the other hand the South had no patience with state rights and *laissez faire* if they implied abandonment of Federal subsidies, loans of credit, and internal improvements. Of these the South believed she had not had anything like her just share and she meant to have a lot more.

[23] St. Louis *Post-Dispatch,* January 15, 1877.

How to get what the South wanted was a more difficult question. Reformers, exposers, and muckrakers were extremely busy in Washington that winter. Boynton himself enjoyed quite a reputation as a reformer. A swarm of congressional investigators and their agents were unearthing gross and shameful corruption in the Departments of Interior, War, Navy, and Justice. Washington was a city of besmirched reputations, and the soiled names included Grant's own family as well as his official family. Former and future speakers of the House, Colfax, Blaine, and Garfield, were among those involved. The phenomenon of moral deterioration was nationwide, not local, and Washington merely epitomized it. The continental looting by the big railroad and mining operators made the better publicized pilfering of Washington politicians seem petty by comparison. Perhaps the offense most discredited by the exposures was the corrupting of politicians to secure government subsidies and grants to big corporations—particularly railroads. Congressmen were understandably sensitive on the subject. Any effort to revive the earlier practices would encounter difficulties. Both Republicans and Democrats had officially forsworn further subsidies.

For all the work of the reformers, however, it was still the Washington of U. S. Grant. Many of the politicians who helped the Gilded Age earn its name were still in office and the old era would not close until March 4—and it might not close entirely even then. General Boynton and Colonel Kellar did not create the atmosphere of Washington during the last months of Grant's rule. But they could not help breathing it and living in it. And it was in that atmosphere that the Compromise of 1877 was framed. It would have been remarkable indeed if the solution of so grave a national crisis, involving the interests and ambitions of so many men and such powerful forces, could have been reached in this atmosphere and remained untouched by it.

By the end of the first week of their collaboration in Washington, Boynton and Kellar had explored the situation sufficiently to arrive at a plan of action. It was of such a nature that it had to be referred to higher echelons—the very highest, in fact. The proposal is contained in a letter from Boynton to William Henry Smith, dated December 20, 1876.

> What we want for *practical* success [wrote the General] is thirty or thirty-six votes. West Tennessee, Arkansas, a large Kentucky element, Louisiana, Texas, Mississippi, and *Tom Scott* want help for the Texas & Pacific Road.
>
> These are strong arguments for making that project an exception to the republican policy of opposition to subsidies — provided the aid is within proper bounds, & properly secured.
>
> The argument may be briefly stated in some such form as this.
>
> 1. It is fair that the South should have a road at the hands of the government as the North has received aid for one.
>
> 2. The country needs a competing line.
>
> 3. The Texas line is below the snow line, has much better grades than the upper route, & has better country for a longer distance from its western terminii [*sic*].
>
> 4. The government needs it to supply its southwestern posts, and to help solve the Indian question.
>
> 5. It has important international bearings running along the border of and topping the richest mineral regions of Mexico.
>
> If such arguments and views commend themselves to Governor Hayes, and Tom Scott, and the prominent representatives of the States I have named could *know* this, Scott with his whole force would come here, and get those votes in spite of all human power, and all the howlings which blusterers North and South could put up. I have never had the least relations with the Texas Pacific lobby. But I know its power here, and see or think I see a way of using it to the best material interests of the country.
>
> If Governor H. feels disposed toward this enterprise as many of the best and most honest men of the republican party do — there would certainly be no impropriety for some recognized friend of his giving *Scott* to understand it. He would go to work without any suggestion whatever.[24]

[24] Boynton to Smith, December 20, 1876, Smith Papers. This is the second of two letters Boynton wrote Smith on this date.

Boynton asked Smith to show his letter to Medill of the Chicago *Tribune* and reported that Kellar was leaving immediately to talk the plan over with Richard Smith in Cincinnati. The general was eager to have the opinion of the inner circle of W.A.P. associates as well as the reaction of Governor Hayes.

Before examining the reaction to the "Scott Plan," as it came to be called, it will be necessary to explore the numerous and wide-ranging forces behind it.

CHAPTER IV

Apotheosis of Carpetbaggery

IN THE WINTER of 1876–1877 Thomas A. Scott was still near the zenith of his Napoleonic career as railroad empire builder. The seat of the Scott empire was Philadelphia, home of the Pennsylvania Railroad. The biggest freight carrier in the world and probably the most powerful business corporation in America at the time, the Pennsylvania moved 31,000,000 tons of freight and reported net earnings of $22,000,000 in 1876, a depression year. It stood astride the heart of the iron, coal, steel, and petroleum districts of the country and stretched out mighty arms in all directions. Vice president of the Pennsylvania for many years, Tom Scott was elected president in 1874 upon the death of his friend J. Edgar Thomson. At the time of his election he had just rejected the presidency of the New York Central and was already president of the Texas & Pacific. He had previously served as president of the Union Pacific and the Atlantic and Pacific, headed two large regional combinations, one in the West and one in the South, and been a director of the Kansas Pacific, the Denver and Rio Grande, and other roads.[1]

Tom Scott first sprang into national prominence at the beginning of the Civil War as Assistant Secretary of War, aged thirty-eight. He earned the admiration and gratitude of President Lincoln by taking over supervision of all government railways and transportation lines and laying the foundation of a working system. According to those who knew him best, Scott was a man of extraordinary charm — affable, friendly, and strikingly handsome. "It was pleasant," wrote his friend John W. Forney, "to note how quietly he met the

[1] New York *Tribune*, May 22, 1881. An obituary of Scott.

leaders of armies and the leaders of the Senate, and how in every circle, no matter what the theme, he was unconstrained and self-poised." According to Forney, Scott "dispatched business with electric facility"; his speeches were "so many flashes of intellect . . . his sentences short, terse, and clear"; and he enjoyed "the capacity of getting rid of difficult questions in a moment."[2]

The uses to which the railroad emperor sometimes put this tremendous power are suggested by a less friendly source. "There is no power in one State," wrote Wendell Phillips, "to resist such a giant as the Pennsylvania road. We have thirty-eight one-horse legislatures in this country; and we have a man like Tom Scott with three hundred and fifty millions in his hands, and if he walks through the States they have no power. Why, he need not move at all: if he smokes, as Grant does, a puff of the waste smoke out of his mouth upsets the legislatures."[3] An illuminating story is told to indicate his power in this respect. After the Pennsylvania legislature had taken the final vote on two railroad bills that Scott was backing a member rose and asked, "Mr. Speaker, may we now go Scott free?"[4]

After his wartime experience as czar of the national railroad system, Scott began to think in continental terms and to dream of making the Pennsylvania the foundation of a huge transcontinental and nationwide monopoly. In 1870 he organized the Pennsylvania Company and as president operated and managed all the numerous lines leased and controlled by the Pennsylvania Railroad lying west of Pittsburgh and connecting it with Chicago and St. Louis. The following year he persuaded the Pennsylvania Railroad to take the lead in the Southern Railway and Security Company for the purpose of controlling tottering systems of the Southeast below Richmond and converting them into traffic feeders for the parent corporation. Turning westward toward the Pacific Coast the same year, Scott thought

[2] Quoted in Edward L. Eames, "The Railroad Men of America," *Magazine of Western History,* X (1889), 209.

[3] Quoted in Henry D. Lloyd, *Wealth Against Commonwealth* (New York, 1898), 147.

[4] Quoted in George H. Burgess and Miles C. Kennedy, *Centennial History of the Pennsylvania Railroad Company, 1846–1946* (Philadelphia, 1949), 344.

he saw an opportunity for a transcontinental connection in the current difficulties of the Union Pacific. He succeeded Oliver Ames as president of the Union Pacific in March 1871, but was disappointed in his hopes of settling the road's troubles and sold out to Jay Gould a year later. One other way lay open to the Pacific — through Texas, New Mexico, Arizona, and California to San Diego — and here also was a means of breaking the transcontinental monopoly that still lay in the hands of the Central Pacific and Union Pacific. The Texas & Pacific Railway Company had been chartered by Congress in March 1871 to build such a road and endowed with the last big grant of public lands the government handed out to railroads. Tom Scott was elected president of the Texas & Pacific in 1872. For the next six years the expansionist ambitions of the Philadelphia railroad king were focused mainly upon the Southwest.[5]

With the southern route to the Pacific, the "32nd parallel route," the illustrious names of John C. Calhoun, Jefferson Davis, and John C. Frémont had been associated in one way or another. The project dated back a quarter of a century in origins to the railroad fever of the early fifties. On February 16, 1852, the Texas legislature chartered a company called the Texas Western, later changed to the Southern Pacific Railroad, to connect with a line from Vicksburg to Shreveport and build westward to El Paso through Marshall and Fort Worth. In spite of a land grant of sixteen sections to the mile of road completed, and the reservation of unsold land in a strip 140 miles across the state, the company managed to complete only 50 miles by 1862. In 1853 a second company, the Memphis, El Paso, and Pacific, was chartered to construct a line north of the other and parallel to it from the Arkansas border westward along the south bank of the Red River through El Paso to the Pacific. It was endowed by the state with an equally large grant of land, but was even less successful in construction, completing only 5 miles and grading 57 miles by the outbreak of the Civil War.[6]

[5] *Ibid.*, 343–348; New York *Times*, May 21, 1881.

[6] Charles S. Potts, *Railroad Transportation in Texas* (Austin, 1909), 32–34; *Texas Western Railroad Company in Connection with the Southern Pacific Railway* (Cincinnati, 1855), 1–6.

Next came the turn of the most romantic plunger of the Gilded Age, the millionaire Abolitionist John C. Frémont. In 1867 he bought up the remains of the old Memphis, El Paso, and Pacific and acquired from Texas the promise of a magnificent principality of 18,200,000 acres of land. Against the land grant he issued $10,000,000 worth of securities and sent agents abroad to sell them. Employing flagrant misrepresentations and fraud, the agents disposed of $5,343,000 worth of bonds, almost all of them to French investors. Upon learning of the crookedness of his agents Frémont took pains to correct some, but not all, of their misrepresentations. The failure of the company in July 1870 plunged Frémont into financial disaster and criminal proceedings by defrauded French bondholders and involved his name in scandal from which it was never fully cleared. The only concrete results of his activities in Texas were six miles of iron rails and three locomotives. By judicial procedures that were later the subject of much criticism, Justice Joseph P. Bradley, acting in Newark, New Jersey, as judge for the United States Circuit Court of the Western District of Texas, appointed John A. C. Gray receiver of the company and turned over its property to him.[7]

At the time the receiver was appointed there was already a bill before Congress to incorporate a new company to build over the same route. Among the incorporators were John C. Frémont, Thomas A. Scott, Grenville M. Dodge, James L. Alcorn, Republican senator from Mississippi, and Joseph R. West, Republican senator from Louisiana. The original act of March 3, 1871, chartering the new company under the name Texas Pacific, was amended the following year and the name was changed to Texas & Pacific Railway Company. As amended, the act empowered the new company to build westward from Marshall through El Paso to San Diego, following roughly the 32nd parallel, and authorized it to purchase the stock and franchises and consolidate with any existing lines along that route. In addition Congress granted to the company twenty alternate sections of land on each side of the road for every mile

[7] Allan Nevins, *Frémont, Pathmarker of the West* (New York, 1939), 587–601; New York *Sun,* April 12, 1878.

completed in the territories of New Mexico and Arizona and ten sections on each side in California. The grant amounted potentially to some 16,000,000 acres. Construction was to begin at both ends, each to complete fifty miles within two years, and the whole was to be completed in ten years.[8]

A few weeks after the Texas & Pacific bill passed Congress a railroad lobby forced a bill through the Texas legislature over the governor's veto granting $6,000,000 in 8 per cent bonds to the two virtually defunct Pacific roads — the Memphis and El Paso and the Southern Pacific and providing that the two-months-old Texas & Pacific should succeed to all the rights and privileges granted the two old companies. The bonds were exchangeable for public land at the rate of twenty-four sections for every mile of road. Since the two roads were already entitled to sixteen sections per mile, they held potential claim to a gift of over 22,000,000 acres of state lands. In his veto message the Republican governor indignantly exposed the graft, showing that it would entail a heavier annual tax than was demanded to support the state government. According to a Texas historian it was the worst measure of Reconstruction "and perhaps the worst ever passed by any Texas legislature."[9]

Shortly after Tom Scott became president of the Texas & Pacific, he set out to acquire the property and franchises of the Memphis and El Paso and the Southern Pacific, as permitted in his charter and the Texas act. The way was opened in the case of the Memphis and El Paso by orders handed down by Justice Bradley sitting as judge of the District of Western Texas. For a consideration of $150,000 in cash to the receiver Gray and thirteen acres of the enormous land grant to each $100 of bonds to satisfy the claims of a large part of the French bondholders, Scott acquired for his company title to the entire property, roadway, land grant, and reserva-

[8] The Texas & Pacific charter as amended is in *Annual Report of the President of the Texas & Pacific Railway Company* (New York, 1872), 13–28; Lewis H. Haney, *A Congressional History of Railways in the United States, 1850–1887* (Madison, Wisconsin, 1910), 123–128.

[9] Charles W. Ramsdell, *Reconstruction in Texas* (New York, 1910), 307–308; Potts, *Railroad Transportation in Texas*, 95.

tion, and other powers and privileges conferred by Texas on the old Memphis and El Paso. The purchase, as Scott correctly pointed out to his stockholders, was enormously advantageous to the Texas & Pacific.[10]

One of Scott's first acts as president was to acquire the valuable services of General Grenville M. Dodge as chief engineer of the Texas & Pacific. Already a man of national prominence, General Dodge was famous as chief engineer of the Union Pacific from 1866 to 1870. He was considered one of the ablest railroad lobbyists of his day. Dodge had retired from Congress in 1869 after serving one term as a representative from Iowa, but kept a hand in national politics. In 1868, 1872, and 1876 he was a delegate to the National Republican Conventions. Scott had tested his capacities as a lobbyist by employing him to win a fight with John W. Garrett of the Baltimore and Ohio over the location of a terminal station in Washington. An intimate associate of General Grant, Dodge discouraged the President's desire to make him Secretary of War in 1869.[11] One of the congressional committees investigating the Crédit Mobilier scandal in 1873 censured the general as the recipient of $24,500 from a fund of the Union Pacific denominated "special legal expenses." Dodge admitted that he was sent to Washington by Scott, then president of the U.P., to secure the passage of a bill, that he did secure it, and was paid for his services, but denied any use of money to influence congressmen.[12]

General Dodge moved his family to Marshall, Texas, in 1872 and threw into his new task the energies that had pushed the first iron rails halfway across the continent. To perform the construction work, he and Scott organized a new company known as the California and Texas Railway Construction Company, modeled in some of its

[10] *Fourth Annual Report of the Board of Directors of the Texas and Pacific Railway Company to the Stockholders, August 10, 1875* (Philadelphia, 1875), 7–9.

[11] Jacob R. Perkins, *Trails, Rails and War, The Life of General G. M. Dodge* (Indianapolis, 1929), 246–247.

[12] Wilson Committee in *House Reports,* 42 Cong., 3 Sess., No. 78, p. xvii; *Pacific Railway Commission Investigation* in *Senate Executive Documents,* 50 Cong., 1 Sess., No. 51, pp. 3810–3811.

features on the Crédit Mobilier of America. The chief stockholders consisted of Scott, Dodge, a favored few of the Texas & Pacific stockholders, and J. Edgar Thomson, then president of the Pennsylvania. The officials of the Texas & Pacific then contracted with themselves as officials of the construction company to build and equip the road. Texas & Pacific stockholders were induced to exchange their stock for construction company shares, as Scott explained, "so that the Construction Company thus became the owner of the entire capital of the Railway Company, except what was held by the members of the Board, as necessary to qualify them to serve as Directors."[13] Reformers declared that an investigation such as was made of the Crédit Mobilier would show that after the passage of the bill chartering the Texas & Pacific "a large number of members of Congress became directly or indirectly interested" in the construction company. But no investigation was made and no facts were produced to sustain the charges.[14]

In their dealings with the government of Texas, Scott and Dodge valued the services of ex-Governor James W. Throckmorton, attorney for the road. An old frontiersman and Indian fighter, Throckmorton had been one of the original incorporators of the Memphis and El Paso. He was an old-line Whig, a Union Democrat in 1860, governor of the state after the war until removed by the Radicals, and afterward a leader of the Democratic party.[15] "I look upon Throckmorton as more valuable to us than any man we have here," General Dodge wrote Scott. "He appears to be devoted to our interests and stands well among the people."[16] The nature of the governor's duties are suggested by a letter he received from Dodge in March, 1873: "How about the Memphis & El Paso Reservation? Will we get this in addition to what the state proposes? . . . It seems to

[13] *Fourth Annual Report of the Board of Directors of the Texas and Pacific Railway Company,* 9–10; Perkins, *Trails, Rails and War,* 248.

[14] New York *Sun,* February 22, 1875.

[15] Claude Elliott, *Leathercoat, The Life History of a Texas Patriot* (San Antonio, 1938), 220–222, 229.

[16] Grenville M. Dodge to Thomas A. Scott, November [?], 1874, letterbook, Box 382, in Grenville M. Dodge Papers, Iowa Historical and Memorial Building, Des Moines, Iowa.

me that you ought to get a fighting force in the legislature and attack everything that comes up until they do us justice. Let them feel us. Attack the extension of time, or try to attack it."[17]

Scott took off to San Diego to make some show of construction work in the West, and Dodge got construction going in Texas in October 1872, using key men from the old Union Pacific outfit. The first objective was fixed by the Texas bond grant, which stipulated that the two roads Scott had acquired must make a junction near Fort Worth by January 1, 1874, in order to earn the $6,000,000 state grant. This meant completing a parallelogram of rails in the northeast corner of the state between Texarkana and Whitesboro in the north and Marshall and Fort Worth in the south. It was a fortunate coincidence that the most valuable part of the land grant the road might earn lay in that region. Dodge wrote Oliver Ames in the fall of 1872 that he had "about 500 miles of road here covered with workmen, shall have nearly 100 miles of it ready for track January 1st."[18] By the following May he had pushed construction westward to Dallas in the south, from a point near Texarkana to Sherman in the north, and connected Texarkana with Marshall. Difficulties slowed the work from the start. Low water in the Red River necessitated the hauling of materials overland 60 to 90 miles from north Louisiana. Then in the spring of 1873 an epidemic of yellow jack crept up from New Orleans to Shreveport and Dallas, depots for construction material, and both towns were put under shotgun quarantine. The fever seized upon the Texas & Pacific construction camps also, decimating the working force and finally leaving Dodge with only one engineer and convict laborers, who preferred yellow fever to prison. Construction came to a virtual standstill.[19]

In the meantime Scott had sailed for Europe to float a bond issue for cash to satisfy the creditors of the construction company and enable it to continue work. Prospects for the bond issue appeared

[17] Dodge to James W. Throckmorton, March 31, 1873, in *ibid.*

[18] Quoted in Perkins, *Trails, Rails and War*, 253.

[19] *Ibid.*, 254; *Third Annual Report of the Board of Directors of the Texas and Pacific Railway Company to the Stockholders, August 11, 1874* (Philadelphia, 1875), 5–7.

to be good. Then came the news of the failure of Jay Cooke and Company and the ensuing "Black Friday" of September 19 that opened the great panic of 1873. Hopes for the bond issue immediately evaporated. Personally involved in some of Jay Cooke's ventures and greatly overextended in his Western speculations, "Scott nearly collapsed mentally and physically, as well as financially," when the crash came. He appealed desperately to Dodge, but the general informed him that the company owed more than a million dollars in Texas and the South and that it would take a half million more to complete construction to Fort Worth in order to earn the Texas bond subsidy. Returning to Philadelphia, Scott found that he was facing ruin. His creditors, however, elected to leave his business in his own hands and permit him to extricate himself if he could.[20]

State subsidies and private credit exhausted or frozen, the only hope Scott had for saving the Texas & Pacific and his own fortunes lay in the Federal Treasury. Unless he could secure Federal subsidies in addition to the land grant, the Texas & Pacific Railroad was doomed to failure. For counsel and assistance in this delicate business, Scott, like the Ames brothers and other officials of the Union Pacific before him, turned to the leading authority on the subject, General Dodge.

Dodge was not encouraging at first. He pointed out that construction in Texas had been hasty and makeshift and was in no condition to undergo inspection by a government commission. Moreover, the Crédit Mobilier investigation had discredited subsidies among the voters and politicians, and both major parties were on record as opposing the policy in the future. Dodge went to see President Grant about the matter but was evidently not satisfied with the interview. "You should see the president yourself," he wrote Scott, "and before he sends his message to Congress. I have had my say with him. Suppose you back it up by suggesting that nothing be said in the message that strikes directly or indirectly at any of the great interests. He might say a kind word for both the northern and southern roads,

[20] New York *Times,* May 22, 1881; Glenn C. Quiett, *They Built the West: An Epic of Rails and Cities* (New York and London, 1934), 320–321.

regretting that the panic had crippled them. At any rate, he should not follow the hue and cry in the west declaring against aid of any kind."[21]

General Dodge set to work with the methods by which he had accomplished great things in the past. Besides his influence with President Grant, there was a large paid lobby at Washington and passes for members of Congress over the Pennsylvania Railroad. "I suppose all the members there have passes," he wrote Scott. "If not I think it would be a good idea to supply those who are of any importance to us."[22] But the old methods did not seem to work as they once did. The trouble was, concluded Dodge, that a deep tide of public opinion had turned against such legislation as the Texas & Pacific wanted. "I do not believe that any plan can be put forward with the hope of success," he told Scott, "until the drift of opinion is different from what it is today."[23] He sought to court public favor through the press of the Northwest, where friendly editors had once eaten out of his hand. "I have tried some of the leading press in the Northwest," he reported, "but they do not take very kindly to it; the fact is the Granger and anti-monopoly element are very powerful and control everything." He observed that "every convention in the Northwest is putting resolutions in their platforms against that class of legislation, so that our fight has got to be made by the combined South and what votes we can get from the middle and eastern states."[24] The main hope lay in mobilizing the South. "The west, northwest and southwest under this raid of the Grangers will be solid against us. . . . We should combine the South and bring it up solid under the leadership of Alexander H. Stephens."[25]

At this point Dodge and Scott set forth on the path which was eventually to cross with that of Governor Hayes and bring them into close touch with the work of Boynton and Kellar. Both groups, the politicians and the railroad men, were seeking favor at the hands of

[21] Perkins, *Trails, Rails and War*, 255–256.
[22] Dodge to Scott, June 16, 1874, letterbook in Box 346, Dodge Papers.
[23] Quoted in Perkins, *Trails, Rails and War*, 257.
[24] Dodge to Scott, June 16, 1874, letterbook in Box 346, Dodge Papers.
[25] Quoted in Perkins, *Trails, Rails and War*, 258.

the South, and both believed themselves able to render services of substantial value to the new rulers of that region. Scott and Dodge, however, had a good two years' start on Boynton and Kellar in the business of reaching an understanding with the Southern leaders.

The campaign by which General Dodge organized the South for the support of the Texas & Pacific was an elaborate and well-financed affair. He had to deal with both Carpetbaggers and Redeemers, but mainly with the latter, for after 1875 only three Southern states remained in Carpetbagger control. He developed a new strategy in his campaign of which he was justly proud. It is best described in a letter he wrote Frank S. Bond, vice president of the road. "There was no success here," he wrote from Washington, "until I changed my whole policy, by reaching men from their homes not in Washington, and let me say to you that all the men who have been brought to us have been brought in that way and not by men who have been here in Washington in our interest and under our pay. . . . The people behind the press at home is what has done this work, and we must continue it in this way. . . . The owners of the road should make up a purse [for] the expenses of this work and it should be put in charge of some very competent man right at Philadelphia who should do nothing but work this up." [26]

The success Dodge enjoyed in bringing the Southern press into line is suggested by clippings from forty-two Southern newspapers published in one of the numerous pamphlets released by the Texas & Pacific in 1875, entitled *The Press and the People.* A sampling indicates that the journals he enlisted were influential and important papers and that they were scattered from one end of the region to the other. The Richmond *Enquirer* declared that "there has been no question since the war so full of interest to the people of the South as the construction of this line." The Norfolk *Day-Book* thought that "Norfolk and her seaport will be greatly benefited thereby. . . . *We want the road.*" "Give us the road, Mr. Scott; give us the road anybody," pleaded the Richmond *Dispatch.* "We are ruined and impoverished, you are rich and prosperous," prayed the

[26] Dodge to Bond, March 1, 1875, letterbook in Box 346, Dodge Papers.

Dallas *Herald*. "Place us on an equal footing with the North in governmental appropriations." The *Methodist Recorder* saw in the Texas & Pacific "the direct Gospel Line to Mexico. Nothing will better prepare the way of the Lord towards that country than a well equipped railway." At the other end of the continent and of the Texas & Pacific route the San Bernardino *Argus* identified itself with the stricken Confederacy and declared it too was exploited by a pitiless "North." "San Francisco and northern California," said the editor, "have reaped a rich harvest from the aid granted to former enterprises, whilst southern California like the Southern States has paid the tribute." [27]

The triumph of which Dodge was most proud was the capture of the National Grange itself, the very seat of the opposition. In July 1874, he secured an endorsement of the Texas State Grange on a circular begging "the co-operation of the various state granges in presenting such a memorial to Congress . . . as will secure favorable consideration and prompt action" on the Texas & Pacific bill. The Kentucky Grange concurred in this action in the fall and so did numerous local lodges.[28] Finally the National Grange, meeting in Charleston under Southern influence, endorsed the Texas & Pacific and petitioned Congress for "reasonable aid to the company." [29] Writing to Vice President Bond of his coup, Dodge boasted, "The fact that I was enabled to carry the National Grange shows what can be done by careful hard work." [30]

The Texas & Pacific forces descended next upon the legislatures of the Southern states seeking formal resolutions or endorsements. Again their methods seemed irresistible. State action usually took the form of a joint resolution of the two houses "instructing the senators and requesting the representatives" in Congress to vote for

[27] All newspaper quotations in this paragraph are taken from *Press and the People*, 25–47.

[28] *Resolutions of the Legislatures, Boards of Trade, State Granges, Etc., Favoring Government Aid to the Texas & Pacific Railway* (Philadelphia, 1874), 35–38.

[29] *House Miscellaneous Documents*, 43 Cong., 2 Sess., Doc. No. 89 (February 20, 1875).

[30] Dodge to Bond, March 1, 1875, letterbook in Box 346, Dodge Papers.

the Texas & Pacific subsidy. Resolutions were passed by the Texas and Mississippi legislatures in this form in the spring of 1874. Missouri, Tennessee, and Alabama followed suit in January and February, 1875. Florida's action took the form of a petition to Congress. In Arkansas, Georgia, North Carolina, and South Carolina favorable action was taken by one of the branches of their legislatures.[31] The only state legislatures of the former Confederacy failing to oblige Dodge with resolutions were those of Louisiana, still under the Carpetbaggers, and Virginia, where the influence of the Baltimore and Ohio and other of Scott's rivals was strong. The stiff opposition encountered in the West made the compliance of the Southern legislature all the more striking. "All the conventions out here," wrote Dodge from Council Bluffs, "so far both republican and democrats have put clauses in their platforms against subsidies or loans of credit, except the Iowa Rep. convention." [32]

The names of the old Confederate chieftains carried too much prestige to be neglected by any interest that sought Southern favor in the days of Redemption. Dodge once hoped to use Alexander H. Stephens as a front for his Southern drive and did acquire his warm support. Favorable co-operation was secured from both Stephens and Jefferson Davis. Public letters from one old captain to another appeared in the Southern press. General Pierre Gustave Toutant Beauregard addressed one to General John B. Gordon taking to task Senator John W. Johnston of Virginia for resisting the movement in his state to endorse the Texas & Pacific in spite of "the irresistible array of facts going to show that the bill asking Government aid before the last Congress had the endorsement of the public sentiment of the South and Southwest, through legislative bodies, chambers of commerce and boards of trade, of I believe, all the Southern States." [33] And ex-Senator R. M. T. Hunter of Virginia penned

[31] *Press and the People,* 6–10. The distinction between "instructing" the senators and "requesting" the representatives was due to the election of the senators by the state legislatures.

[32] Dodge to Frank S. Bond, July 28, 1875, letterbook in Box 346, Dodge Papers.

[33] Beauregard to Gordon, September 9, 1875, in Richmond *Dispatch,* September 17, 1875.

another to L. Q. C. Lamar contending that "the question is large enough and of an interest sufficiently common to animate the whole south to common deliberation and common efforts, for it is one not only of a large pecuniary interest, of trade and commerce, but of empire also." [34]

Chambers of commerce, boards of trade, and cotton exchanges of the Southern cities were the most outspoken and articulate allies of the Texas & Pacific forces. And it must be admitted that the railroad spokesmen held out to the civic bodies attractive and plausible inducements. They pictured their movement as a concert of cities united to break the strangling grasp of a Northern monopoly that diverted traffic with the West through New York and Chicago, discriminated against them in freight rates, retarded their recovery, drained the lifeblood of commerce from the veins of the region, and blighted the Gulf and South Atlantic ports. Impressed by such arguments, the chambers of commerce in New Orleans, Memphis, Nashville, Louisville, Augusta, Atlanta, Richmond, Macon, and Vicksburg petitioned Congress for passage of the Texas & Pacific bill.[35]

In an ingenious and shrewd manner the railroad propagandists dovetailed the aspirations of the Southern cities with those of the Middle West. St. Louis, Kansas City, Cincinnati, Cairo, and other cities of the upper Mississippi Valley were currently engaged in a war of succession with the Northeastern seaports to wrest from them the regency of the Cotton Kingdom. Aided by legislation making them direct ports of entry, by the westward shift in cotton growing, by new railroad developments, as well as by greater geographical access, the Middle Western merchants were aggressively dominating the Southern markets with their "Knights of the Bag" and driving out their Eastern competitors. They were therefore eager to please their Southern customers and especially willing to encourage a movement to weaken Eastern control.[36] Their chambers of commerce willingly petitioned Congress in behalf of the Texas & Pacific bill

[34] Hunter to Lamar, in *Railway World,* II (February 12, 1876), 103.

[35] *Press and the People,* 14.

[36] George Woolfolk, "The Cotton Regency: The Northern Merchants and Reconstruction, 1865–1880" (Ph.D. thesis, University of Wisconsin, 1947), 229, 313–314.

along with those of the Southern cities. "The whole South and West," declared the St. Louis *Daily Globe,* "should act as a unit in this matter." And the Kansas City *Times* went so far as to assert that "the South and Southwest are a unit on the subject."[37]

It was perfectly clear to Scott and Dodge, however, that they did not have the Southern field to themselves. Disputing that field and the control of Congress as well was the Central Pacific and its general agent and vice president, Collis P. Huntington. The Californians had organized the Southern Pacific Company in 1865 to build south from San Francisco in order to shut out competitors from the state. On the alert when Congress chartered the Texas & Pacific, their lobby managed to squeeze into the act a clause authorizing the Southern Pacific to build south via Los Angeles and connect with the new road at or near the Colorado River, the boundary between Arizona and California. Since this construction would make it necessary for Scott to parallel the Southern Pacific line for a couple of hundred miles from Fort Yuma to San Gorgonio Pass, it was assumed that rather than attempt that he would depend upon the California monopoly for access to the coast. Not content with the scheme to stop Scott at the California border, Huntington sought also to prevent him from challenging the transcontinental monopoly by building a competing line from Texas. If that line was to be built, Huntington was determined that his own Southern Pacific would build it. To give a thin disguise to the monopoly, Huntington, who was the most prominent official of both Central and Southern Pacific companies, resigned as president of the latter and separated the management of the two firms. In command of Huntington's Washington lobby, performing the services for him that General Dodge performed for Scott, was General Richard Franchot, who, according to Huntington, "had a good many people in his employ." The primary objective of the Central Pacific lobby was to defeat Scott's efforts to obtain a Federal subsidy and complete his Texas & Pacific line. Huntington had already started to build south from San Gorgonio Pass to head off Scott, but more than that he

[37] Quoted in *Press and the People,* 37, 39.

was asking Congress for permission to continue his construction eastward from the California border over the route assigned the Texas & Pacific to meet Scott on his way west. He pointed out that Scott had not been able to get so far as Fort Worth and was still some 1500 miles from San Diego, where no construction had been completed. Moreover, Huntington promised to complete his construction without the benefit of any financial subsidy such as Scott demanded, though he hoped to get the benefit of Scott's land grant.[38] "I propose to say to Congress," wrote Huntington to David D. Colton, " 'We will build east of the Colorado to meet the Texas P. without aid,' and then see how many members will dare give him aid to do what we offer to do without. My only fear then would be the cry that the C.P. and the S.P. was all one and would be a vast monopoly, etc." [39]

Both Scott and Huntington recognized the South as the strategic battleground of the war to control Congress. "Scott is making the strongest possible effort," observed Huntington in September 1875, "to pass his bill the coming session of Congress. He gets every little gathering in the South to pass resolutions favoring the Texas Pacific bill . . . then he is promising a connection with all the broken-down roads in the South with a promise of money to help them all if his bill passes." [40] Since Scott was "promising everything to everybody," and the Southerners were "so very poor that many of them will hold to Scott in hopes he may do something for them," Huntington was alarmed at the strides his rival was making.[41] "I get letters from Washington nearly every day," he reported to Colton, "that almost everybody is for Scott's Texas Pacific bill, and that he,

[38] Lewis B. Lesley, "A Southern Transcontinental Railroad into California: Texas and Pacific versus Southern Pacific, 1865–1885," in *Pacific Historical Review,* V (1936), 52–60; Stuart Daggett, *Chapters on the History of the Southern Pacific* (New York, 1922), Chapters I–VIII.

[39] Collis P. Huntington to David D. Colton, November 8, 1875, in Chicago *Tribune,* December 27, 1883. Many of Huntington's letters to Colton are also printed in a government document (*Senate Executive Documents,* 50 Cong., 1 Sess., Doc. #51, Part 8, pp. 3707 ff.), but names are frequently deleted.

[40] Huntington to Colton, September 27, 1875, in Chicago *Tribune,* December 27, 1883.

[41] Huntington to Colton, December 12, 1875, *ibid.*

Scott, is sure of passing it, but he won't do it."[42] In the meantime Huntington was taking strong countermeasures. "I have set matters to work in the South that I think will switch most of the South off from Tom Scott's Texas and Pacific bill," he wrote in the spring of 1875. "I am having articles written and set afloat."[43] By November he could report, "I am getting the South well waked up on Scott's Southern-Northern project."[44]

The antagonists swapped blow for blow in the Southern press and on the platform. In reply to the Texas & Pacific charge that the Southern Pacific and Central Pacific were really one and the same and that both were part of a gigantic monopoly, the Huntington spokesmen replied that the Texas & Pacific was but another name for the Pennsylvania Railroad and that Scott was merely seeking access to the Pacific Coast for the Philadelphia monopoly. Was not that the meaning of a proposed branch to St. Louis, western terminus of the Pennsylvania-controlled system, and of the existing connection at Texarkana with the St. Louis and Iron Mountain Railroad? It was a scheme to "slew" the whole line northward and by-pass the South. After all, why should Scott wish to build a line in the South to compete with his own road in the North? And what assurance did the river port cities of the lower Mississippi have that their promised branches would not be forgotten once their political support had served its purpose? Scott's Texas & Pacific, with all its fancy features, large pretensions, and small achievements, looked to some Southerners more like a "carpetbag" line than it did a "trunk" line. Were not the features of land grabbing, "construction company," state bond issues, pressure lobbies, salaried Scalawags, and corrupted legislatures familiar to all Southerners who had followed the history of Carpetbag "developers" in Alabama, Georgia, and North Carolina? Then why should the great Philadelphia Carpetbagger deserve any more support from the South for his Southwestern jobbery than less powerful Carpetbag operators earned

[42] Huntington to Colton, December 27, 1875, *ibid.*
[43] Huntington to Colton, April 7, 1875, *ibid.*
[44] Huntington to Colton, November 24, 1875, *ibid.*

for their schemes in the Southeastern states? What was the difference, other than the fact that Scott had more money than the others? Were they not all Carpetbaggers?

The suspicions implanted in the South by Huntington's men found reflection in a convention of Southern railroad promoters and civic leaders held in Memphis on November 19, 1875. Delegations from Arkansas, Tennessee, Mississippi, Louisiana, South Carolina, Alabama, and Missouri were in attendance. The main business before the meeting, aside from much oratory, was a movement to make sure that the Texas & Pacific did not by-pass the South and locate its terminus to the northward. Judge J. W. Clapp, temporary chairman, implored the convention "to lay down as a sine qua non that Memphis shall have her branch." And Jefferson Davis, who "was greeted with long repeated and vociferous cheers . . . favored Vicksburg as the eastern terminus on the Mississippi River." Spokesmen of New Orleans were present to defend her interests. The upshot was a resolution asking the aid of Congress for the Texas & Pacific and for "the construction of such railways as will connect the eastern terminus with the cities of Memphis and of Vicksburg, and New Orleans."[45]

As the Texas & Pacific scheme snowballed over the years, the branch-road aspect assumed more and more importance. So far as Scott's purposes were concerned the branches were only an additional concert of interests organized for pressure on Congress. These interests included holders of shares in bankrupt companies or "paper roads" with neither rails nor rolling stock; hundreds of landlocked towns scattered along proposed routes and dreaming of the "great day"; congressmen through whose districts the routes ran; eight states and three territories directly touched by trunk line and branches, and the hinterland of Eastern states whose traffic would be tapped. Together they constituted a formidable network of civic hopes and private cupidity.

[45] Memphis *Avalanche,* November 20, 1874; St. Louis *Globe-Democrat,* November 20, 1875; *Scott's Texas Pacific Bill. Ought it to be Passed?* (n.p., n.d.), in John Crerar Library, Chicago.

On the map the southern branches resembled the prongs of a huge trident whose shaft stretched across from the Pacific and whose three easternmost points speared the Mississippi River at the equidistant points of Memphis, Vicksburg, and New Orleans. A fourth branch left the projected trunk line of the Texas & Pacific in western Texas and wandered off in the general direction of St. Louis. The map facing this page indicates the proposed eastern branches as well as their strategic connections.

The Memphis branch of the Texas & Pacific, a line of more than 300 miles diagonally across Arkansas from Marshall, Texas, would parallel a line already in operation. The existing line was capable of handling what traffic there was. Built by private capital and none too prosperous, it would be thrown into competition with a line subsidized by the government. The new line, moreover, would shorten the existing route only a very few miles. The significant thing about the projected Memphis branch was the company incorporated to build over its route, the "Memphis, Pine Bluff & Shreveport Railway (Projected) Company." Among the company's directors were the two Carpetbagger senators from Arkansas, Stephen W. Dorsey, whose term of office expired March 3, 1879, and Powell Clayton, whose term was up March 3, 1877. Senator Dorsey served as president of the company. Two other directors of prominence were Colonel Andrew J. Kellar of Memphis, able colleague of General Boynton in the delicate Washington mission of 1876–1877, and Thomas A. Scott himself. The Memphis, Pine Bluff & Shreveport was, in short, a replica of one of Beriah Sellers's pipe dreams — but with more influence in the U. S. Senate than Mark Twain's hero managed to muster.[46]

The Vicksburg branch, containing what Davis considered the proper terminus of the Texas & Pacific and for which he spoke in the Memphis convention, was a line of 170 miles across northern Louisiana from Shreveport to Vicksburg. The line was pictured as

[46] Henry V. Poor, *Manual of the Railroads of the United States, 1875–76,* 714–715; *Railroad Gazette,* IX (January 19, 1877), 30; New York *Times,* January 22, 1877; Chicago *Tribune,* January 17, 1877.

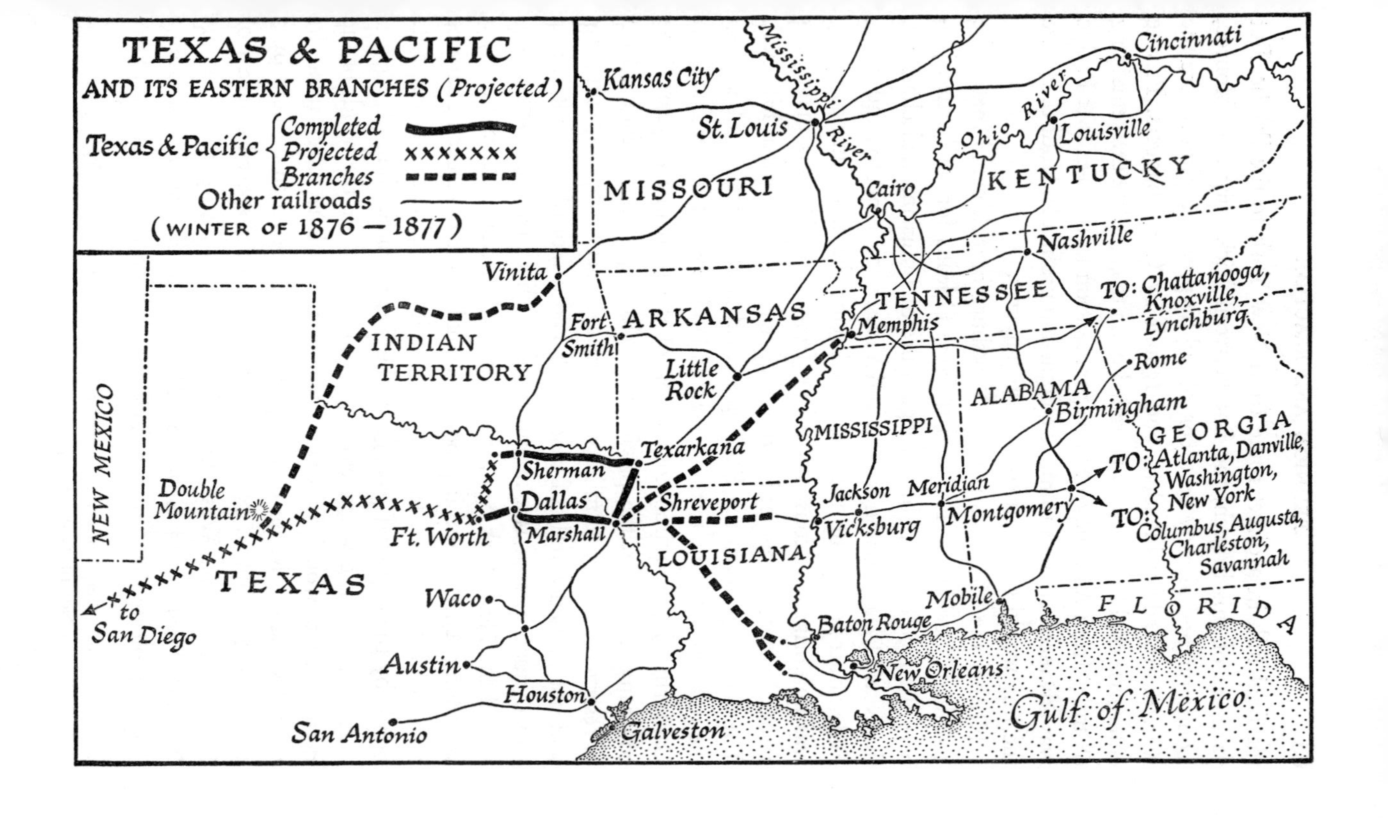
TEXAS & PACIFIC
AND ITS EASTERN BRANCHES (Projected)
Texas & Pacific
Completed
Projected
Branches
Other railroads
(WINTER OF 1876 — 1877)
Kansas City
St. Louis
Mississippi River
Cincinnati
Ohio River
Louisville
KENTUCKY
MISSOURI
Cairo
Nashville
TENNESSEE
TO: Chattanooga, Knoxville, Lynchburg
Vinita
Fort Smith
ARKANSAS
Memphis
INDIAN TERRITORY
Little Rock
Rome
ALABAMA
Birmingham
GEORGIA
NEW MEXICO
MISSISSIPPI
Texarkana
Sherman
TO: Atlanta, Danville, Washington, New York
Double Mountain
Dallas
Shreveport
Jackson
Meridian
Ft. Worth
Marshall
Vicksburg
Montgomery
TO: Columbus, Augusta, Charleston, Savannah
LOUISIANA
TEXAS
Waco
Mobile
FLORIDA
to San Diego
Baton Rouge
Austin
New Orleans
Houston
Gulf of Mexico
San Antonio
Galveston

the final link in a direct route from New York to the Pacific. But 72 miles of this branch, the line between Vicksburg and Monroe, Louisiana, had already been completed by private capital before the war, destroyed by invaders, and rebuilt by Carpetbaggers. Private enterprise could reasonably be relied upon to complete the remaining 98 miles from Monroe to Shreveport as soon as the Texas & Pacific was advanced enough to make completion profitable. Until that time the line would be of dubious worth anyway.

Neither the Memphis nor the Vicksburg branch could match the so-called "Backbone" Railroad to New Orleans for unabashed jobbery. In 1869 the Republican legislature of Louisiana had chartered the New Orleans, Baton Rouge, and Vicksburg Company, and in the Federal act setting up the Texas & Pacific the Louisiana company was authorized to construct a line from New Orleans diagonally across the state for 320 miles to connect with Scott's road at Marshall. The act also granted the Backbone Road twenty sections of land to the mile on the same terms it granted land to the Texas & Pacific in California, but required completion of the road in five years. The company was given the privilege of selecting its land from a strip of reserved territory 80 miles wide. Since the act of 1871 the company had not graded a mile of roadbed or laid a foot of rail, but it had issued quantities of stocks and bonds. "This imaginary road," observed the New York *Sun,* "was regarded in Louisiana as merely a swindling scheme, and it probably would never have been heard of again had it not been for the opportunity afforded to galvanize its bonds by the expected passage of the Texas Pacific bill." [47]

A government guarantee of 5 per cent interest on the bonds of the defunct road would naturally have a miraculous effect upon its worthless paper. Much of this paper was reported to be held by a Carpetbagger ring in New Orleans and to be a special concern of Senator Joseph R. West, one of the original incorporators of the Texas & Pacific, and Governor William Pitt Kellogg. The Dodge Papers indicate that Senator West took a keen interest in the move-

[47] New York *Sun,* January 16, 1877; *House of Representatives Reports,* 45 Cong., 2 Sess., Report No. 1018, pp. 1–3.

ment for a Federal subsidy.[48] General Dodge hoped that Scott was not "under such obligations" as to require him to incorporate the Louisiana branch in his bill, for "the cleaner the bill is left . . . the stronger it will be." However, he added, "If Louisiana has strength enough to put that section in then we can have no objection to it."[49] After all, Senator West of Louisiana was chairman of the Senate Railroad Committee. In 1876 a rival company, the New Orleans Pacific Railroad, was organized to build over the same route and sought to replace the Carpetbagger company as builder of the New Orleans branch of the Texas & Pacific and as recipient of Federal subsidies in Scott's bill. Directed by "prominent citizens of New Orleans who have the confidence of the people," endorsed by the president of the New Orleans Cotton Exchange, and aligned with the Democrats and Redeemers, the new company pressed its cause upon Congress and upon Scott with growing confidence as hopes for Louisiana's Redemption and the Carpetbaggers' downfall gained ground.[50] But whether the cause of the Carpetbaggers or that of "home rule" won out in Louisiana in 1877, the Texas & Pacific would have strong support in the state.

General Dodge adopted the same pragmatic view toward a fourth branch seeking incorporation in the Texas & Pacific bill that he had toward the others. This was projected to start at Double Mountain, a point some 200 miles west of Fort Worth on Scott's unfinished route, and wander for 436 miles northeastward through unsettled Texas plains and through the unsettled Indian Territory to Vinita, where the Atlantic and Pacific and the Missouri, Kansas and Texas lines intersected. Forth Worth was already connected by rail to Vinita by way of Dallas, or would be as soon as Dodge pushed his trunk line that far west. The branch was thoroughly indefensible from the viewpoint of railway economics or common sense, for the greater part of it would run through country where trade and settle-

[48] Dodge to Scott, December 25, 1874, letterbook in Box 346, Dodge Papers.

[49] Dodge to Scott, December 4, 1874, *ibid.*

[50] See petition in *Congressional Record,* 44 Cong., 2 Sess. (January 30, 1877), 1118.

ment were forbidden by law. When an alteration in the branch was proposed, however, a large group of Missouri interests threatened to desert the Texas & Pacific coalition. "This matter will have to be settled immediately," Dodge informed Scott, "or it will burst us. We cannot get along without Missouri. . . . They claim that they control 25 votes every one of which will be against us if this change is made."[51] So the "Vinita Branch," connecting St. Louis—and the 25 votes—with the Texas & Pacific and its congressional fortunes became a permanent part of the Scott coalition. "Each branch," observed the *Nation,* "represents so many Congressional Districts and so many votes, and it represents so many thousand tons of iron which are to be manufactured in so many other districts which have so many more votes."[52] It was inevitable that General Boynton should learn of this coalition of Southern interests in his search for a solution to the political crisis.

Overshadowing all of Scott's earlier demonstrations of pressure and publicity was the National Railroad Convention held at St. Louis on November 23 and 24, 1875. Invitations were issued by a mass meeting of St. Louis citizens who appeared as the formal sponsors of the convention and made preparations for entertainment of the delegates.[53] Claiming it to be "the largest convention of representative men ever held in the West," convention officials listed 869 accredited "delegates" attending as representatives of 31 states and territories. Texas sent a delegation of 159, Kentucky 74, Georgia 54, Tennessee 30, Louisiana 26, and the other Southern states smaller numbers. Mayors or officials of 76 cities and towns and representatives of 22 trade organizations, 4 state granges, and the National Grange were recognized as members. Decorating the assembly hall were banners reading, "The Grange Railway—The Texas Pacific," "Westward the Star of Empire Takes its Way," "Twenty Millions

[51] Dodge to Scott, January 12, 1875, letterbook in Box 346, Dodge Papers.

[52] *Nation,* XXIV (January 11, 1877), 24.

[53] *Southwestern Pacific Railroad: Address to the People of the United States Calling a National Convention in Saint Louis on the 23d of November, 1875, to Take Action in Favor of a Southwestern Pacific Railroad, Together with Letters from Leading Citizens Upon the Same Subject* (St. Louis, 1875).

of People Seek an Acceptable Route to the Pacific," "There is the East—There is India." One delegate from Tennessee "rejoiced to see General Sherman and General Johnston walk up and shake hands" and suggested that "any Commanding General on either side in the late war will be requested to take a seat upon the platform." Whereupon another member protested that "if a motion of this sort were to prevail, there wouldn't be room enough on the platform to accommodate all the Generals here present." A motion was carried, in spite of "several voices in the negative," inviting Jefferson Davis to take a seat on the platform. Davis declined with thanks, saying, "I am Chairman of the Mississippi delegation; my functions are to be performed off the platform."[54]

For the more history-minded delegates the convention awakened echoes of similar conventions in the past and stirred memories of historical movements of which the St. Louis convention was, in truth, a continuation. In November 1845, three decades earlier, the Southwestern Convention assembled at Memphis, presided over by John C. Calhoun. The great Carolinian, in his last bid for the Presidency, sought to ally the South and West upon a program of internal improvements that included work on the Mississippi and other Western rivers and harbors as well as a system of railroads connecting the Mississippi Valley with the South Atlantic seaports. Then in October 1849 a Pacific Railroad Convention met in St. Louis, with Stephen A. Douglas as president and Thomas H. Benton a prominent participant. Its purpose was to crystallize sentiment for a Federal subsidy of a railroad to the Pacific Coast by a central route, with Chicago, St. Louis, and Memphis as the eastern termini. In the 1840's as in the 1870's the eastern terminus of the Pacific road was a point of controversy. Another convention five days after the adjournment of the St. Louis meeting of 1849 met in Memphis to canvass the problem of the eastern terminus.[55] The same question was the

[54] *Proceedings of the National Railroad Convention at St. Louis, November 23 and 24, 1875, in Regard to the Construction of a Southern Transcontinental Railway Line from the Mississippi Valley to the Pacific Ocean* (St. Louis, 1875), vii–viii, 45–57; St. Louis *Globe-Democrat*, November 24, 1875.

[55] Robert R. Russel, *Economic Aspects of Southern Sectionalism, 1840–1861* (Ur-

primary concern of the Memphis convention of 1875 that met four days before the St. Louis convention of that year. In both cases the upshot was a compromise upon multiple termini.

Southern members of the 1875 convention recalled that a railroad to the Pacific had been one of the South's great objectives in the sectional struggle of the fifties. In at least three of the Southern Commercial Conventions between 1852 and 1859 the Pacific railway was placed first over all remedies for the region's troubles. "This was the great panacea," said the New Orleans *Delta* after the convention of 1853, "which is to release the South from its bondage to the North, which is to pour untold wealth into our lap; which is to build up cities, steamships, manufactories." [56] The railroad to the Pacific was part of the struggle for control over the Western territories, and part of the contest for sectional balance of power; it was behind the Kansas-Nebraska Act and the repeal of the Missouri Compromise. And like nearly all else in the fifties it was deeply involved in the slavery controversy. The main barrier to the southern route was removed in 1853 by the Gadsden Purchase, which opened the Gila River route. Congress remained deadlocked over the Pacific railroad question, however, until secession. Then while the South was absent from the Union the route was chosen without regard to her interests.

Isaac H. Sturgeon, who participated in the calls for the St. Louis conventions of both 1849 and 1875, pointed out that the Pacific route was still a great sectional issue, but he hoped that in 1875 the issue would be used to reconcile instead of embitter the divided sections. Other members reminded the convention of Jefferson Davis's report of 1855 demonstrating the superiority of the 32nd-parallel route over that adopted by the Union Pacific and Central Pacific. And Mr. Davis was on hand to defend his report.[57]

---

bana, Illinois, 1924), 124–126; *Proceedings of the National Railroad Convention at St. Louis,* 110.

[56] Robert R. Russel, *Improvement of Communication with the Pacific Coast as an Issue in American Politics, 1783–1864* (Cedar Rapids, 1948), 25–26. The *Delta* was being ironical, of course.

[57] Sturgeon quoted in *Southwestern Pacific Railroad: Address to the People of the United States Calling a National Convention,* 10–11.

The president of the convention of 1875 was Stanley Matthews of Cincinnati, kinsman of Governor Hayes, uncle of Henry Watterson, counsel of Colonel Scott, and later a prominent figure in the Compromise of 1877. In an "Address to the People of the United States," signed by Matthews, the convention heartily endorsed the plan of Federal subsidy desired by the Texas & Pacific. This plan took the form of a government guarantee of 5 per cent interest in gold on the railroad bonds issued up to the limit of $40,000 per mile. And the mileage, including the various branches, ran over 2000. Matthews's "Address" did not neglect the interests of the allied branches of the Texas & Pacific, which were the concern of the preliminary Memphis Convention.[58] There was a resemblance between the St. Louis railroad convention and the great national conventions of the political parties in the way local interests, sectional alliances, and personal pressures were woven together.

Another historic note struck by Scott's convention was that of Manifest Destiny, a Southern emotion of the fifties. One veteran of the Mexican War recalled "the mineral wealth that lay there untouched and under the clumsy management of Mexican machinery" and said that "a railway to Mexico would bring us the trade of sixty millions a year." Another delegate called the Texas & Pacific "the road to India," "the track of Columbus" by which "Christian civilization" was "marching westward with the star of empire" until "it shall have encircled the globe."[59]

Stanley Matthews pictured Scott's project as an act of economic statesmanship and a panacea for the national depression. "It will rekindle the fires and start the machinery in furnaces and foundries East and West," he said, "giving profitable employment to an army of idle men, either in the construction of the work or in the preparation of material." But most important of all, it would bring the real reconstruction that the South needed and awaited. "It will resurrect and rehabilitate the South, by pouring through that fertile but distracted region of our country a perpetual tide of the world's com-

[58] *Proceedings of the National Railroad Convention at St. Louis,* 16–18.
[59] *Ibid.,* 37, 64–65.

merce, vitalizing its railroad system, and reviving its paralyzed industries." Scott's bill "would be the great healing act of Federal legislation, giving assurance that the people of the Union and their common representatives . . . know no sections in the country, no divisions among the people." [60]

"Our promised land is before us," declared Colonel E. N. Hill of Arkansas; "we stand upon its borders ready to enter in and take possession." And it looked as if Moses were coming along this time. "That this is so," added the Colonel, "we owe, as I said before, to the energy, ability and will of Thomas A. Scott. Let us, then, one and all, 'hold up his hands' in the work, each of us to the best of his ability." [61] The convention appointed a committee to lay its conclusions before the Forty-fourth Congress.

Meanwhile, General Dodge had been giving careful attention to the task of "organizing" (as he put it) the new Congress. He had failed to carry the Forty-third Congress, but felt more confident about the Forty-fourth, which would expire March 4, 1877. "I have been looking after the organization of the next House," he wrote Vice President Bond, "and the Southern members should be brought right up to the point of determining that whoever are officers of the next House shall be friends of the Bill. I have already made a good many friends among the new Senators. We shall be far stronger in the Senate next winter than we are today." [62] He was somewhat concerned, however, over the current preoccupation of Southern politicians with Redemption and partisan matters that diverted their attention from the business at hand. "I do not like the way in which the Southern Democrats talk," he confided to Bond. "They are looking forward to the Presidency and unless we can concentrate them on the Officers of the House and on the Committee your fight will be a hopeless one. If they have interest enough in the T & P to make a stand in the organization of the House, to get a man for

[60] *Ibid.*, viii–x, 23.

[61] *Ibid.*, 119.

[62] Grenville M. Dodge to Frank S. Bond, March 1, 1875, letterbook in Box 346, Dodge Papers.

speaker who will be friendly to us, to get the Pacific RR Committee formed in our favor, we can go through."[63]

With the discernment of an expert in the business, Huntington was keeping a close watch on the maneuvers of his rivals. "Scott is prepared to pay, or promises to pay, a large amount of money to pass his bill," he told Colton, "but I do not think he can pass it, although I think this coming session of Congress will be composed of the hungriest set of men that ever got together, and that the devil knows what they will do."[64] He confessed that he was puzzled about the nature of his strategy against Scott. "Just what effort to make against him is what troubles me," he wrote. "It costs money to fix things so that I would know his bill would not pass. I believe with $200,000 I can pass our bill, but I take it that it is not worth that much to us."[65]

The announcement of the appointments for the Pacific Railway Committee of the House of Representatives in December 1875 almost caused Huntington to despair of victory. Among those members recognized as "Scott men" were Lamar of Mississippi, chairman of the committee, Throckmorton of Texas, attorney and former land commissioner for the Texas & Pacific, John D. C. Atkins of Tennessee, and Gilbert C. Walker of Virginia. Huntington considered John K. Luttrell of California unreliable. "He must have *solid reasons* or he will go back on you," he told Colton. On the other hand Dodge did not think he could do anything with John A. Kasson of Iowa, whom he had once defeated for Congress; he believed Thomas C. Platt would "be influenced by Jay Gould," and thought Garfield might be reached through pressure on his constituents.[66]

"The Texas Pacific seems to own almost every one in the whole country," wrote Huntington despondently. "I hear in very many of the large towns there are parties holding stock in this construction

[63] Dodge to Bond, July 28, 1875, *ibid.*

[64] Collis P. Huntington to David D. Colton, November 20, 1874, in Chicago *Tribune,* December 27, 1883.

[65] Huntington to Colton, January 17, 1876, *ibid.*

[66] Quoted in Perkins, *Trails, Rails and War,* 257.

company and they are all in Washington working for the T. P. bill. . . . Scott is working mostly amongst the commercial men. He switched Senator Spencer of Alabama and Walker of Virginia this week, but you know they can be switched back with the proper arrangements when they are wanted; but Scott is asking for so much that he can promise largely to pay when he wins, and you know I keep on high ground."[67] The Californian descended from "high ground" sufficiently to contest with the Texas & Pacific forces the control of the House Railroad Committee. "They have considerable money," he informed Colton, referring to the Scott lobby, "as they have convinced several parties that I thought we had sure. I am doing all I can, but it is the liveliest fight I was ever in. I sent a man to Richmond, Va., Saturday, and one to Albany today, to get resolutions passed by the Legislatures against subsidies. If I can get them it will control two members of the Railroad committee, and [I] want them very much."[68] The struggle for control of the committee continued to be close, with no great advantage on either side. "The Railroad Committee of the House was set up for Scott," wrote Huntington, "and it has been a very difficult matter to switch a majority of the committee away from him, but I think it has been done." He was never sure, however, for as he told Colton, "Scott is very able, and then he promises everything to everybody, which helps him for the day in this fight."[69]

Scott was watching Huntington as closely as his rival was watching him. In April 1876, he wrote Chairman Lamar that the "men of the Northern Pacific have joined Mr. Huntington in his endeavor to take away the land grant and destroy the Texas and Pacific Com-

[67] Huntington to Colton, January 29, 1876, in Chicago *Tribune,* December 27, 1883. The men whom Scott had "switched" were Senator George E. Spencer, a Carpetbag Republican from Florida, and Gilbert C. Walker, Democratic Congressman from Virginia. Of Walker, Huntington wrote Colton, "He is a member of the Forty-fourth Congress, ex-Governor of Virginia, and a slippery fellow, and I rather think in Scott's interest, but not sure. I gave him a pass over the C.P. and got one for him over U.P.; so do the best you can with him, but don't trust him much." Huntington to Colton, October 19, 1875, in *ibid.*

[68] Huntington to Colton, February 14, 1876, *ibid.*

[69] Huntington to Colton, March 4, 1876, *ibid.*

pany. . . . Under these circumstances, it has been deemed advisable that this little game should be blocked."[70] In the race for speakership in December 1875, Scott had swung his support to Samuel J. Randall of Pennsylvania. "The charge that Tom Scott wanted me had its effect," Randall confided to a friend. "The energy of his friendship is shown by the votes of Louisiana, Tennessee & Missouri in our caucus. The three states which have within their limits the three forks of the route at Eastern End."[71] Randall was defeated by Michael C. Kerr of Indiana, however, and did not believe Scott's assistance was helpful. Actually he was known to oppose subsidies, and the South was doubtful of him. He was elected speaker on the opening of Congress in December 1876, after Kerr's death, but it is questionable that Scott expected any great advantage from Randall's speakership.

By the time of the Presidential election crisis in December 1876, the two powerful railroad lobbies had fought each other to a virtual deadlock. Each was blocking the plans of the other. There had been several meetings between the principals in an effort to reach a compromise that would satisfy both Scott and Huntington, but up to December 20, the day General Boynton wrote William Henry Smith his letter proposing a Republican understanding with Scott, no agreement had been reached.[72]

While Scott found his efforts virtually checkmated in Congress, it was a different story in the South. For there his forces could almost boast of a clean sweep. It is true that there were a few defections, that the conservative Senator Johnson of Virginia was unfriendly, that other congressmen co-operated with Huntington, and that a few of the "lame duck" Carpetbagger congressmen were wavering or unreliable in their adherence, but they were exceptions. Nor

[70] Thomas A. Scott to L. Q. C. Lamar, April 13, 1876, in Lamar and Mayes Papers, Mississippi State Department of Archives and History, Jackson, Mississippi.

[71] Samuel J. Randall to C. F. Black, December 5, 1875, quoted in Albert V. House, Jr., "The Political Career of Samuel Jackson Randall" (Ph.D. Dissertation, University of Wisconsin, 1934), 66–67.

[72] See letters from Huntington to Colton on May 1, November 15, and December 20, 1876, in Chicago *Tribune,* December 27, 1883.

should it be cynically assumed that Scott's Southern adherents were necessarily brought into his fold by "improper" inducements. General Dodge's letter to Frank S. Bond on his method of "reaching men from their homes, not in Washington," and his statement that "all the men who have been brought to us have been brought in that way and not by men who have been here in Washington under our pay" is strong evidence on this point.[73]

So skillfully had Dodge and his lieutenants integrated the Texas & Pacific with deeply felt needs and indigenous impulses of the region that they had made the movement seem almost native to the South. For one thing the railroad subsidy accommodated itself perfectly to the ground swell of reviving Whiggery in the region. It rejuvenated the Cotton Kingdom's old *drang nach Westen,* the ante-bellum impulse to expand the Southern system southwestward and make colonies of the territories between Texas and California. It realized in a more tangible form than they took in the fifties the dreams of the old planter statesmen of a transcontinental railroad over Jefferson Davis's chosen route. It promised "justice to the South" by offering some of the Federal largess and subsidies that had been lavished upon more fortunate regions during the South's period of estrangement or banishment. And it tied together almost as many local and private interests as did one of the great national tariff bills of the time. The election of ex-Governor John C. Brown of Tennessee in 1876 as a new vice president of the Texas & Pacific gave the company an additional Southern flavor and further modified its Carpetbagger character.

It was a simple enough matter to demonstrate, as the *Nation* did in an article on "The South and the Texas-and-Pacific Job,"[74] that the region's economy had many more pressing needs at the moment than a road to the Pacific. There was little outlet to the westward for the South's products, and there was no immediate need for opening up new territory for settlement. By comparison the Southern demands for Mississippi levee construction, flood control, and river

[73] See above, p. 94.

[74] *Nation,* XXIV (February 8, 1877), 82–83.

and harbor improvements were much more urgent. The South had by no means abandoned its demands for the latter improvements and its spokesmen frequently mentioned them in connection with the Texas & Pacific bill. But the other improvements had behind them no such organized lobby, no such wealthy Northern friends and allies, and no such skillful organizers and publicity managers as General Dodge. The hope was frequently expressed that the railroad bill would open the way to the others, and many Southerners who supported Scott's bill were more interested in levees, harbors, and other needs. "True, the construction of the Texas and Pacific Railroad cannot do all this desirable work," said one of the committeemen appointed by the St. Louis Convention to present its views to the Senate Railroad Committee. "But we think no public measure known to the practical men of this age can go so far towards accomplishing the matter." The Texas & Pacific movement canalized and gave vent to the exuberant Southern Whiggery even if it did not satisfy the impulse.

An inkling of the intensity of feeling aroused in the South is to be found in a Democratic paper of Vicksburg that called for the defeat of any candidate whatever who opposed Scott's subsidy, "*even if beaten by a Radical*"—that is, a Republican.[75] That was going pretty far in Mississippi in 1877. The Galveston *Daily News* thought that "next to the settlement of the presidential question, the southern transcontinental railroad is the matter of greatest moment before the present congress."[76] And the New Orleans *Times,* instead of putting the Southern demands second to the Presidential dispute, saw in that crisis an opportunity to get what the South wanted. Observing "the great change which has been made in the calculations of all parties by the presidential complication," the *Times* believed that the crisis had "made a 'new departure' of some sort necessary to both parties in the North, in order to secure the favor of the

[75] Vicksburg *Democrat-Commercial,* October 5, 1877, quoted in Albert D. Kirwan, "The Political History of Mississippi, 1875–1925" (Ph.D. dissertation, Duke University, 1948), 79. Italics mine.

[76] Galveston *Daily News,* January 25, 1877.

South."[77] As it turned out, there were many Southerners who were eager to fish in the troubled waters of the national crisis for sectional advantages.

"What did the South want?" The most seasonable and pat answer to the question Garfield and Boynton were asking was, "The Texas & Pacific." That answer was implicit in Boynton's letter to William Henry Smith regarding the "thirty-six votes." But Colonel Kellar was on hand to remind Boynton that the Texas & Pacific was not the whole answer. It merely stood for a large category of the South's wants.

[77] New Orleans *Times,* February 24, 1877.

CHAPTER V

The Scott Plan

AS SOON AS William Henry Smith received Boynton's letter proposing the enlistment of the lobby of Tom Scott in Governor Hayes's cause he took it to Joseph Medill. The proposal placed the editor of the Chicago *Tribune* in a rather embarrassing position, for his paper had been one of the most outspoken critics of Scott's methods and of the Texas & Pacific subsidy bill.

"I do not want to decide on my course without thinking over it one night at least," Medill told Smith. "The *Tribune* has been so decided in its course in discussing the railroad question, that I must take time in arranging work in support of a difficult policy. Gen. Boynton's plan is one of grave importance, and the results cannot at once be measured. I assume that you will send this letter to Gov. Hayes. When you do so please say for me that I do not think the price too high for the end proposed to be accomplished."[1]

Smith promptly forwarded Medill's reactions to Boynton, who was evidently quite pleased with the result. "Yours of the 22d gave me much satisfaction," he replied to Smith. "Your statement of Mr. Medill's interest, & his position was particularly gratifying. My idea is not that we need say anything in favor of the Southern road *now,* but only to ascertain Gov. H's views regarding certain important improvements were likely to be somewhere near what I indicated, & in case they were whether such papers as the Tribune & the Gazette would, in consideration of the great stake it might assist us in gaining, stand with him. *Then* to let some one — who might be

[1] Medill, quoted in William Henry Smith to Rutherford B. Hayes, December 22, 1876, Hayes Papers.

deemed just the right one tell Scott privately what the policy of Gov. H is to be, then let him, of his own accord, & in his own interest, set the immense machinery he controls to work to keep democrats within proper bounds when the joint convention begins to act. He knows *how* to work. I do not know him, & have no relations —even indirect—with his lobby. But I know its *power*. He can easily see that with Tilden in & a hostile Senate he could do nothing even if T. was friendly; while with Hayes in & friendly, the House under the influences we hope to have prevail would work with H. in such a matter."[2]

As for the embarrassments involved for editors and politicians in a sudden change of policy, Boynton foresaw no insuperable difficulty. "This need not, in fact could not be an open thing," he thought. "But the knowledge that Gov. H. feels as we suppose he does can be made by Scott to go a great ways toward securing the 36 votes." As for the Southern politicians, they need not "even appear to come over to a republican administration in the first instance." They could take high ground in merely saying, "'Let the republicans do wrong if they will, we will not countenance revolution starting in our own party, & no vote of ours shall aid it.'" Then there were the gentlemen of the press. "As to the Tribune, or other republican papers advocating the Southern road, there is no necessity for a word till Gov. Hayes sends his first message. If then (as we hope will be true) a new era of candid co-operation seems on the part of the South [to be] opening it will be easy to say: There is after all, & under the new administration, an equity in this thing. It is a good thing to do. That is the way I shall turn the corner if we get to it. When I hear definitely the response you are to obtain, as you say, to my first letter, I will then write you at once as to prompt & practical work on the general plan."[3]

In the last sentence Boynton was referring, of course, to the response of Governor Hayes. Smith had forwarded to Hayes two of Boynton's letters, both dated December 20. "The letter from

[2] H. V. Boynton to Smith, December 26, 1876, Smith Papers.
[3] *Ibid.*

Gen. Boynton, which I enclose is of great interest," he wrote Hayes. "In continuance of the practice which has always obtained in my correspondence and intercourse with you, viz: of concealing nothing — of giving without reservation all the facts in my possession whether agreeable or otherwise — I send also a supplemental letter from Gen. B." He enclosed also Medill's reaction to Boynton's proposal quoted above.[4] Much depended upon Hayes's response, of course, and both Smith and Boynton awaited it with great interest.

It had been only two weeks since Governor Hayes had entered in his diary a solemn vow. "I am determined," he wrote on December 7, "that no selfish ambition or interest shall influence my conduct in the face of these tremendous events. Whatever, on the whole, is best for the country, that I will do if I can know it, regardless of consequences to myself."[5] Rutherford B. Hayes was a thoroughly respectable and rather devout Victorian gentleman of the old school, with not a known blemish on his public record. Those were the qualities for which the Republicans, bent on repentance and reform, were looking when they nominated him in 1876. Unable to go the whole way and nominate an out-and-out reformer like Bristow, they agreed on Hayes as about as far as they could go in that direction. And Hayes had mildly deplored Republican sins of the past and acknowledged the need for reform. He frequently consulted Schurz, a leader of anti-Grantism, and eventually took him into his cabinet. For that matter, however, so was General Boynton a reformer, more of one than Hayes, in fact. He had helped to expose Blaine's dealing with Tom Scott, written muckraking articles on the rackets, rings, and deals of Grantism, and taken charge of General Bristow's pre-convention drive for the 1876 nomination. Then there were the gentlemen below the Potomac and Ohio rivers who were involved in this matter. They might call themselves reformers too, though "Redeemers" seemed more appropriate. "Reform" was

[4] Smith to Hayes, December 22, 1876, Hayes Papers.

[5] Hayes Diary, December 7, 1876, in Williams (ed.), *Diary and Letters of Hayes,* III, 388.

their stock-in-trade, however, and together with "White Supremacy" their rallying cry. Their purpose, they said, was to throw out the rascals, clean up the corruption that had stained the names of their states, and restore "home rule." Some of them were as thoroughly respectable, Victorian, and devout as Governor Hayes.

All of these gentlemen — Republicans and Democrats, Northerners and Southerners — found it necessary to come to terms with the dominant forces of the age in which they lived if they hoped to carry out their purposes. They were able to give those purposes a more attractive appearance in their public pronouncements than in their private correspondence. In public they spoke of the reconciliation of estranged sections, the solution of a national crisis, or the avoidance of violence and civil war. But if the votes necessary for the attainment of those purposes — whether the ones published or the ones more privately discussed — happened to lie in the control of a Gould, a Huntington, or a Scott, then some sort of accommodation had to be reached.

That was the way things were in the Gilded Age.

Governor Hayes's first reaction to the Scott Plan was guarded and tentative, but by no means negative. "Enclosed I return you the letters," he wrote Smith on Christmas Eve. "I do not wish to be committed to details. It is so desirable to restore peace and prosperity to the South that I have given a good deal of thought to it. The two things I would be exceptionally liberal about are education and internal improvements of a national character. Nothing I can think of would do more to promote business prosperity, immigration, and a change in the Sentiments of the Southern people on the unfortunate topic. Too much politics, too little attention to business is the bane of that part of our country." He requested that Smith meet him at Xenia, Ohio, the following Tuesday, which was the day after Christmas.[6]

The outcome of the conference at Xenia between Smith and Hayes is not known. But on January 3 the Governor wrote his friend, "I am not a believer in the trustworthyness [*sic*] of the forces

[6] Hayes to Smith, December 24, 1876 (presumably a copy), Hayes Papers.

you hope to rally. After we are in, I believe a wise and liberal policy can accomplish a great deal. But we must rely on our own strength to secure our rights. With firmness it can be done."[7]

Smith appears to have been puzzled by this, for he said in reply: "I am at a loss for an interpretation of the opening sentence—'I am not a believer in the trustworthiness of the forces you hope to rally.' Does this refer to the Southern forces or to the Republican forces in the North who just now I am more particularly engaged in rallying? I shall assume the former, & content myself with the single remark—That there can be no harm in furthering a great cause in searching for latent patriotism in the South. . . . As to the Southern matter: That I shall pursue on my own responsibility."[8] There the matter rested for the time being.

In the meantime, however, there began to appear strong indications that Hayes's confidence that the Republicans could rely on their own strength "to secure our rights" was not justified by facts. Medill showed Smith a confidential letter from the Washington correspondent of the *Tribune* giving "a list of 17 doubtful Republicans," including Senators George F. Edmunds, Conkling, and Blaine, who could not be depended upon in the matter of the electoral vote count. Smith forwarded the information to Hayes, suggesting that "all of the influence possible shd. be brought to bear on Edmunds."[9] About the same time ex-Governor Edward F. Noyes of Ohio, a trusted advisor of Hayes, wrote him of "indications that a few Republican Senators are 'weakening,'" and mentioned particularly Conkling and Thomas W. Ferry, acting president of the Senate.[10] Ferry had appointed Conkling a member of the Senate committee that was to act with a committee of the House to establish a tribunal for the purpose of deciding the Presidential election. Conkling was therefore in a position to wreck Hayes's cause. He had a strong influence in Congress, particularly with the remaining Carpetbagger members, and was known to be disgruntled at the poor

[7] Hayes to Smith, January 3, 1877 (ditto), *ibid.*
[8] Smith to Hayes, January 5, 1877, *ibid.*
[9] Smith to Hayes, December 30, 1876, *ibid.*
[10] Edward F. Noyes to Hayes, December 26, 1876, *ibid.*

showing he made against Hayes for the nomination and to suspect Hayes of intending "reform" mischief if he actually became President.

Most alarming of all was a letter from Senator John Sherman, written January 3, giving confidential information on Conkling's course in the committee on the electoral tribunal. "Mr. Conkling has openly stated in the committee," he told Hayes, "his position that the President of the Senate has no right *to count* the votes, and that, as the case stands, he will not vote that you have either Florida or Louisiana."[11] After a talk with Sherman two days later, Garfield noted in his diary that "Sherman is satisfied that Conkling is going to break with the party on the Presidential question. How many Senators he can carry with him is not certain."[12] Whether Conkling broke with the Republicans or not, his abandonment of the claim that the Vice President could count the electoral votes left the party no constitutional leg to stand on. In that claim Hayes was a strong believer himself,[13] and now that it had been undermined he was practically forced into some sort of compromise. On top of this blow came the news that President Grant had rather openly expressed his skepticism of Republican claims to Louisiana.

In view of this critical state of affairs around the first of January, several of Hayes's friends urged that he either come to Washington himself or send a representative in whom he had complete confidence. "I want to say things I cannot write," said William E. Chandler, urging Hayes to have someone "in Washington immediately 'spying out the land.'"[14] William Henry Smith agreed that such a mission was necessary and suggested either Stanley Matthews or General James M. Comly.[15] President Grant settled the matter by requesting General Comly for the mission. Of all the numerous war comrades with whom Hayes had kept touch, Comly, who had succeeded him as colonel of the Twenty-third Ohio Regiment, was

[11] John Sherman to Hayes, January 3, 1877, in Williams, *Life of Hayes,* I, 521.
[12] Garfield Diary, January 5, 1877, Garfield Papers.
[13] Hayes to Sherman, January 5, 1877, in Williams, *Life of Hayes,* I, 522.
[14] Chandler to Hayes, December 29, 1876, Hayes Papers.
[15] Smith to Hayes, December 30, 1876, *ibid.*

said to have been "his most devoted friend."[16] He was living in Columbus and editing the *Ohio State Journal.*

Arriving in Washington on January 2, General Comly set out to fill a very crowded calendar. In one of the four days he was in the city he made twelve calls and received fifteen callers. Although his appointments included the President, several cabinet members, leaders of the Senate and House, and numerous other dignitaries, the first man he sought out and the one with whom he appears to have spent most time was General Henry Van Ness Boynton. Hayes apparently did not know Boynton personally, and it is evident from the amount of space devoted to the man in Comly's twenty-page report of his mission that one of his assignments was to find out what manner of man Boynton was. On the way out of the Ebbitt House to meet him, Comly was waylaid by a couple of excited Carpetbaggers from South Carolina, one of them with a heavy load of liquor aboard, the other with "an utter contempt for nicety in political morals," both talking at once, "barroom fashion." "They were so boisterous and violent," he complained, "that the attention of the whole room was drawn to us, and I could scarcely conceal my disgust." Shaking them off finally, he joined General Boynton and was relieved to find him in complete agreement with himself on the ungentlemanliness of Carpetbaggers. Republicans of the new order appeared to view Carpetbaggers with as much distaste as did Redeemers. Boynton plunged immediately into an analysis of the threatening split in the Republican party. He had "grave doubts of Senator Conkling" and some of his Carpetbagger friends, particularly Senator George E. Spencer of Alabama, and thought that Boss William A. Shepherd of the notorious Washington ring was "at the bottom of most of the mischief in that quarter." Shepherd's fear was that his enemy Bristow and the reformers were going to "run Hayes and his Administration, if Hayes got in." Comly reported that Boynton "talked freely and frankly on the situation, giving me many valuable hints as to leading men on both sides."[17]

[16] Williams, *Life of Hayes,* II, 421–422.
[17] James M. Comly to Hayes, January 8, 1877, copy in Hayes Papers.

The subject of the Scott Plan was not mentioned in the report Comly wrote of the interview for Hayes, which merely supplemented oral reports. He had several other interviews with Boynton which the written report did not cover. His analysis of Boynton himself is of especial significance only in light of the Scott proposal. "Several very interesting and suggestive interviews with Gen. Boynton," wrote Comly, "led me to count him one of your most discreet and reliable friends—chastened, I may say, by devotion to Bristow, and restrained by detestation of 'Boss' Shepherd. Grant is the common focus of these divergent likes and dislikes, so that Boynton dislikes and distrusts Grant half because of his love for Bristow, and half because of his hate for Shepherd."[18]

Grant dismissed all White House callers and devoted two hours to his interview with General Comly. The primary purpose of Comly was to eliminate the threatening breach between Grant and Hayes. He came right to the point by assuring the President, as he told Hayes, that "there was not one chance in a million that you would appoint Bristow to a Cabinet position in view of the fact that he had made himself so personally obnoxious to the President and to so large a section of the Republican party." Much gratified, the President "showed strong emotion" and at that point "*drew the friendly cigars from his pocket,*" which Comly considered "the best symptom any one can have."[19]

Less reassuring were Comly's talks with the inner circle of Hayes's advisors in Washington—Attorney General Alphonso Taft, Postmaster General James N. Tyner, Senator Sherman, Garfield, and Dennison. Tyner gave him convincing "proof that there was already active danger in the attitude of Senator Conkling toward the counting business." He was also told that Simon B. Conover, Carpetbag senator from Florida, had paid three visits to Tilden during the Christmas holidays, and he collected other reports of Carpetbagger defection. The Carpetbagger contingent was a particularly difficult problem. In view of the numerous reports of Hayes's overtures to their enemies, the Redeemers, and his evident *rapprochement* with

[18] *Ibid.* [19] *Ibid.*

them, the Carpetbaggers naturally suspected that they were being sold out, and this fact made them more susceptible to Conkling's control. It was decided at a council of Hayes's close friends that the Carpetbaggers would have to be "seen." Comly begged off from the assignment. Sherman said, "I will do anything I can, but I'll be damned if I do that." Whereupon, "Attorney General Taft solemnly winked one eye (this is literally reported, also)," wrote Comly, "and said mysteriously that he had a great deal to do with those fellows in the Department of Justice," and that "he might count on considerable influence with them." Comly learned a great deal more, some of which he did "not feel at liberty to write, even here," but the general tenor of his report to Hayes was not very reassuring.[20]

Evidence of Republican disunity and defection continued to pour into Hayes's office after Comly was suddenly called home to Columbus by an illness in his family. On January 12 Carl Schurz sent the governor an article from *Harper's Weekly* that dealt with the disgust with which righteous Republicans viewed the chicanery of the Louisiana returning board of their own party. Schurz believed that *Harper's* conclusion about "the impression produced by those doings upon a very large number of conscientious Republicans, is unfortunately correct." The senator assured Hayes that there were "grave doubts in the minds of that class of citizens," and that considering the "suspicious circumstances" surrounding the Louisiana board's action and its evil reputation, "those doubts are not unnatural."[21]

And on January 13 William E. Chandler, one of the most zealous workers among the Southern returning boards and Carpetbaggers, and more optimistic than some about keeping the Southern Republicans in line while Comly was in Washington, wrote in an extremely pessimistic vein. "Practically," he pointed out, "if there are 10 Republicans in the Senate who are weak & yielding & will not sustain the correct constitutional theory, in other words, who do not want to have Hayes President, we are gone. The House is revolu-

[20] *Ibid.*
[21] Carl Schurz to Hayes, January 12, 1877, Hayes Papers.

tionary. If the Senate does not stand Republican we cannot inaugurate our President." Then on the following day Chandler wrote that "the evidence is convincing that Senator Conkling is against us," and worse still, "he is bitter, determined, excited, and I now think means to defeat Hayes & Wheeler." According to his information, and he was well informed, "there are *today* [January 14, 1877] Senators enough who will go with him to defeat us. This is the outlook tonight of those who know the situation best."[22]

So it was that the rosy Christmas-time prospect of splitting the Democratic party had been clouded before the middle of January by the ugly threat of a split in the Republican party.

The threat of schism in the Republican party was only one of three simultaneous but separate developments that, taken together, were pushing Hayes and his advisors toward a new departure in strategy and dispelling the calm confidence Hayes had expressed. The second of these developments was an intensification of the threat of violence as a solution to the election dispute that reached a climax in the first two weeks of the new year. Even in December the Grant administration was taking seriously reports of the organization of "rifle clubs" and secret military preparations in various Northern states. "Advices from all parts of the North and West," said Halstead's paper, "establish, beyond question, the existence of a secret political society composed exclusively of Democrats, and having for its purpose the inauguration [of Tilden]—by force, if necessary. The administration was evidently first appraised of this startling fact yesterday morning, and a conference was at once called at the White House." The secret organization was said to be strongest in Indiana, Ohio, and New York, but was "spreading rapidly throughout all the Northern states." Democratic congressmen were "daily in receipt of letters from their constituents, breathing the most determined spirit of resistance to Hayes's inauguration."[23]

Mainly confined to the Northern states, the spirit of violent resistance had its strongest Southern exponent in Henry Watterson's

[22] Chandler to Hayes, January 13 and 14, 1877, *ibid.*

[23] Cincinnati *Commercial* quoted in Memphis *Avalanche,* December 20, 1876.

Louisville *Courier-Journal.* Declaring that "the Democracy constitutes the popular majority," that paper took the position that "it is nonsense to suppose that they will quietly yield what they consider the fruits of a hard-earned victory."[24] In a signed article written from Washington January 7 Watterson called for "the presence of at least ten thousand unarmed Kentuckians in this city on the coming 14th of February," the day for opening and counting the electoral vote. "Less than this will be of no avail," he thought. In fact the Democrats should "send a hundred thousand petitioners to Washington" in order "to present the memorial in person."[25] John G. Thompson, Democratic sergeant-at-arms of the House, had already proposed to appoint 100,000 men as deputies and have them on hand to execute the determination of the majority to assure Tilden's election.[26]

January 8, Jackson Day, was appointed by the Democrats for rallies all over the country to demonstrate the party unity for Tilden. According to the New York *Times* the ward and county meetings to select delegates to the state conventions of the eighth were "a general chorus of threats," "full of wild talk." The Toledo, Ohio, meeting was reported "redolent of blood and violence."[27]

At a great Democratic rally on January 8 held at Ford's Theatre, the scene of Lincoln's assassination, Henry Watterson repeated his call for the presence of 100,000 citizens in Washington "exercising in their persons the freeman's right of petition." Should Tilden prove to have a majority "then — and this as 'Old Hickory' would say it and mean it — 'by the Eternal!' he shall be inaugurated." Joseph Pulitzer of the New York *World* outdid the Kentuckian by offering "to bare his breast to the bullets of the tyrant and rush headlong upon his glittering steel."[28] In Indianapolis the papers reported an "immense mob" listened to George W. Julian, a former Abolitionist Republican who had become a Democrat. He recalled that "a cen-

[24] Louisville *Courier-Journal,* January 4, 1877.
[25] *Ibid.,* January 8, 1877.
[26] New York *Times,* January 7, 1877.
[27] *Ibid.,* January 7 and 8, 1877.
[28] Washington *National Republican,* January 9, 1877; New York *Times,* January 9, 1877.

tury ago our fathers took up arms in defense of their right to a voice in the government. We assert the right now," declared Julian, "when we ask that the will of the people be registered as the supreme law, and that whoever may defy it by overt acts shall receive the same treatment which the nation awarded to the men who appealed from the ballot to the bayonet in 1861. . . . Millions of men will be found ready to offer their lives as hostages to the sacredness of the ballot as the palladium of our liberties."[29]

The Democratic rally of Ohio was held in Columbus, under Governor Hayes's very nose. In spite of a violent snowstorm the attendance at "The People's Indignation Convention" was good. The audience demonstrated "a good deal of enthusiasm when anything defiant and warlike was spoken," particularly when General Thomas Ewing appealed to the revolutionary doctrine that "resistance to tyranny is obedience to law." The convention adopted a resolution declaring that any attempt to settle the disputed election by decision of the president of the Senate, the method favored by Hayes, should be "resisted by the people to the last extremity, even should that extremity be an appeal to arms."[30]

From Indiana came a report that the Democratic governor had declared his intention of "putting the state militia of Indiana at once on an efficient war footing," and Republican authorities in Pennsylvania were said to be making "warlike preparations." Grant responded to these manifestations by an announcement that his authority was "as supreme in the District of Columbia as if it were a garrisoned fortress, and any demonstration or warlike concentration of men threatening the peace of the city or endangering the security of public property or treasure of the Government would be summarily dealt with, should the public safety demand, by a declaration of martial law."[31]

[29] New York *Tribune,* January 9, 1877.

[30] *Ibid.,* January 10, 1877; New York *Times,* January 9, 1877; George W. Morgan, Mount Vernon, Ohio, to Samuel J. Tilden, January 15, 1877, Tilden Papers (New York Public Library). Morgan helped frame the resolution.

[31] New York *Tribune,* January 9, 1877; New York *Times,* January 12, 1877; Washington *National Republican,* January 13, 1877.

In Congress the Democrats were attempting to impeach President Grant for alleged misuse of the military to intimidate voters in the election of 1876. Ill-tempered charges and snarling rejoinders marred the debates over this and the disputed election question in both houses. Demonstrations took place in the galleries and some members were said to be carrying arms on the floor. "The same influence now rules the House and *its galleries* that did in 1860–61," Senator Sherman wrote Hayes, "and I feel that we are to encounter the same enemies that we did then." [32]

The third development bearing upon the political crisis was primarily economic. During the critical weeks between Christmas and the middle of January the struggle between the Texas & Pacific and the Southern Pacific forces reached a climax. Both sides marshaled all their powerful resources for a showdown in Washington before the old Congress expired on March 4. The new Congress would mean new committees, an unusual number of new members, and a vast amount of reorganization and "fixing" by the railroad lobbies. "I am having the roughest fight with Scott that I ever had," Huntington reported to Colton on December 20 (the day Boynton made his proposal for a union of Hayes and Scott forces), "but I hope to drive him into something that we can accept." [33] It was Huntington's belief that he could bring sufficient influence to bear upon the House Committee on Pacific Railroads to block the passage of Scott's bill until the Pennsylvanian would be compelled to agree to some acceptable compromise. A succession of conferences between Huntington and Scott, two of them in Philadelphia in November and others later, resulted in no agreement. The difficulty lay in Scott's confidence that he could control the House committee. "Scott and I had an open break last week," wrote Huntington. "He said he would pass his bill through the committee and I could not prevent it." [34]

[32] John Sherman to R. B. Hayes, January 18, 1877, in Williams (ed.), *Diary and Letters of Hayes,* III, 405.

[33] Huntington to Colton, December 20, 1876, in Chicago *Tribune,* December 27, 1883.

[34] Huntington to Colton, November 15 and December 25, 1876, *ibid.*

Garfield, one of the committeemen opposing Scott's bill, recorded in his diary almost daily meetings of the House Committee on Pacific Railroads or its subcommittee during this period. These meetings sometimes occurred in the special committee room and occasionally at Willard's Hotel in the room of Lamar, chairman of the committee and proponent of Scott's bill. At a meeting on December 20 Garfield found the Scott members "determined to push Scott's bill through," but managed to thwart them. "I resisted them by amendments and quietly delayed until the hour of adjournment," he noted.[35] A second attempt to force committee acceptance of the bill likewise came to grief. These failures convinced Tom Scott that it was time to come to terms with his antagonist. "So after trying it twice and failing," wrote Huntington to friend Colton, "he [Scott] came to my room and we agreed on a bill nothing like what we want, but as good as we can get."[36] The substance of the bargain was that Huntington would call off his opposition to Scott's subsidy and Scott would concede the building of the western end of the line in California to the Southern Pacific; that Huntington would agree to Scott's demand that the new railway "should always remain an open highway," and on the other hand Scott was to support a Federal subsidy for Huntington.[37]

When the House committee members learned of the agreement they postponed discussion of the subject until after the holidays and recommitted the bill and its amendments to a subcommittee consisting of Lamar, Garfield, and a few others. Garfield noted in his diary on December 30 that he had "worked with Mr. Lamar on amend'ts to the compromise bill of Scott and Huntington until nearly four o'clock."[38] The agreement between principals was naturally the occasion of some embarrassment for the politicians. Scott's friends had been for years picturing Huntington's transcontinental

[35] Garfield Diary, December 20, 1876, Garfield Papers.

[36] Huntington to Colton, December 25, 1876, in Chicago *Tribune,* December 25, 1876. On Scott's side the compromise was predicted in G. M. Dodge to James A. Evans, November 6, 1876, letterbook in Box 384, Dodge Papers.

[37] *Railroad Gazette,* IX (January 20, 1877), 18; Railway *World,* III (January 20, 1877), 62.

[38] Garfield Diary, December 30, 1876, Garfield Papers.

system as an unpardonable monopoly that the Texas & Pacific would break; while Huntington's friends had been pouring merciless criticism upon Scott's cry for subsidies, and the Californian was offering to build the same road without a penny of subsidies. Now the politicians were expected to vote for a friendly alliance between the antagonists, by which Scott permitted the despised monopolist to build part of the line calculated to break his monopoly, and Huntington accepted part of the despised subsidy without which he had already offered to build the road.

When the House subcommittee informed the press that it was working on a "compromise bill," the announcement was greeted with some disrespectful levity. "It is the result of a bargain," declared the New York *Sun,* "for a division of the expected spoils between Tom Scott on the one hand, and Huntington. . . . We doubt if the world ever saw anything to compare with what has taken place in Washington in relation to this stupendous job." As the *Sun* pictured the "deal," Huntington "comes in and cries halves, threatening to smash the job entirely if he does not get an interest in it. . . . Scott became thoroughly scared, weakened on every point that Huntington claimed, and now we are told that the House subcommittee have agreed upon a compromise bill! Faugh! . . . Taken altogether it would seem that the new compromise Texas Pacific bill is intended to promote the most nefarious railroad jobbery yet attempted in this country."[39] It was, of course, but part of the embarrassment to which politicians are heir when former enemies suddenly make friends. The politicians made the most of the situation.

On January 11, a few days after Comly returned to Columbus, the members of the Pacific Railroad Committee composed their differences — or those of the principals — and a majority voted to instruct Chairman Lamar to report to the House for passage a bill granting Federal aid for the completion of a southern road to the Pacific.[40]

The compromise bill was interpreted by the press as not only a truce in the Scott-Huntington war, but an aggressive alliance of

[39] New York *Sun,* January 9, 1877.
[40] Garfield Diary, January 11, 1877, Garfield Papers.

their forces. "The two great schemers have joined hands," observed the New York *Times.* In previous sessions of Congress the greater part of the resources of each had been expended in fighting and blocking the other, so that any cause that identified its fortunes with one of the warring antagonists ran the risk of incurring the opposition of the other. "This time the two powerful lobbies," said the *Times,* "which have been for a long time arrayed against each other will unite for the compromise bill, as the differences which separated them have been composed by C. P. Huntington and Tom Scott."[41] The alliance was an uneasy and unstable one. In the very letter in which he informed Colton of the agreement, Huntington gave instructions for knifing Scott if the combination failed of its purpose. Colton was to have engineers survey 100 miles of line beyond the Colorado River in Scott's country at once. "Get the necessary legislation from Arizona," Huntington told him, "so that if the bill does not pass we can lay in 1877 say 100 to 140 miles of road in Arizona. When that is done the question of who builds the S.P. Road will be settled, or at least we shall command the situation."[42] The truce was obviously regarded as valid, in case the bill did not pass, only until March 4. So long as it did last, however, the combination was a formidable and, some thought, well-nigh irresistible one. While it lasted, at any rate, those forces that worked in cooperation with Scott's lobby needed no longer to fear the opposition of Huntington and might reasonably expect help from that quarter as well.

On the evening of January 3, while General Comly was in Washington on his mission, James A. Garfield "went to Willard's Hotel and worked with the special Committee on the Pacific Railroad at Lamar's room until nine o'clock. Then spent an hour at Foster's with General Conley [*sic*] on the political situation."[43] Comly reported to Hayes upon the intertwining of economics and politics in the conversation at Foster's. "Garfield came in later," he

[41] New York *Times,* January 5 and 13, 1877.

[42] Huntington to Colton, December 25, 1876, in Chicago *Tribune,* December 27, 1883.

[43] Garfield Diary, January 3, 1877, Garfield Papers.

wrote, "from a meeting of the Pacific Railroad committee, of which Lamar is chairman. Both Garfield and Foster intimated regret that the Republican party was so squarely committed against further subsidies as to prevent them from advocating the building of the Texas Pacific R.R. by the help of Congress." The two congressmen outlined with evident enthusiasm certain practical political benefits to be derived from co-operation with Scott and his Southern friends. "They thought a large following might be gained for the Republican party in the South by favoring this road, and both asserted that Texas might be made a Republican State by advocating the road. . . . Both said they had no doubt of being able to build up a strong Southern following for a Republican Administration by advocating such Southern public improvements as had been granted to the North during the war."[44]

The course of Governor Hayes's reflections on the Boynton proposal after he questioned the "trustworthyness" of the plan in his letter to William Henry Smith on January 3 took no written form that has been unearthed. That the problem remained on his mind seems indicated by an entry in his diary on January 5. Looking forward to his inaugural address, he wrote, "I must urge a liberal policy towards the South especially in affording facilities for education and encouraging business and emigration [*sic*] by internal improvements of a national character."[45] The phrase "internal improvements of a national character" recurs in subsequent reflections on the subject of his inaugural,[46] but it does not clarify his attitude on the Scott Plan.

The question was, as Joseph Medill framed it, was "the price too high for the end proposed to be accomplished"? Perhaps the answer might depend upon how broadly the "end" was conceived. Medill had certainly phrased it attractively. "Indeed," he had written, "I shall not think any price too high that will secure protection to the

[44] James M. Comly to Hayes, January 8, 1877, Hayes Papers.

[45] Hayes Diary, January 5, 1877, in Williams (ed.) *Diary and Letters of Hayes,* III, 400.

[46] Hayes to Carl Schurz, January 29, 1877, *ibid.,* 410.

lives of the poor Negroes, and peace to the South."[47] Still, he had not considered it worth the embarrassment, on further reflection, of changing his editorial policy. He continued to attack Scott's bill as a plan "to plunder the American people again for the benefit of Crédit-Mobilier companies,"[48] and contented himself with promising that Hayes's administration could "do a thousand-fold more for the South than Tilden's."[49] William E. Chandler offered light on Hayes's problem of political ethics in a letter of January 13. Complaining of "difficulties" that "may prove fatal to a good and righteous cause," Chandler added, "Pres. Lincoln used to say that 'all there is to honest statesmanship is controlling and directing *individual meannesses* for the public good.'"[50]

How Governor Hayes rationalized the ethical question involved is not known. Nor is it known to what extent he went in his commitments regarding Scott and the Texas & Pacific. It is quite probable that he did not go any further than he did in the letter saying that while he did "not wish to be committed to details" he would be "exceptionally liberal" to the South in the matter of "internal improvements of a national character." In view of the governor's known record for extreme cautiousness and circumspection when it came to political commitments, it is surprising that he went that far. More characteristic is his subsequent letter to Smith questioning the "trustworthyness," presumably of the railroad forces. Whether he intended that as a retraction or not, his friends did not so interpret it for they proceeded on the contrary assumption. And the governor was kept fully informed of their progress. William Henry Smith went to Columbus for another talk with Hayes around the first of the new year, and General Boynton found his report of the interview quite satisfactory for the purpose of their plans.[51]

General Boynton wrote that he had been "working very hard at

[47] Quoted in William Henry Smith to Hayes, December 22, 1876, Hayes Papers.
[48] Chicago *Tribune,* January 8, 1877.
[49] *Ibid.,* January 3, 1877.
[50] William E. Chandler to Hayes, January 13, 1877, Hayes Papers.
[51] The visit to Columbus is referred to in both Boynton to Smith, January 14, 1877, Smith Papers; and Smith to Hayes, January 23, 1877, Hayes Papers.

the matter we have written about. But it is a big job, & there ought to be more help here. If Col Kellar could have remained, or if Gen Comly had not been called back at once, it would have been easier." On January 14, however, he was elated to report great progress to Smith.

"Since your letter came after your visit to Columbus," he wrote, "I have been bothered to find how, in a perfectly *safe* way, to put Tom Scott in possession of the facts I had. But at last it is done. Gen Dodge with whom I am on confidential terms came here, & I first sounded him, & finding him all right in the political features of our plan, I broached the R.R. matter. Seeing how he felt about that, I went further, & of his accord he sent for Scott, who came down last night & I surmised, from my general knowledge of the man (I never knew him personally before) he saw the vital importance of the knowledge to him."[52] Scott and Dodge came to Boynton's house by appointment, and the three men had "a most satisfying talk" on the afternoon of January 14. "Col Scott feels sure," continued Boynton, "that the attitude of Gov H towards the South & his willingness to help them in their material interests can be so used here among prominent Southern democrats as to effectively kill all measures looking toward revolution. He will go to work in the matter *personally* & with the skill & *directness* for which he is justly celebrated. The talk we had was a long one, covering all the ground, & I am sure you would have been much pleased & encouraged by it. From today there will be no lack of help, for Scott's whole powerful machinery will be set in motion at once, & I am sure you will be able to detect the influence of it in *votes* within ten days. Scott is for Ferry's declaring the result [of the electoral count] without flinching, & I believe it must come to that in the end. If we can commit the South (a part of it) against revolutionary resolutions it is the short way out of the muddle—perhaps the shortest in any

[52] Boynton to Smith, January 14, 1877, Smith Papers. Boynton wrote two letters to Smith on January 14, both covering the same ground. Why he did this I have not been able to make out. There are no inconsistencies between the two accounts, though each has a few details not in the other. I have made no attempt to distinguish between the two in citation. They are both in the Smith Papers.

event. In a day or two I will write definitely how Scott finds the field. I cannot write more & get this off tonight. This is a short letter, but it weighs a *ton*." [53] In a supplementary letter of the same date Boynton emphasized that Scott felt "the *very greatest confidence*" in his ability to influence the Southerners in the desired direction. "It is as if our army had made a juncture with his on the field of battle," added the General. "I feel quite confident now in the result."

In Columbus General Boynton's stock took a sharp rise shortly after the events described above. Comly wrote him requesting his views on the crisis in Washington. Boynton responded with a seventeen-page letter containing an astute and detailed analysis of the political situation and the factors underlying it, and Comly passed it on to Hayes.[54] The governor returned the letter with the following comment: " 'Tell General Boynton for me, that is the best letter I have seen — more than that tell him I do not think it would have been possible for anybody to write a more consummately perfect & comprehensive review of the situation. Tell him it is the best letter he ever wrote — better than he has ever published.' " In delivering this message to Boynton, Comly remarked, "It is really the first time in my life that I ever heard the Gov. so far enthused as to 'gush.' He could hardly say enough," reported Comly.[55]

In Washington rumors of an understanding between the Southerners and the friends of Hayes were plentiful. The *Nation* of January 18 reported discouraging results of an attempt to discover the nature of the understanding: "As to what overtures have actually been made by Mr. Hayes's friends to the Southerners, although there is a general agreement that something of the kind has taken place, it is impossible as yet to get any definite information." A prominent Republican, "though willing enough to state his views and opinions as to almost everything else, manifested a sudden reticence when this topic was approached." In fact, said the *Nation,* "The introduction of the subject is fatal to conversation." [56]

[53] *Ibid.*

[54] Boynton to Comly, January 25, 1877, Hayes Papers.

[55] Quoted in Boynton to Benjamin H. Bristow, February 2, 1877, Benjamin H. Bristow Papers (Library of Congress).

[56] *Nation,* XXIV (January 18, 1877), 39.

Southerners were reticent or, at first, downright bellicose in their denial of rumors of an agreement with the Republicans. "There will be no selling out by Southern Congressmen," declared the Charleston *News and Courier*. "The South may be sold out, but will not sell out. That is sure!" Quoting this with hearty approval, Watterson's *Courier-Journal* added: "Take this as a text, Mr. Halstead. You know you can't buy the South for Hayes, for you have just tried it."[57] Watterson continued to uphold his reputation as the most belligerent of the Southern congressmen for several more days. "The *Courier-Journal*," said his paper on January 24, "has freely expressed the opinion that armed resistance was better than submission to usurpation. What we said on that score represented the feelings of thousands of men in Kentucky who know what war means, and who are ready to carry out their sentiment by shouldering a musket."[58] Shortly thereafter, however, the paper changed its tone and became a voice of moderation.

On January 26 General Boynton added the following note in a letter to William Henry Smith: "You could not guess in some time who was the first man to surrender without hesitation to Scott after the talk I wrote you about. You will hardly believe it but it *was* Watterson!"[59] January 26 was the day on which the House of Representatives adopted the Electoral Commission Bill as a means of settling the election dispute, and it is possible that Watterson dropped his belligerent tone on that account, though ten days earlier he had expressed bitter opposition to the bill. At any rate, Watterson was converted from the most bellicose and uncompromising of all the Southern congressmen and editors to one of the leading advocates of peace and deplorers of hotheads. Whatever the reason, the change was sudden and it was the cause of some comment. "The Louisville *Courier-Journal,* much to public astonishment," observed Joseph Medill's Chicago *Tribune* with satisfaction, "is one of the fairest Democratic papers."[60]

[57] Louisville *Courier-Journal,* January 3, 1877.
[58] *Ibid.,* January 24, 1877.
[59] Boynton to Smith, January 26, 1877, Smith Papers.
[60] Chicago *Tribune,* February 13, 1877.

CHAPTER VI

The Rift in the Democratic Ranks

OTHER ARMIES than those of Hayes and Scott, to borrow Boynton's phrase, "made juncture on the field of battle" during the last session of the Forty-fourth Congress. The combination between the Texas & Pacific and the Southern Pacific forces has already been explained. Another powerful combination was effected by an alliance between the Central Pacific men and the forces of the Union Pacific. The latter company was at that time under the management of Sidney Dillon and Jay Gould. In command of the Central Pacific contingent was Huntington.

In spite of bitter fights of the past, the Union Pacific and Central Pacific companies found several common interests that drew them together in 1876. In the spring of that year General Dodge, then a Union Pacific director, observed that the two roads were "mixed up together in so many fights and combinations that neither feels like encroaching upon the other even by implication."[1] At the very time he was concluding his alliance with Tom Scott, in December 1876, Huntington took steps to bind Gould and Dillon to his cause by offering the Union Pacific a large block of Central Pacific stock on favorable terms. He cautioned Colton at the time of "the importance of the public not knowing anything of this arrangement with the U.P."[2]

The most urgent legislative problem the Union Pacific and Central Pacific had in common was the large debt they owed to the

[1] Grenville M. Dodge to James A. Evans, April 20, 1876, letterbook in Box 384, Dodge Papers.

[2] Collis P. Huntington to D. D. Colton, December 25, 1876, in Chicago *Tribune*, December 27, 1883.

Federal government and their combined effort to forestall impending steps to collect that debt. The debt originated in government subsidy bonds issued to aid construction of the roads. These bonds amounted to $27,236,512 for the Union Pacific, $25,885,120 for the Central Pacific, and smaller amounts for branch roads. They were in the nature of loans to mature in thirty years at 6 per cent interest, payable semi-annually. The law specified as means of liquidating the debt transportation services rendered the government by the debtor railroads and, after the roads were completed, 5 per cent of their annual net earnings. By raising legal obstructions, claiming that interest payments need not start until maturity of the bonds, and disputing the meaning of the terms "date of completion" of the road and "net earnings," the railroad companies contrived to block and postpone collection of interest or any plan of funding the principal and to foil the government's attempts to solve the dispute. Annual returns up to 16 per cent on capital stock and handsome dividend payments stood in striking contrast to the railroads' claim that they were unable to meet their obligations to the government. Since the companies were taking no steps to meet their obligations and since interest at the time the bonds matured promised to be nearly double the principal, Congress with good reason became alarmed that the entire debt might be lost to the government by default. To prevent this, two bills were introduced in 1876 calculated to bring the companies to terms. One passed the House, but was blocked in the Senate. A second, introduced by Allen G. Thurman, Democratic senator from Ohio, had strong support and bade fair to succeed.[3]

Gould, Dillon, and Huntington combined forces to press upon Congress a substitute more to their liking than the distasteful Thurman bill.[4] Huntington's preference was for a scheme by which the government would reimburse itself by buying back from the companies land it had originally given them, paying twice the amount regu-

[3] Lewis H. Haney, *A Congressional History of Railways in the United States, 1850–1887* (Madison, Wisconsin, 1910), 84–97; *Railway World,* III (February 3, 1877), 107.

[4] Grenville M. Dodge to Jay Gould, February 12, 1877, letterbook in Box 384, Dodge Papers.

larly charged for pre-emption of public lands. Since this would raise the price of the lands retained by the railroads, and since the lands offered the government were the poorest in the companies' possession, there was much to be said for the scheme from the railroad point of view.[5] Huntington instructed Colton to "have the newspapers take the ground that this land ought to be taken by the Government and held for the people, so that when they wanted it they could have it, etc. Something that the demagogues can vote and work for."[6] Since the prospects of such a land-sale bill were admittedly not bright, an alternative bill providing for a railroad "sinking fund" to retire the debt was agreed upon by Huntington and Gould.[7] The bills were sponsored by two Southern senators, one a Republican and one a Democrat. The Republican Senator from Louisiana, Joseph R. West, chairman of the Senate Railroad Committee, introduced the railroad land-sale bill but it made no progress.[8] Sponsor of the sinking-fund bill favored by the Pacific roads was Senator John B. Gordon of Georgia, whom Huntington characterized as "one of our men."[9]

On January 12, 1877, Gordon introduced the sinking-fund bill, and one week later his colleague West reported the bill out of committee with certain amendments.[10] In supporting his bill and attacking Thurman's, Gordon viewed "with unfeigned alarm" any measure "in any degree violative of vested rights," or of "the sanctity of contracts." His rule regarding the government's conduct was, "not her interest first, and her good name afterward, but her interest and her honor one and inseparable."[11] Democratic Senator Francis M. Cockrell of Missouri regretted that Gordon did not remain in his seat after his speech long enough to explain how long it would take his sinking fund of $1,500,000 a year to liquidate the railroad debt when the interest alone was accumulating at the rate of $3,305,531

[5] Haney, *Congressional History of Railways,* 96–97.

[6] Huntington to Colton, June 24, 1876, in Chicago *Tribune,* December 27, 1883.

[7] Dodge to Gould, February 12, 1877, letterbook in Box 384, Dodge Papers.

[8] *Congressional Record,* 44 Cong., 1 Sess. (May 26, 1876), 3342.

[9] Huntington to Colton, March 14, 1877, in Chicago *Tribune,* December 27, 1883.

[10] *Congressional Record,* 44 Cong., 2 Sess. (January 12, 1877), 589; (January 19, 1877), 736.

[11] *Ibid.* (February 7, 1877), *Appendix,* 107, 109.

a year. Senator West offered an explanation that was not very convincing.[12] In spite of stiff opposition, particularly from Northern Democrats, General Dodge assured Jay Gould that their friends in Congress would push the bill through, or at any rate "they would give us pretty nearly the Gordon Bill."[13] The Gould-Huntington combination was thought to be invincible.

If the weight of the Union Pacific–Central Pacific combination could be thrown behind that of the Southern Pacific–Texas & Pacific lobby in the Presidential election crisis and be made to support the works of Dodge, Boynton, and Kellar, the aggregate of influence would be terrific. The Texas & Pacific group was affiliated with the Central Pacific–Union Pacific alliance by ties with each of the partners to the combination. Since the distinction between the Southern Pacific and the Central Pacific was largely nominal and since their lobbies and leadership in Washington were practically identical, the agreement in December 1876 between Scott and Huntington meant an affiliation with both Central and Southern Pacific.

The Union Pacific, although it "did not show its hand openly," according to General Dodge, had been a secret ally of the Texas & Pacific so long as both roads were fighting Huntington. An additional connection of importance between the two companies was established in 1875 when Dodge returned to the Union Pacific board of directors. He was thus serving simultaneously as general engineer of the Texas & Pacific and director of the Union Pacific. Upon informing the vice president of the Texas & Pacific of his decision to become a director of the Union Pacific, Dodge promised that "in our fight next winter [before Congress] I shall endeavor to have that organization with us."[14] Dodge was in an excellent position to promote co-operation in Washington between the two companies, since he organized and in large measure directed the lobbies of both on the scene. During the summer of 1876, while he was hard at work organizing the Texas & Pacific forces for the coming session of

[12] *Ibid.*, 1308–1309.
[13] Dodge to Gould, February 12, 1877, letterbook in Box 384, Dodge Papers.
[14] Dodge to Frank S. Bond, March 1, 1875, letterbook in Box 346, *ibid.*

Congress, General Dodge, "after consulting Mr. Gould fully and at his suggestion," made arrangements of salary and contingent fees for the Union Pacific with lobbyists "to look after our interests during the balance of that session, the vacation and during the present session until March '77." [15] During that period the general remained in close touch not only with Scott and Bond of the Texas & Pacific but with Dillon and Gould of the Union Pacific. His correspondence with these executives reveals, besides numerous common interests in railway legislation, a common concern for a solution of the national election crisis in favor of the Republican candidate.

"When Gould, Scott, Huntington, and their confederates are seen acting together, though professedly hostile," observed Charles A. Dana's New York *Sun,* a Tilden paper, "there is good ground for suspicion." The activities of this "formidable lobby" recalled to the editor "the closing days of the session of 1873, when the great corporations swarmed in the House of Representatives to save the Crédit Mobilier statesmen from expulsion." The motives of the railroad combination seemed "perfectly plain" to the *Sun.* "One-third of the Senate, and about one-half of the present House," it observed, "will disappear from Congress after the 4th of March. Most of them will probably never return to public life. The venal, loose, and speculative patriots will . . . look upon this as their last chance, and be glad to profit by any opportunity to better their fortunes." [16] The Chicago *Tribune* and the New York *Times* made the same analysis of the railroad combination's political tactics, but added as another motive of the combination the desire to seize advantage of the Presidential election crisis as a cover for the movements of their lobby and their friends in Congress.[17]

In the opinion of General Dodge the prospects of favorable action on the Texas & Pacific bill, as of January 17, were encouraging. The movement was "very popular" in Washington, "much more so than ever before," he thought. Could the bill be brought to a vote before

[15] Dodge to Sidney Dillon, December 14, 1876, letterbook in Box 382, *ibid.*
[16] New York *Sun,* February 16, 1877.
[17] New York *Times,* January 5, 1877; Chicago *Tribune,* January 8, 1877.

March 4 he believed it would command a majority in both houses. The real difficulty lay in bringing the bill to a vote, for that meant crowding the measure into a congressional calendar already overcrowded to the bursting point with the business of solving the election crisis. To accomplish that would require all the skill of a master and all the power of an imposing lobby.[18]

On January 24, in the midst of the debate over the Electoral Commission bill, L. Q. C. Lamar arose in the House to report two bills from the Committee on the Pacific Railroad. One of these was the new Texas & Pacific bill upon which Scott and Huntington had reached a compromise. But Lamar first reported a Northern Pacific Railroad bill, and its reception foreshadowed the fate of the Texas & Pacific measure.

Required by law to complete its construction by July 4, 1877, in order to earn a huge Federal land grant of some 36,000,000 acres, the Northern Pacific fell into financial difficulties that prevented it from meeting these requirements. Lamar's bill would remove the requirement and grant the company an additional eight years to complete its main line to Puget Sound and earn the land grant. William S. Holman of Indiana, Democratic chairman of the House Committee on Appropriations, was immediately on his feet to challenge Lamar. Incorrigible foe of monopoly, land grants, speculation, and government subsidies to private capitalists, Holman was the Democrat who had introduced the resolution committing his party against subsidies of any kind and carried it over Southern opposition in December 1875. Now he was maintaining that the Lamar bill in effect actually appropriated government property and that House rules required the discussion of all such appropriations by a committee of the whole House, a requirement that would seriously impede the progress of the bill. Lamar denied that his bill amounted to an appropriation. Democratic Speaker Randall, however, rejected Lamar's construction and upheld Holman's. Lamar then asked that his bill be considered by the committee of the whole on the following Tuesday. This required unanimous consent, and Holman immediately objected. Garfield

[18] Dodge to J. M. Eddy, January 17, 1877, letterbook in Box 384, Dodge Papers.

and John A. Kasson of Iowa, another Republican, joined Lamar in imploring Holman to withdraw his objection. It was another clash between Northern Democrats and a combination of Republicans and Southern Democrats, for Lamar had been supported in committee by Walker of Virginia, Atkins of Tennessee, and Throckmorton of Texas.[19]

Lamar's argument was that defeat of the bill would injure "meritorious stockholders, widows, orphans, and trustees." Holman was unmoved. "The investments made by widows and guardians of orphan children are already lost," he declared, and the only beneficiaries of the bill would be "the leading capitalists who heretofore have had control of this whole enterprise." He then unloosed a terrific blast on the subsidy seekers. "This whole subject of subsidy by the Federal Government," he said, "in all its forms, has uniformly ended in fraud, not only upon the Government, but upon the people, and has been a most fruitful source of dishonesty and of national humiliation, and the sooner the whole system is put an end to the better it will be for the Government, the public honor, and the people. Its continuance will be ultimately fatal to the integrity on which our free institutions rest." Holman refused to withdraw his objection, and "Sunset" Cox of New York and another Northern Democrat joined in blocking further debate.[20]

Immediately following this chilling prologue, Lamar reported the Texas & Pacific bill. In view of its political repercussions it deserves close analysis. The bill removed the penalty of forfeiting the land grant that the Texas & Pacific had incurred by failure to comply with the law, and divided construction of the trunk line between the two major companies involved. Scott's company was to build westward from Fort Worth to a point one hundred miles west of El Paso. There it was to make juncture with the Southern Pacific, which was to build eastward from Fort Yuma and westward to San Diego. Land grants originally made to the Texas & Pacific on the western

[19] *Congressional Record,* 44 Cong., 2 Sess. (January 24, 1877), 922–923.

[20] *Ibid.,* 44 Cong., 1 Sess. (January 24, 1877), 922–923; also (March 2, 1877) 2131.

part of its route were to be turned over to the Southern Pacific. In case either company failed to construct the part of route agreed upon, it was required to forfeit its grant to the other, but not to the United States. Each of the four eastern branch lines—to New Orleans, to Vicksburg, to Memphis, and to Vinita—was incorporated in the bill. The two trunk-line companies were to deposit with the Secretary of the Treasury their bonds up to $40,000 per mile of road, the four eastern branches $30,000 per mile, and the San Diego branch $35,000 per mile. All bonds were payable in gold fifty years from their date with 5 per cent interest. The United States was to guarantee payment of interest on all bonds in gold for the half century. This guarantee covered 1187 miles of trunk line at $40,000 a mile, a possible 1248 miles of eastern branches at $30,000 a mile, and 130 miles of the San Diego branch at $35,000. A total of $89,470,000 of bonds was thus guaranteed for $4,473,500 annual interest, or for the fifty years an aggregate interest of $223,675,000. The totals were distributed as follows:[21]

Guaranteed Bonds per Mile	*Railroads*	*Least Estimated Length*	*Amount Bonds on the Least Estimate*	*Maximum Authorized Length*	*Amount Bonds on Maximum Estimate*
$40,000	Texas & Pacific and Southern Pacific trunk line	1,187	$47,480,000	1,187	$47,480,000
35,000	San Diego branch	100	3,500,000	130	4,550,000
30,000	Vinita branch	325	9,750,000	436	13,080,000
30,000	Memphis branch	260	7,800,000	305	9,150,000
30,000	Vicksburg branch	98	2,940,000	170	5,100,000
30,000	New Orleans branch	337	10,110,000	337	10,110,000
		2,307	$81,580,000	2,565	$89,470,000

Interest per year on least estimate	$ 4,079,000
Interest per year on maximum estimate	4,473,500
Aggregate interest for fifty years on least estimate	203,950,000
Aggregate interest for fifty years on maximum estimate	223,675,000

The security proposed for this enormous loan was somewhat better defined than the security for the smaller loan to the Union Pa-

[21] House of Representatives *Reports,* 44 Cong., 2 Sess., Report No. 139, Parts I and II. The table is taken from p. 4 of Part II, the Minority Report.

cific and Central Pacific, but in view of the current experience of the government with those defaulting companies there was reason to take exception to security proposed for the new transcontinentals. First there were the proceeds from the sale of land grants. But the congressional grants were actually a reservation of the government's own property yet to be earned by the companies and could hardly be regarded as security. Only that part of the Texas grant west of Fort Worth was offered, and it as well as the Federal grant was of very uncertain value. As for the value of the railroad property, the small sinking fund, and the portion of net earnings, offered as security, that would depend on the unproved ability of the several companies to earn substantially more than operating and repair expenses in great stretches of sparsely settled territory. The Vinita branch was aptly described as a "tunnel" several hundred miles long through territory closed by law to settlers. The cost of government transportation over the subsidized roads, to be reserved by the treasury as security, was good so far as it went, but the amount was undetermined and would probably not be very large. Champions of the bill stressed the security provided by the retention in the Federal Treasury of $5000 of bonds per mile, interest guaranteed by the government, pending construction of the roads. The value of this security had the curious feature of depending on the very guarantee it was proposed to secure, a feature that justified more than any other the opinion of the Minority Report on the bill that the whole scheme was "a fabric of credit floated upon credit without capital." For the government was, in effect, asked to create a property by a liability of its own, then accept what it created as security against its liability, but without requiring any definite amount of capital stock to be furnished by the subsidized corporations to contribute to the security of the government.[22]

Another interesting feature of the security offered the government by the railroads was that it did not include the completed and most profitable portions of the roads, nor their land grants and earnings. Should the government be forced to foreclose and take over the mort-

[22] *Ibid.*, Part II, p. 5.

gaged roads, therefore, it would find itself in possession of scattered and unconnected fragments, the longest of which lay between Fort Worth and Fort Yuma, but without control over a continuous route between important termini. This was also true of the branch roads, to which the bill reserved rights granted, or to be granted, by state legislatures to operate existing lines. The existing lines so operated would not be subject to government control or foreclosure.

The whole matter of the branch roads seems to have got out of hand as the Texas & Pacific faction evolved and attracted new support. Originally attached as riders to gain local support, the branch roads, now five in number, had come to overshadow the trunk line in mileage by the time Lamar reported the bill: 1378 miles of branches to 1187 miles of trunk line. To General Dodge they were a source of embarrassment. Writing Frank S. Bond about the bill, Dodge confessed that he was "sorry all these *branches* are in it. I fear we will have hard work holding members up to the subsidies in the States." [23] On the other hand it would have been awkward politically to abandon the branch roads. Senator Dorsey of Arkansas introduced the Texas & Pacific bill in the Senate, and Dorsey was the president of the railroad company that hoped to build the Memphis branch.[24] Colonel Kellar, one of the directors of Dorsey's road, described Dorsey's Senate bill as "substantially the same" as the bill Lamar reported in the House.[25]

"It is substantially a proposition," concluded the two Northern Democrats and three Republicans, who signed the Minority Report on the bill, "to build this road and the branches on Government credit without making them the property of the Government when built. If there be any profit, the corporations may take it; if there be loss, the Government must bear it." [26] All things considered — the peculiarities of the security proposed, the one-sided nature of the financial arrangements, and the proliferation of branch-road schemes

[23] Dodge to Bond, December 20, 1876, letterbook in Box 382, Dodge Papers.
[24] *Congressional Record,* 44 Cong., 2 Sess. (February 14, 1877), 1549.
[25] Kellar in Memphis *Avalanche,* February 21, 1877.
[26] House of Representatives *Reports,* 44 Cong., 2 Sess., Report No. 139, Part II, p. 8.

— this characterization of the bill was not inaccurate. One critic suggested that for an amount of money equal to the maximum contemplated by the bill the government could construct the Isthmian canal. The maximum amount, incidentally, represented more than twice the total of all Federal expenditures for railroads, canals, and wagon roads from 1789 to 1873.

Lamar related the Texas & Pacific bill to the national political crisis by presenting it as a means of "reconciliation" between the sections, "material reconstruction" of the South, and a way of restoring "mutual respect and affection" at a moment when those sentiments were desperately needed. Conscious that he was speaking in "the midst of serious political perplexity and threatened danger," the Mississippian offered the bill as "one of the simplest and yet surest means of reconciling the interests and harmonizing the sentiment of this whole country." [27]

Lamar was perfectly aware by this time that harmonizing the sentiment of his own party, the Northern and Southern wings of it, was impossible so far as this and similar subsidies were concerned. Even if Holman of Indiana had not so recently reminded him of the Northern Democratic position by his blast against subsidy seekers, Lamar could have easily anticipated the coming reaction. It was well known and deeply resented among Southerners that Holman, just one year to the day before Lamar reported his bill, on January 24, 1876, had introduced a resolution instructing the Committee on the Judiciary to investigate the Texas & Pacific Company with a view to justifying procedure for the forfeiture of its franchise. A preamble to the resolution declared that it had been "alleged that improper and fraudulent means were resorted to to influence legislation" incorporating the company in 1871 "by persons interested in the passage of said act, and that contracts and combinations were subsequently entered into by said company, in violation of the terms of said act." [28] The resolution could have been aimed at Southern

[27] *Ibid.*, Part I, p. 8.

[28] *Congressional Record,* 44 Cong., 1 Sess. (January 24, 1876), 598. The resolution was allowed to pass without a division of the House, but died in committee.

Republicans such as Senator Alcorn of Mississippi and Senator West of Louisiana, who were among the original incorporators of the Texas & Pacific, or at Senators Dorsey and Clayton of Arkansas, who were officials of one of the branch road companies. But if the Texas & Pacific movement had been predominantly Southern Republican in origin, it had become increasingly Southern Democratic as Redemption progressed, and by 1876 it was overwhelmingly so. Holman's resolution was a slap in the face of the leaders of the Southern wing of his own party, and it drew embarrassing attention to collusion between the Redeemers and their public enemies, the Carpetbaggers. Coming on the eve of the Presidential campaign, the resolution also served notice that the Northern Democrats, led by Randall, Holman, Hewitt, and Cox, were determined to wage a reform fight and that they would refuse to begin their fight by yielding to a Southern demand for a revival of Grantism.

It came as no surprise that Holman took the floor as soon as Lamar completed his report of the Texas & Pacific bill and raised the same points of order and objections he had used to block the Northern Pacific bill. Franklin Landers, another Indiana Democrat, then introduced a substitute for Lamar's bill, pruning from it all the branch roads, eliminating subsidies to Huntington, and drastically revising the financing plan in the direction of increased security for the government.[29] The House refused Lamar's request for unanimous consent that his bill be made a special order in the committee of the whole on the state of the Union for February 3 and from day to day until disposed of. The bill was then placed at the bottom of the calendar of the committee of the whole, with thirty-four bills preceding it. To gain consideration for the bill before the end of the session it would be necessary to carry a motion suspending the rules of the House, a motion requiring a majority of two thirds to pass. Undaunted by this apparently insuperable obstacle, the Texas & Pacific men organized their forces to make the attempt. One great difficulty in the way was that the House calendar was already crowded with

[29] *Ibid.*, 2 Sess. (January 24, 1877), 924; for Landers's description and defense of his bill see *ibid.*, Appendix, pp. 196–201.

the Electoral Commission business. Another was that the press of the country was making a concerted outcry against the railroads, particularly the Texas & Pacific men, and watching every move of their lobby.

Republican papers of New York and Chicago merely intensified a long-standing campaign against the Southern transcontinental road, a campaign that the press of the Southwestern cities claimed was animated by motives of sectional jealousy and interest. The New York *Times,* which kept up a running editorial attack, called Lamar's bill "the most outrageous job now before the country," and "an attempt to reopen a system of national expenditures on a scale more extravagant than that which was applied to the Union and Central [Pacific] Companies, in spite of the warning which the bad faith of these companies has given to the American people." If these completed, well-equipped, and prosperous Pacific roads pleaded inability to pay a smaller debt to the government, why should Congress gamble a second time against heavier odds and for larger stakes when there was no emergency such as justified the first experiment? The *Times* reminded the Democrats of their endorsement of Holman's resolution repudiating the entire subsidy system, pronounced the security proposed in the new bill "worthy of Col. Sellers," and declared that there was "no swindle that might not claim Mr. Lamar's endorsement" if his bill was allowed to pass.[30]

The strictures of the New York *Times,* the Chicago *Tribune,* and their like could be discounted as the voice of partisanship and sectional bias. It was a different matter with Edwin L. Godkin's *Nation.* The weekly spoke for the Northern liberals and intellectuals, mainly of Republican background, who had abandoned the Republicans because of their disgust with Grantism, railroad jobbery, and Carpetbagger corruption. The liberals had joined with the Democrats to fight for reform. They preached "reconciliation," readmission of the Southern states, "home rule," and an end to Reconstruction. In advocating "the free and cordial readmission of Southern men to partici-

[30] New York *Times,* January 13, 22, 28, February 14, 1877. The Chicago *Tribune,* January 8, 16, 1877, made similar attacks on the bill.

pation in the work of government," these liberals, said the *Nation,* had been "very largely actuated by the hope of finding in Southern politicians like Mr. Lamar himself and Senator Gordon of Georgia, powerful assistance in ridding the Government of the corrupt and jobbing practices," practices from which "both North and South have been suffering during the last ten years." "It seems, therefore," said the *Nation,* "almost incredible that they should be seen rising up in company with Mr. Tom Scott and his kind to help to fasten the yoke of the rings more firmly than ever on the neck of the Northern reformers." The Southern wing of the reformers seemed to have joined the enemy.[31] The editor was particularly concerned "to remind Mr. Lamar of the injurious consequences of his advocacy of so scandalous a job," for Lamar was "by force of his abilities the representative, *par excellence,* of the South in the new order of things. . . . Mr. Lamar is strangely careless if he overlooks the fact that suspicion of bribery will just as naturally rest on the supporters of a Texas and Pacific as of a Union Pacific job, and that this suspicion, if confirmed in his case, will extend to the entire delegation from the reconstructed South, than which there could hardly be a greater misfortune. The unmercenary traditions of Southern statesmen will not save him or them; on the contrary, the poverty of the South caused by the war will make it *a priori* probable that Southern Congressmen are corruptible."[32]

As an indication of Democratic cleavage over railroad subsidies the New York *Sun* was more significant than the *Nation.* It was popularly believed in Republican as well as Democratic circles that Tilden had a personal hand in shaping Dana's editorial policy on politics. So far as the *Sun* editorials on the Scott lobby were concerned, the rumor was verified to the satisfaction of Attorney General Alfonso Taft by one of his secret service men.[33] And none of the metropolitan dailies was more relentless than the *Sun* in following the maneuvers of the Scott lobby nor more merciless in expos-

[31] *Nation,* XXIV (1877), 82–83.
[32] *Ibid.,* 65–66.
[33] Alfonso Taft to R. B. Hayes, February 14, 1877, Hayes Papers.

ing politicians — Southern Democrats among them — who were used by the lobbies. The editor pronounced the bill that Lamar reported "the most nefarious railroad jobbery yet attempted in this country."[34] The alert Washington correspondent of the *Sun,* A. M. Gibson, who collaborated with Hewitt to prepare the Democratic campaign textbook of 1876, was the first to warn Tilden that the railroad lobby was undermining Democratic unity by working on the Southerners. Thereafter he kept a sharp eye on the manipulations of Scott, Dodge, and Gould, and reported their doings regularly.

It was in some ways ironical that Samuel J. Tilden should have been pushed to the front as a leader of a national movement of opposition to the railroad monopolists. A manipulator and speculator among Western railroads on his own in the past, Tilden had at various times during his legal career served as counsel for Scott, Gould, Fisk, Oakes Ames, and W. C. Whitney.[35] Yet the New Yorker had acquired such a reputation as an enemy of railroad subsidy seekers that the Democratic Cincinnati *Enquirer* in opposing his nomination branded him as "a most pitiless foe of the interests of the West and South," and an "unscrupulous oppressor of the great struggling industries" of those sections. "No Republican administration could be more hostile to them than would his," declared the *Enquirer.*[36] So persistent were reports that Tom Scott was seeking the defeat of Tilden that a few weeks before the nominating convention Scott sent the New York governor a long telegram denying the story and reminding him of their "pleasant relations of many years."[37]

Whether there was any foundation for the story in fact or not, the newspapers repeated reports throughout the Presidential election crisis that Tilden was directing Northern Democratic opposition to the Texas & Pacific bill. Seeing in the story another opportunity for widening the North-South rift in Tilden's ranks, the Washington *National Republican* played it up during the electoral vote count.

[34] New York *Sun,* January 9 and February 16, 1877; for other attacks see the *Sun,* February 6, 13, 1875.

[35] Flick, *Tilden,* 164–165.

[36] Cincinnati *Enquirer,* June 5, 1876.

[37] Thomas A. Scott to Samuel J. Tilden, June 1, 1876, Tilden Papers.

"The Southern Democrats have become furious," said the editor on the day after Lamar reported his bill, "since they learned that Mr. Tilden has instructed the Northern dough-faces to kill the Texas Pacific for this session. What object Mr. Tilden has in attempting to deprive the South and the country of the great and lasting benefits which would arise from this important enterprise we do not know."[38] The *National Republican* followed this up with a full-column, front-page editorial praising the Lamar bill as "undoubtedly the greatest, as it surely is the most beneficent measure now before the public," and denouncing opposition to it as "lunatic" and "willfully blind."[39] Lest the contrast between Republican friendliness and Northern Democratic hostility to their interests escape Southern congressmen, the editor remarked that "there is a great deal of cupidity about the Northern dough-face's love of the true interest of the South. If not, why did Mr. Tilden order that the Texas Pacific bill should not be allowed to pass?"[40]

As a matter of fact the Northern Democracy required little assistance from the Republican press in clarifying the cleavage between its aims and views and those of the Southern Democracy. The contrast was brought home daily to Southern congressmen in the columns of the Washington *Union*. Montgomery Blair had launched the daily *Union* on December 7, 1876, with the liberal backing of William W. Corcoran, a wealthy banker. In addition to fulfilling the long-felt need for a Democratic daily paper in the national capital, the *Union* served a more immediate need as the voice of the Tilden forces in the contested election struggle. Within two months the paper became the largest morning daily in Washington and was quoted widely over the country as a leader in the Tilden battle. Manton Marble and Jeremiah S. Black lent a hand with editorials, but the main burden fell upon Blair as editor-in-chief. For three months he devoted virtually all his time to the paper.[41]

[38] Washington *National Republican,* January 25, 1877.
[39] *Ibid.,* January 30, 1877.
[40] *Ibid.,* February 23, 1877.
[41] William E. Smith, *The Francis Preston Blair Family in Politics,* 2 vols. (New York, 1933), II, 482–484.

A member of the famous Blair family that had figured in almost every important political event from 1828 to 1876, son of Francis P. Blair, once editor of Andrew Jackson's Washington organ and kitchen-cabinet member, Montgomery came of a stanchly Jacksonian background. A borderlander who lived successively in Kentucky, Missouri, and Maryland, Montgomery Blair became a Free-Soiler, served as counsel for Dred Scott, and went over to the Republican party on the slavery issue. During the Civil War he was Lincoln's Postmaster General and strong defender, and after the war he befriended President Johnson, fell out with the Radicals, and drifted back into the Democratic party. Blair played a leading part in securing Tilden's nomination by organizing support for him in the Southern and border states, and after the election Tilden appointed him one of his counsel before the Electoral Commission. No doubt the wish helped father the thought, but Blair pictured Tilden to the country as belonging to the old antislavery, Free-Soil, Unionist school of Silas Wright, Van Buren, and Preston King, and Tilden's victory to him meant the triumph of the Jacksonian element in the Democratic party.[42] Blair had a profound sympathy for Southerners of the Jacksonian school, men of Andrew Johnson's sort, and had left the Republican party largely because of its Southern policy. But among the Redeemers who had captured control of the Southern Democracy he thought he saw a rejuvenation of Whiggery, the emergence of conservatives in Democratic clothing. Blair blamed this element for defeating his nomination to Congress from the Sixth Maryland District in 1874. Southern conservatives and proslavery men had captured the party of Jackson in the fifties and driven the Blairs from the home of their fathers. Now that he had returned to the old party, Montgomery was determined that what had happened in the fifties should not recur in the seventies.

Within a week of the launching of the *Union,* Blair struck a hard blow at the combination of railroad lobbies, particularly the Texas & Pacific group, and charged that they were working on Congress to rob Tilden of his victory. He followed this with an editorial on

[42] *Ibid.,* 469, 473–475; Washington *Union,* December 18, 1876.

January 5 charging that Lamar had adopted the Republican theory that the Vice President had the right to count the electoral votes, and that leading Southern Democrats were deserting Tilden and secretly supporting Hayes.[43] Blair's editorial was reported to have "caused considerable excitement" in Washington. Lamar wrote Blair a card "which meant fight, or it meant nothing," but was dissuaded from sending it. Instead he sent Judge Jeremiah S. Black to the editor with a denial that he supported the Republican theory of settling the election dispute. Lamar believed that the attack was "meant as punishment for his support of the Texas Pacific Railway."[44] Blair printed as "a correction" the denial that Judge Black brought him, but he continued to believe and say that Lamar and other Southern Democrats were betraying Tilden and secretly dealing with Hayes. "It is painfully evident to me," he wrote Tilden, "that you will be defeated by the lobbies of Congress who are largely in the ascendant over both parties"—and particularly over the Southern Democrats. "There was in fact," he continued, "an active co-operation whether arranged or not is immaterial between the Radicals & the men of the Lamar order in the H. of Reps. This will appear more fully I believe hereafter."[45] Meanwhile the *Union* kept up a running attack on the suspected Southern leaders, even going so far as to repeat the strictures of the *Nation* on Lamar.

The effect of Blair's campaign against Southern conservatives was to widen the sectional rift in Tilden's ranks and smooth the path to an understanding between Southerners and Republicans. While Blair was calling Southerners bad names, the Washington *National Republican*, sometimes referred to loosely as "the administration organ," was calling them "a brave people who hate scheming knavery and sneaking whitelivered pusillanimity" and who were "willing and ready to throw off the coils of friendship and evil

[43] Montgomery Blair to S. J. Tilden, November 25, 1877, Tilden Papers. Blair reviews the whole controversy in this letter. Also Washington *Union*, January 5, 1877.

[44] St. Louis *Republic* quoted in Edward Mayes, *Lucius Q. C. Lamar: His Life, Times, and Speeches, 1823–1893* (Nashville, 1896), 303.

[45] Montgomery Blair to Samuel J. Tilden, February 8, 1877, Tilden Papers.

advice the Bourbon Northerners have been lavishing for party purposes upon them for the past twenty years. . . . They see in President Hayes a man who will bring peace to their distracted country."[46]

Southerners took up Blair's aspersions and returned them in kind. Colonel Kellar replied with considerable bitterness in his Memphis paper. While the Washington *Union* pretended to speak for the national Democracy, said Kellar, "the real work of this latest journalistic abortion is that of inducing the Northern Democrats to defeat, primarily the Texas and Pacific Railroad measure, and secondarily every project designed to rebuild the shattered fortunes of the Southern tier of states." The South could not be bound to the Democratic party by sympathy and sentiment alone, warned Kellar. "The *Union* speaks for that class of Democrats who argue with themselves that gush alone is necessary to hold the South in partisan tracks. . . . The tendency of so many of our public men to cultivate the emotional and scout the practical is so well understood by such men as the Blairs, Woods, Holmans and Randalls that it is relied upon in all cases, and too frequently with success." It was only because Lamar had "labored earnestly in behalf of the Texas and Pacific" that Blair was "indecently assailing him, and giving editorial prominence to the sneers of the *Nation*."[47] And to William Henry Smith the colonel complained of the *Union's* attack "on those Southern democrats of national faith whom it charges with defeating 'their' president."[48] More and more Tilden came to be pictured as "their" President, not the South's.

The Texas & Pacific group picked January 29 as the day on which to make their drive to gain a two-thirds vote to suspend the House rules and fix a day for the consideration of the Lamar bill. Southerners believed that while the Northern Democrats would desert them they could depend upon sufficient Republican support to carry the difficult maneuver.[49] Remarking that "the Democratic party will be

[46] Washington *National Republican,* January 4, 1877.
[47] Memphis *Avalanche,* February 15, 1877.
[48] Andrew J. Kellar to William Henry Smith, February 9, 1877, Smith Papers.
[49] New Orleans *Times,* January 30, 1877; Memphis *Avalanche,* February 3, 1877.

put on trial today," the *National Republican* urged Republican congressmen to vote with the South. "It would be proper," said the editor, "under the circumstances, to force upon the Tilden wing of the Democratic party the responsibility of defeating the passage of the bill. This responsibility has been heretofore evaded, because an open offense to the majority of the Democratic party could not safely be offered by the minority until the hoped for inauguration of Tilden."[50] It was indeed a strategic moment to force into the open and place on record by roll call the underlying cleavage among Democrats, for it was the day on which the Electoral Commission bill became law and the House was to proceed with the election of its five members of the tribunal.

The railroad lobbies turned out in full force for the trial of strength on the twenty-ninth, crowding into the House chamber itself in violation of the rules. According to the *National Republican* there were "at least one hundred outsiders behind the members' desks," and one member protested that he could not move twenty feet in any direction from the Speaker's desk without running into a half-dozen lobbyists.[51] "The disgraceful scene enacted Monday in the House of Representatives would not have been possible in the legislative halls of any other nation in the world," declared the Chicago *Tribune*. "The floor of Congress was actually invaded by hired and professional lobbyists, who openly resorted to all the devices of their trade to coax, buy, or bully Congressmen to give their proposed robbery of the National Treasury precedence over the needed and rightful legislation of the nation." It was considered a "special impertinence" that the lobbyists were demanding that Congress give precedence to a bill subsidizing a new Pacific road over several bills seeking to make the old Pacific roads pay their debts.[52] Disturbance created by the lobbyists finally threatened to drown out proceedings of the House, and Speaker Randall on the request of a member had them evicted from the floor, many with "violent protests."[53]

[50] Washington *National Republican*, January 29, 1877.
[51] *Ibid.*, January 30, 1877.
[52] Chicago *Tribune*, January 31, 1877.
[53] New York *Times*, January 30, 1877.

As it turned out, a division of the House over the Lamar bill was evaded by a rule which gave over the day to the committee on the District of Columbia. Randall upheld the rule and the embarrassment of the Democrats, for which the Republicans hoped, was postponed. The lobby was reported by the New York *Times* to be "by no means discouraged by the delay" and determined to return to the attack "when the bustle and confusion of the last days of the session make this easier than now." [54]

It is not suggested for a moment that all the differences that divided Southern and Northern Democrats can be traced to the Texas & Pacific fight, nor for that matter is it intimated that Tom Scott, or Dodge, or Gould, or Huntington, was a *deus ex machina* dangling national destiny on the strings of a lobby. The railroad struggle illustrated and dramatized the cleavage, but it was only one among numerous issues that caused bad blood between the sectional wings of the Democratic party.

Over the years the Northern Democrats had developed a sensitive conscience and a defense psychology about their ex-Confederate brethren. During the war they had taken a good deal of punishment on account of the record of the copperhead or pro-Southern wing of the party, and afterward the Republicans sought constantly to identify the party of their rivals with disloyalty and treason. Several Northern Democrats performed valiant service to the South of the Redeemers by defending her against the slander and bloody-shirt propaganda of Republicans.[55] But party officials generally were inclined to lean over backward to avoid anything that would lend color to Republican propaganda that the Democrats were controlled by "rebels." A standard feature of the bloody-shirt campaign was the charge that a Democratic victory would result in a Southern "raid on the Treasury" in the shape of appropriation bills and improvements to recoup war losses. Such raids would "destroy national credit" and "bankrupt the nation." The anxiety to avoid any such

[54] *Ibid.*, February 3, 1877.

[55] Albert V. House, Jr., "Northern Congressional Democrats as Defenders of the South During Reconstruction," *Journal of Southern History*, VI (1940), 45–71.

imputation was therefore added to the strong "reform" impulse against railroad jobbery and subsidies to double the resistance of Northern Democrats to demands for internal improvements in the South — however needed or justifiable. Oversensitivity to the charge of rebel domination also served to justify the denial of positions of honor and leadership to Southern Democrats. Perhaps this also served to advance the ambitions of certain Northern politicians. At least a suspicion of the sort was entertained among Southern politicians.

One old chestnut familiar to all bloody-shirt campaigners was the prediction that a Democratic majority would pay off all "rebel" claims for war damage, as well as the Confederate war debt and compensation for emancipated slaves. The only basis for the charge was some $60,000,000 worth of claims for war damage filed by "loyal" Southerners. Some of the claimants probably had dubious war records, and only a fraction of the claims were ever paid. But so persistently did the Republicans hammer away at the charge that Tilden felt constrained before the end of the campaign to issue a public denial that he would ever under any circumstances pay either claims, debts, or compensation to any "rebel" or "disloyal person." [56] The statement was of course resented and remembered in the South. Republicans revived the issue after the election with a bill for an amendment to the Constitution forbidding the payment of war damage claims to anyone save those who "gave neither aid nor encouragement to the enemy." A preamble to the bill declared that "fears have been and still are entertained by the people" that the government would be compelled "at some time in the future to pay a large amount for damages" and that the amendment was necessary "in order to allay such fears." Three times during the disputed election crisis — on December 18, January 8, and January 22 — a roll call on the bill was forced on the House, and each one served to emphasize the sectional cleavage among the Democrats. Of the 118 Northern Democratic votes in the House only 7 were

[56] Tilden, "War Claims and the Rebel Debt," in John Bigelow (ed.), *Writings and Speeches of Samuel J. Tilden* (New York, 1885), II, 380–383.

cast with the Southern Democratic votes in opposition on the first division, 16 on the second, and 11 on the third.[57]

The Republicans followed a similar strategy in urging a resolution providing for an investigation of public schools in all states to discover whether Negro children were denied equal privileges and instructing the committee to report a bill enforcing equality. Undoubtedly numerous discriminations between the races existed in public schools, and not all of them were in the South, but it is improbable that the main purpose of the Republican resolution in January 1877 was to correct those abuses. On a motion to suspend the rules and adopt the resolution the Northern Democrats split, 30 voting with the Republicans in favor of the motion, 25 with the Southern Democrats against it, and the rest not voting.[58]

Relations between the two wings of the party were not improved by the critical tone adopted by certain Tilden supporters toward the methods used to "redeem" some of the Southern states in 1876. Northern reformers feared that the red-shirt tactics of the Redeemers would embarrass Tilden. Colonel William T. Pelton, Tilden's nephew, had been openly critical of Hampton's candidacy, and the national committee of the party had refused any financial aid to the hard-pressed Democrats of South Carolina. After the election, when it appeared that Hampton was elected and Tilden defeated in South Carolina, and when the suspicion was growing that the Redeemers had betrayed Tilden, Northern critics revived the attack upon the political morals of their Southern brethren. The New York *World* pressed home this attack on Hampton and his supporters with unusual bitterness, charging that Southern Democrats were "degrading the character of American citizens."[59] Replying in the same tone, the Charleston *News and Courier* declared that South

[57] *Congressional Record,* 44 Cong., 2 Sess. (December 18, 1876), 275; (January 8, 1877), 489–490; (January 22, 1877), 813. Since each of the votes was on a motion to suspend the rules and required a majority of two thirds to pass, the nonvoting Northern Democrats naturally assisted in a less conspicuous way in defeating the motion.

[58] *Ibid.* (January 8, 1877), 488–489.

[59] New York *World,* February 23, 1877.

Carolinians had "hazarded everything for the National Democracy" and that "in return, no single thing was done by the National Democracy to help us in our mortal struggle. So with every other Southern State." While the South furnished 131 of the 196 votes claimed for Tilden, the Northern minority, thought the Charleston editor, showed no sense of gratitude and assumed instead a tone of arrogant superiority. It was time for the South to look to its own interests.[60]

All of this was, of course, grist to the mill of Boynton, Kellar & Company, who were constantly endeavoring to exploit these differences between Northern and Southern Democrats. And there were additional differences on which they could work, differences of the economic sort that divided the sectional wings of the party over the Texas & Pacific.

In their efforts to gain support for internal improvements other than railroads, Southerners ran up against the same unfriendly resistance from their own party that they encountered over the Texas & Pacific bill. And by contrast they often met with friendliness and co-operation from Republicans. "Our sectional interests and material development are about the last things the [Democratic] party is disposed to consider," remarked the New Orleans *Times*. Louisianans found that the party leaders of the North were as indifferent or hostile toward the Mississippi levee bill as they were to the Texas & Pacific measure, and "strangely neglectful" of both.[61]

From the viewpoint of public interest and immediate practical need there was much more to be said for government aid to Mississippi levee construction than for subsidies to a new Pacific railroad. Although there was no such skilled professional lobby behind the levee demand as there was supporting the railroads, it is probable that in the Lower Mississippi Valley popular demand for flood control was greater and more deeply felt than the better organized demand for railroad subsidies. Delta spokesmen placed levees above party and urged Southern congressmen to press the demand "not as Democrats

[60] Charleston *News and Courier,* February 27, 1877.
[61] New Orleans *Times,* January 28, 1877.

or Republicans, but as agents of a great and fertile region sorely needing the assistance of the Government to recover from the misfortunes and the prostration of the past sixteen years." The bill for which they asked was a modest enough affair compared with the amounts the railroads were seeking. It called for an appropriation of $4,202,000 to be spent in closing crevasses, repairing levees, and reclaiming flooded lands. With the exception of $75,000 for Illinois and $500,000 for Missouri, the money was divided among four states of the South, $100,000 going to Tennessee, $447,000 to Mississippi, $1,280,000 to Arkansas, and $1,800,000 to Louisiana.[62]

In view of the large Democratic majority in the House, the Delta congressmen entertained high hopes at the beginning of the first session, not only of a sympathetic hearing but of favorable action on the levee bill. Over a period of two years their indignation had time to grow as they watched their pretended friends from the North sidetrack the bill "on one absurd pretext or another," so they felt, throughout both sessions. Petitions and resolutions from the legislatures of Louisiana and Arkansas were of no avail. Then at the end of the second session, "determined to exact some recognition of Southern interests no matter at what inconvenience to others," the Delta men made a final attempt with a motion to suspend the rules and pass the bill.[63] The roll call seemed to confirm the view that the perfidious Democracy of Yankeedom was indifferent to Southern needs. The motion was defeated by a vote of 72 to 113. Of the 118 Northern Democratic members of the House, only 14 rallied to the aid of the Southern Democrats in support of the bill, and of the 14 only 6 came from sections north of the border states. On the other hand, from the minority side of the House—the seat of Carpetbaggery, "Negro domination," and Radical rule—came 26 votes in support of Southern levees.[64] Once again the Southern Democrats of Whiggish leanings had found their friends in the camp

[62] *Congressional Record,* 44 Cong., 2 Sess. (March 3, 1877), 2232.

[63] *Ibid.,* 44 Cong., 2 Sess. (January 12, 1876), 378; (January 17, 1876), 443; (January 31, 1876), 771; (May 8, 1876), 3038. New Orleans *Times,* January 28, 1877.

[64] *Congressional Record,* 44 Cong., 2 Sess. (March 3, 1877), 2232.

of their professed enemies and their enemies in their own house.

It is an old maxim in American history that the people of the Lower Mississippi Valley owe their first allegiance to the great river and only a secondary loyalty to any other power. In 1876 Captain James B. Eads, the famous engineer, won the acclaim of a hero from the Delta people by freeing the mouth of their river from the control, not of Spaniard, English, or French, but of mud. By Herculean labors and inexpensive methods he had constructed jetties of willow mattress that turned the current and cut through the mud bars blocking the mouth of the river a channel deep enough to admit ocean-going vessels of deep draft into the port of New Orleans. These labors were impeded by the cry that Eads was a visionary and his project another "Southern raid on the Treasury," if not a downright swindle.[65] With official proof of the success of his work in hand by October, 1876, Eads was blocked for several months during the election crisis from collecting the $500,000 due him by his contract with the government. The main controversy over the payment of Eads hinged upon whether he was to be paid in cash or in United States bonds, then selling above par. His contract could be interpreted either way, and the difference was a small matter of $60,000. But Congressman Holman, Democratic chairman of the Committee on Appropriations, took an uncompromising stand against payment in bonds on his usual grounds of protecting the Treasury from "raids." On the other hand Charles Foster, close friend of Hayes and congressman from his district, took the liberal view and rebuked Holman for his penuriousness. Other Republican members agreed with him, for example Omar D. Conger of Michigan, who urged immediate payment of "this benefactor of the Mississippi Valley, of the United States, and of the World." Captain Eads arrived on the scene, engaged in angry public controversy with Holman, and fired Southern sympathies in his behalf. It was altogether a small matter, to be sure, but in the midst of a party crisis it served once more to drive home to the Southern mind the ambigu-

[65] Florence Dorsey, *Road to the Sea. The Story of James B. Eads and the Mississippi River* (New York, 1947), 181–200.

ities of the South's political allegiance and weaken Southern attachment to Tilden's cause.[66]

The exchange of courtesies and amenities between Republicans and Southern Democrats became more and more open in Washington. Henry Watterson, who was thought to be close to Tilden, boasted on the floor of the House that the Democratic majority had declined "at the instance and request of those who are described by the republican journals as the confederate brigadiers," to institute an inquiry looking toward the impeachment of President Grant. Watterson no doubt had in mind Grant's refusal of recognition to Chamberlain and Packard, Republican claimants to the governorship in South Carolina and Louisiana. "We did not doubt that the President was impeachable," he continued. "But, as he had befriended us in time of need, we took that method of paying the debt. In other words, in his hour of need we simply declined to prosecute."[67]

Republicans were constantly on the lookout for opportunities such as they had improved in the case of the Texas & Pacific bill to widen the sectional cleavage in Tilden's ranks. General Comly reported to Governor Hayes that "Garfield said he had made a serious breach in the Southern Democratic lines by advocating an appropriation for Galveston harbor which was defeated by the objections of Holman."[68] Such gestures did not go unnoticed in the South. The New Orleans *Times* gratefully acknowledged another instance of the sort when the Republican Senate voted a "handsome subsidy" to a steamship line from New Orleans to Brazil, while the Democratic House Committee on appropriations turned it down. "These repeated rejections of similar bills for Southern aid or relief on the part of a strongly Democratic House may prove at last too much for patient endurance," warned the *Times*.[69]

[66] *Congressional Record*, 44 Cong., 2 Sess. (January 27, 1877), 1066–1073; (January 29, 1877), 1086; (February 8, 1877), 1347. *Letter from James B. Eads to Hon. W. S. Holman, January 29, 1877* (Washington, 1877), a pamphlet.

[67] *Congressional Record*, 44 Cong., 2 Sess. (January 24, 1877), 927.

[68] James Comly to R. B. Hayes, January 8, 1877, Hayes Papers.

[69] New Orleans *Times* quoted in Memphis *Avalanche*, March 1, 1877.

In the meantime, Kellar and Boynton and the group that was at work behind the scenes promoting a Southern Democratic defection from Tilden were effectively employing all these instances of party cleavage over appropriation measures to promote the political cleavage they planned. Kellar crowded the columns of his Memphis paper with propaganda of this sort. Describing Congressman Holman as an enemy of the South, Kellar wrote that "he belongs to that class of Northern Democratic swashbucklers who, while pretending great friendship for the South, are thrown into a nightmare whenever anyone suggests the propriety of tossing a dollar in the direction of the 'late rebellious' States." Yet Holman would "smuggle every dollar asked for his 'deestrick' in Indiana."[70] Kellar identified Tilden and his spokesmen in the House, Abram S. Hewitt, Fernando Wood, and Benjamin A. Willis, as well as the whole New York Democracy, which he bracketed with Tammany Hall, as the guiding force behind the policy of "retrenchment" and opposition to internal improvements. "There is not a single measure of relief for the South and Southwest that has not been opposed by Tammany Hall," wrote Kellar, for Tammany and its friends were "equally against the Texas Pacific railroad, Mississippi levees, and improvement of the lower Mississippi River and its tributaries." Yet in this "noble work of reform they reserve for themselves the right to appropriate five millions to improve the harbor of New York."[71]

"You *know* by this time," wrote Boynton to Comly in the letter that Hayes praised so highly, "that many of the Southern men care nothing for Tilden, & that many of them distrust the Northern democrats. This was early apparent here, & the knowledge of it has proved of great consequence."[72] The consequence was that Hayes's friends were able to make use of a sectional cleavage in the Democratic party that had its origins in other issues entirely for the purpose of winning Southern support in the election crisis.

[70] "A.J.K." in Memphis *Avalanche,* January 10, 1877.
[71] *Ibid.,* February 21, 25, 1877.
[72] Boynton to Comly, January 25, 1877, Hayes Papers.

CHAPTER VII

The Crisis Renewed

AFTER nearly a month of labor two bipartisan committees, one of the Senate and one of the House, brought forth jointly an Electoral Commission bill on January 18. The plan it contained was ingeniously contrived to avoid the appearance of giving so much as a hair's weight of advantage to one party or the other. It was entirely noncommittal on all the fine points of constitutional law involved in the dispute. The crucial question of the powers of the new tribunal to go behind the election returns made by officials of the disputed states was neatly sidestepped by assigning the commission "the same powers, if any, now possessed for that purpose by the two houses acting separately or together." If it were asked whether the Commission was forbidden to go behind the state returns — and that was the key to the whole dispute — the answer was, only if Congress is so forbidden.[1]

All-important to the acceptability of the Commission was its carefully balanced composition. It was to consist of fifteen members, five from each house of Congress and five from the Supreme Court. Three of the Senators selected by the Upper House were to be Republicans and two Democrats, while the Lower House was to choose three Democrats and two Republicans. Only four of the Supreme Court justices were designated by the bill: two Democrats, Justices Nathan Clifford and Stephen J. Field, and two Republicans, Noah H. Swayne and William Strong. Among fourteen members of the Commission named, therefore, there were seven Democrats and seven Republicans. Though the choice of the fifth justice was left

[1] *Congressional Record,* 44 Cong., 2 Sess. (January 18, 1866), 713–714.

to the four justices named, it was universally assumed that the place would be filled by Judge David Davis, the only avowed Independent in the Supreme Court. The decision of the Commission on the election returns of the four disputed states was to be final unless an objection should be sustained by the separate vote of both houses, an altogether unlikely possibility.

The vote on the Electoral Commission bill clearly revealed in each house a strong Democratic support and a weak and divided Republican sentiment for the measure. In the Senate 26 Democrats voted for the bill and only 1 against, and in the House Democrats voted 160 for and only 17 opposed to the bill. The Republican senators, on the other hand, were divided, 21 supporting and 16 opposing the measure; while in the House the party voted more than two to one against the bill, or 31 to 69. In both houses together the Democrats cast 186 votes for and only 18 against the bill, while the Republicans cast only 52 for and 85 against.[2] There was considerable justice, therefore, in regarding the adoption of the bill a "Democratic victory."

The reluctance of Republicans to support the Commission plan was understandable. Since the regular returns from the disputed Southern states, by whatever means secured, were all in favor of Hayes, the Republicans had a prima-facie case that placed the burden of proof upon the Democrats. Moreover, there was a Republican President in the White House with a respectable military reputation and an army at his command. Of even greater importance to many of the party was the fact that Thomas W. Ferry, a Republican, was president of the Senate, for a large proportion of the party still clung to the theory that it was his constitutional right and duty to count the disputed votes. It is not surprising that Republican leaders and journals raised against the bill the cry of "capitulation" and "surrender." General Boynton held that it would have been unnecessary for the Republicans to agree to the Commission plan under other circumstances. "If the knowledge which a few of us possessed could

[2] *Ibid.* (January 25, 1877), 913; (January 26, 1877), 1050. Nevins, *Hewitt,* 364, and Haworth, *Disputed Election of 1876,* 217, are in agreement on this count.

have been imparted to all republicans," he wrote Comly, "I think we could still have held them up to a count by Ferry, & could have put it through without violence from the democrats. But the matters to which I refer & of which you know were not such as could be trusted outside of a narrow circle."[3] Boynton was referring, of course, to the understanding with Southern Democrats and the railroad lobbyists. Hayes himself was opposed to the Commission plan, and Senator Sherman and Garfield, who belonged to the "narrow circle" of which Boynton spoke, were among its most outspoken critics in Congress.

Tilden's consent to the Commission plan was given with great hesitance and reluctance but, as Professor Nevins has shown, it *was* given.[4] Colonel Kellar advanced the theory that "the movement in favor of public works in the Southwest, supported by liberal minded Republicans and Democrats so alarmed him, that the compromise plan was a necessity."[5] And Boynton likewise believed that the Democratic opponents of the plan "would have found themselves effectively resisted from within their own party" by Southerners had they attempted to block the movement for compromise.[6] The belief of Boynton and Kellar was corroborated in some degree by Montgomery Blair's suspicions and his advice to Tilden, as well as by the fact that the Southern congressmen voted more solidly for the Commission bill than the congressmen of any other region. The threat of a Southern defection may help explain Tilden's decision, but it is quite unnecessary in explaining the large Democratic vote for the bill. The fact was that the Democrats saw in the Electoral Commission a chance to win.

For all their confidence in the justice of their cause the Tildenites were keenly aware of the difficulty of the position in which they were placed by Republican control of the Presidency, the Senate, and the army. Even if they should proceed on their theory that the election

[3] Boynton to Comly, January 25, 1877, Hayes Papers.

[4] Nevins, *Hewitt,* 351–359.

[5] Kellar to William Henry Smith, February 2, 1877, Smith Papers.

[6] Boynton to Comly, January 25, 1877, Hayes Papers; also Boynton to Benjamin H. Bristow, January 21, 1877, Bristow Papers.

was thrown into the House and declare the Democratic candidate elected, Tilden could hardly be more than a President *de jure*. To establish him in power a party already tainted with rebellion would have probably found it necessary to resort to force, and the outcome of such an enterprise was highly doubtful. As an alternative the Electoral Commission presented several attractions. In agreeing to submit their case to the Commission, the Republicans tacitly abandoned their claim that the president of the Senate should count the disputed votes. Furthermore, in order to seat Hayes in the White House the Republicans would be compelled to win every one of the twenty contested electoral votes, while a victory for Tilden would require a favorable decision on only one of the twenty. Surely, reasoned the Democrats, Tilden would be awarded at least one of the votes. Any fair-minded judge would vote to go back of the corrupt election returns in one or more states, and any such investigation would overturn Hayes's claims. Reliance upon the independence of Judge Davis was probably the decisive factor in Democratic opinion. "I thought at the time and I still think," wrote Abram S. Hewitt, "that the division of parties on this measure was largely controlled by the conviction that Judge Davis would have the casting vote, and that he could be relied upon to see that the will of the people as expressed in the election of Mr. Tilden should not be thwarted." [7]

At about two o'clock on the afternoon of January 25 news arrived in Washington that the Illinois legislature had elected Judge Davis to the United States Senate, and the judge declared himself unavailable for service on the Electoral Commission. The Democrats were shocked and thrown off balance by the news, but it came too late to change the party's course. The bill had already passed the Senate early that morning and the party was irrevocably committed to support the measure in the House a few hours later. The suspicious timing of the election by the Illinois legislature has given rise to much speculation. The legislature had been deadlocked over the election since January 17, with the Republican members unable to

[7] Hewitt, quoted in Nevins, *Hewitt*, 362.

re-elect Senator Logan, the Democrats unable to muster a majority for their candidate, and five Greenbacker Independents holding the balance of power. Davis had received a sprinkling of votes from the Independents from time to time, but suddenly the Democrats joined them and on the fortieth ballot elected Davis by a bare majority. The theory that Republican leaders in Illinois engineered this maneuver is rendered unlikely by the fact that William Henry Smith attributed the election to the manipulations of Tilden and believed that as a result Davis would favor Tilden on the Electoral Commission.[8] Since Smith was in close touch with Republican leaders in Illinois it is unlikely that he would have confided this theory to Hayes if the Davis election had been a Republican plot.

As a result of the elimination of Judge Davis, the fifth judge, and the fifteenth commissioner, would have to be selected from among the four remaining justices of the Supreme Court, all of them Republicans. This unforeseen prospect naturally threw the Democratic camp into despair. When the choice fell upon Justice Joseph P. Bradley, however, the outlook brightened somewhat. Bradley was the author of a well-known decision against the constitutionality of the Enforcement Act, and he had presided for several years over a Southern circuit, where he had won a degree of popularity. Even before Davis was removed from the picture some Democrats considered Bradley an acceptable alternative. Describing him as the man "who first knocked the bottom out of the enforcement act," the Louisville *Courier-Journal* believed that "if Justice Bradley could withstand the party pressure that reached him on that occasion, there does not appear to be any reasonable grounds for supposing that he will succumb to such pressure against his judgment should he be selected as the fifth judge on the electoral tribunal."[9] Hewitt pronounced "entirely satisfactory" a report that John G. Stevens, a mutual friend he had sent to interview the judge, made upon Bradley's open-mindedness and impartiality.[10]

[8] Smith to Hayes, January 24, 1877, Hayes Papers; Chicago *Tribune,* January 26, 1877; Washington *National Republican,* January 26, 1877.

[9] Louisville *Courier-Journal,* January 22, 1877.

[10] Nevins (ed.), *Writings of Hewitt,* 172.

On the other hand certain of the best-informed Republicans took a different view of Bradley's open-mindedness. Before he heard the news of Davis's election Boynton was writing Comly that "if we could get Bradley all would go right I believe."[11] And William E. Chandler assured Hayes after the choice of the fifth judge that Bradley was as safe as "either of the other Republican judges."[12]

Fresh evidence of the corruption of the Louisiana returning board appeared after the appointment of the commissioners, making it seem more difficult than ever for the tribunal to refuse to go behind the state returns. Joseph H. Maddox, an agent of the United States Treasury, testified before a House committee that Governor J. Madison Wells had commissioned him to come to Washington and put the votes of Louisiana up for sale. "He said he wanted at least $200,000 apiece for himself and Anderson and a smaller amount for the niggers," testified Maddox.[13] Even Republican papers admitted that these developments threw "a terrible suspicion over the action of the Louisiana Returning Board, and seriously involved a number of men whom the country has tried hard to think well of."[14]

The first decision of the Electoral Commission was on the Florida vote. This turned upon the question of going behind the returns and would reveal how the members would divide and whether Bradley would side with Tilden or Hayes. The decision was to be announced on Thursday, February 8. On the preceding night John G. Stevens, an intimate friend of Bradley's, visited the justice and read his opinion. About midnight Stevens returned to Hewitt's house, where he was spending the night, and reported that he had just read Bradley's opinion "in favor of counting the vote of the Democratic electors of the State of Florida." Assuming that Tilden was thus assured of victory, Hewitt attended the Commission the following day and listened to the reading of Bradley's opinion, which "until the few concluding paragraphs were reached was

[11] Boynton to Comly, January 25, 1877, Hayes Papers.

[12] Chandler to Hayes, February 4, 1877, *ibid.*

[13] Washington *National Republican,* February 2, 1877. This in a Republican paper, of course.

[14] New York *Daily Graphic,* February 1, 1877.

strictly in accordance with the report of Mr. Stevens." That is, it was for Tilden. Then to Hewitt's astonishment the opinion concluded in favor of Hayes. He could only infer, he later wrote, that the judge had changed his opinion "between midnight and sunrise."[15]

Bradley's vote added to those of the seven other Republicans fixed the division of the Commission along hard-and-fast partisan lines of eight to seven, the pattern that prevailed throughout the following three weeks and was repeated again and again—eight to seven. It is not surprising that as soon as his vote on the Florida case was known Bradley became a target for Democratic suspicion and abuse —"a middle-aged St. Sebastian, stuck full of Democratic darts," the New York *Times* called him.[16] Harsh judgments were passed by men of highest rank in the party, including Justice Stephen J. Field, Bradley's associate on the bench, and Tilden himself. Some of the charges were unfair, some unproved, and some incapable of proof. It is nevertheless necessary to review them for they are essential to an understanding of the growing conviction among Northern Democrats that the Commission was corruptly controlled. They persuaded themselves that the Commission was but a new device for stealing the election, and that they were thoroughly justified in refusing to uphold the tribunal's decision and preventing a completion of the electoral count by a deliberate filibuster. That conviction led to a renewal of the national crisis and once more underlined the sectional cleavage within the Democratic party.

On February 8, the day Bradley's position became known, Tilden told John Bigelow that "one of the justices (Rep.) was ready to give his vote to Tilden for $200,000," that a caller he did not name had brought him the news, and that "this justice in question is reported to be embarrassed from old engagements & obligations." Bigelow immediately concluded that the justice was Bradley, though Tilden declined to identify him. The idea could have been the invention of some busybody or talebearer. It had been only a week,

[15] Nevins (ed.), *Writings of Hewitt,* 173.
[16] New York *Times,* February 17, 1877.

however, since the papers had carried the story that the governor of Louisiana had offered to sell the vote of that state for $200,000 to himself and the same amount for an associate. Tilden told Bigelow that the Florida returning board had been offered to him for $200,-000. "That seems to be the standard figure," remarked Tilden.[17] In such an atmosphere almost any rumor became credible.

On the following day, February 9, ex-Senator John P. Stockton, a Democrat of New Jersey, called on Bigelow after returning from Washington, where the previous day he had had an hour's talk with Judge Bradley. Associated with the justice for years as a railroad attorney, Senator Stockton believed that he had "a more intimate knowledge of Judge Bradley's habit of thought than anyone else"—so he wrote Tilden.[18] Stockton apparently did not confide in Bigelow the reasons for his conclusion, but told him that Bradley was "not particular about the means with which he compasses his ends."[19]

The gravest of the public charges leveled against Bradley were those made by the New York *Sun,* and, if Attorney General Alphonso Taft was correct in crediting the reports of his secret service man, the *Sun* articles were published after they were read and approved by Tilden.[20]

For more than two years the *Sun* had been hammering away at alleged frauds and judicial misconduct by which the Texas & Pacific acquired for a nominal sum the enormous land grants and valuable franchises of John C. Frémont's old Memphis, El Paso, and Pacific Railroad Company.[21] The story dated back to the summer of 1870 when through Cortlandt Parker's aid Justice Bradley as judge of the United States Circuit Court for the Western District of Texas was persuaded to hear a suit asking that a receiver be appointed for the Memphis, El Paso. Although the company was a Texas corpora-

[17] Bigelow Diary, February 9, 1877, John Bigelow Papers (New York Public Library).

[18] John P. Stockton to Tilden, February 8, 1877, Tilden Papers.

[19] Bigelow Diary, February 9, 1877, Bigelow Papers.

[20] Alphonso Taft to Hayes, February 14, 1877, Hayes Papers; also William D. Bickham to Hayes, February 14, 1877, *ibid.*

[21] For early attacks see New York *Sun,* February 6, 13, 1875.

tion chartered in that state, Bradley accepted jurisdiction in Newark, New Jersey, on the ground that a New York attorney of the corporation had waived a hearing in Texas. The Texas officials of the company later claimed that they were not consulted about the matter. Sitting in Newark, Justice Bradley proceeded to appoint John A. C. Gray receiver of the Memphis, El Paso, and Pacific and later granted his request for permission to dispose of the property to another company. Gray subsequently turned over all the franchises and lands of the company to Tom Scott's Texas & Pacific for $150,000 paid to Gray and an agreement to settle the claims of certain French bondholders with small portions of land.[22]

The role of John C. Frémont in these transactions was emphasized by the *Sun* articles. Although it was because of alleged misappropriations of Frémont that the Memphis, El Paso, and Pacific came to ruin and was placed in the hands of a receiver, Frémont was among the original incorporators of the Texas & Pacific[23] and later claimed that the incorporation of the Texas & Pacific was "a continuation of the Memphis, El Paso" and a vindication of his course. The *Sun* charged that Scott and the Texas & Pacific "agreed to take care of the interests of Frémont, Gray, and their friends, in consideration of being allowed to control the new company and of obtaining the support of all the friends of the old company in both Houses of Congress." The *Sun* also charged that the stock and securities of the Memphis, El Paso, and Pacific were used in purchasing support in Congress for the passage of the bill incorporating the Texas & Pacific in 1871 and that "the air of Congress was thick with its bonds, falling like snowflakes and dissolving like dew."[24] These charges excited the

[22] For Bradley's defense of his course see *Forbes et al.* v. *Memphis, El Paso & Pacific Railroad Co., et al.,* 2 Woods 323, and also in *Federal Cases,* Case No. 4, 926, Book 9, p. 408. For an attack on Bradley's decisions see *Closing Argument of Douglas Campbell, Esq., in Regard to the Title of the Texas and Pacific Railway Company to the Property of the Memphis, El Paso and Pacific Railroad Company before the Judiciary Committee of the House of Representatives, April 24, 1878* (Washington, 1878), in Library of the Bureau of Railway Economics, Washington, D.C. Campbell's opening argument is in New York *Sun,* April 12, 1878.

[23] *Annual Report of the President of the Texas & Pacific Railway Company* (New York, 1872), 13–14.

[24] New York *Sun,* February 6, 13, 1875.

interest of Congress and formed the background of Holman's resolution calling for an investigation of alleged fraud in the passage of the Texas & Pacific Act of 1871.[25]

After it became apparent that Bradley had aligned himself with the seven Republican members of the Electoral Commission and that his vote would defeat Tilden, the *Sun* reopened its attack, making it more personal and vindictive than ever. When Bradley assumed jurisdiction of the Texas suits at Newark, "fraudulent and corrupt and collusive as they were at every step," he became a tool of Scott, Gray, and Parker, declared the *Sun*. "He ceased to be his own man and became forever the man of the men who owned and used him then." The justice was not a free agent. "It is a grave mistake to suppose that Mr. Justice Bradley is the fifth Judge" on the Electoral Commission, said the paper. "The fifth Judge is John A. C. Gray of New York, assisted by Col. Tom Scott and Cortlandt Parker." Evidence in the hands of Gray controlled the justice, and Gray "will award the Presidency according to his good pleasure, and he will award it to Hayes, because Mr. Tilden's inauguration would be very bad for subsidy jobs in general, and the Texas-Pacific in particular."[26] The editor later cited Justices Field and Clifford, Bradley's Democratic colleagues on the Commission, in support of the story that Bradley had first written an opinion supporting Tilden and then only the night before the decision had changed his mind. "During the whole of that night," said the *Sun,* "Judge Bradley's house in Washington was surrounded by the carriages of visitors who came to see him apparently about the decision of the Electoral Commission. . . . These visitors included leading Republicans as

[25] *Congressional Record,* 44 Cong., 1 Sess. (January 24, 1876), 598.

[26] New York *Sun,* February 20, 1877. It is an interesting sidelight on the story that Colonel William T. Pelton, Tilden's nephew, claimed to possess evidence reflecting upon Bradley's conduct in the case. Mentioning this fact, Pelton wrote John Bigelow on February 10 urging him to call on John A. C. Gray and "advise him to see that Justice Bradley *does right.*" Bigelow did call upon Gray on February 13. Gray professed willingness to see Bradley, but said that he would first have to talk to Cortlandt Parker. He went to Newark for that purpose and returned to report to Bigelow that Parker was opposed to the idea and agreed with Bradley's position on the Florida case. John Bigelow, *Retrospections of an Active Life* (New York, 1909), V, 299–300.

well as persons deeply interested in the Texas Pacific Railroad scheme."[27] The paper carried the same story in subsequent issues, "that there may be no misunderstanding," and added the detail that "seventeen carriages, more or less, were gathered about his house, having brought there Republican politicians and Pacific Railway men."[28]

Goaded by the repetition of the charges, Bradley was finally provoked into publishing a reply to the *Sun* in the Newark *Daily Advertiser*. "Whether I wrote one opinion, or twenty, in my private examination of the subject," said the justice, "is of little consequence, and of no concern to anybody." He admitted that he "wrote and re-wrote the arguments and considerations on both sides" of the question of going behind the Florida returns, "sometimes being inclined to one view of the subject, and sometimes to the other," the writing being used merely to clarify his mind.[29] Regarding the charge of pressure brought to bear by politicians and railroad lobbyists, Bradley made a sweeping denial. "The whole thing is a falsehood," he wrote. "Not a single visitor called at my house that evening; and during the whole sitting of the Commission, I had no private discussion whatever on the subjects at issue with any persons interested on the Republican side, and but very few words with any person. Indeed, I sedulously sought to avoid all discussion outside the Commission itself. The allegation that I read an opinion to Judges Clifford and Field is entirely untrue." The justice did not reply to the attack on his handling of the Memphis, El Paso, and Pacific receivership.[30]

[27] New York *Sun,* August 4, 1877.

[28] *Ibid.,* August 29, September 1, 1877.

[29] In regard to Bradley's explanation of writing opinions on both sides Professor Nevins observes: "In a world where anything is possible, this is possible. But it is certainly hard to believe. . . . There was no need to write out the arguments, for they lay in printed form before the judges. Bradley's quick, clear mind was one of the last on the tribunal to require such aid. Moreover, the vital question of going behind the returns was not complex and did not require elaborate argument — it was a very simple issue of principle." Nevins, *Hewitt,* 372.

[30] Newark *Daily Advertiser,* September 5, 1877, quoted in Charles Bradley (ed.), *Miscellaneous Writings of the Late Hon. Joseph P. Bradley* (Newark, 1902), 220–222.

Asked to comment on a report that Bradley had "read" him an opinion favorable to Tilden the day before the decision was announced, Justice Field replied to a reporter in California: "Well, sir, all that I care to say with regard to that is that Justice Bradley *read* — " with peculiar emphasis on the word 'read' " — no opinion to me in advance of the formal submission of the opinions to the commission. Beyond that, I think it would be improper for me to say anything. If I should enter upon the subject, I should probably say a great deal more than I wish to say." [31] After Field's death it was stated that he had written Bradley denying that he meant anything "derogatory" by the statement.[32] Field evidently held strong mental reservations, however, for he sent Tilden a clipping of Bradley's statement and remarked that "the language of the letter justifies some of the comments of the Press upon the change of views which the judge experienced shortly before the vote was taken in the Florida case." [33] The New York *Sun* pronounced Bradley's letter an admission of "the truth and accuracy of the fundamental features of the charge brought home to him in the *Sun*," and called for his impeachment.[34] The paper continued a merciless attack and other Democratic journals of the country joined in.[35]

Bradley's accusers never brought forth proof of their charge that the justice yielded to improper pressure in changing his opinion. It is true that there have never been any satisfactory answers to several questions raised by critics of Bradley's procedure in appointing Gray receiver of the Memphis, El Paso, and Pacific and permitting the disposal of the property to the Texas & Pacific. The Supreme Court in the case of *Davis* v. *Gray* [36] cast doubt upon the legality of the transfer of the road. In a minority report on a new Texas & Pacific bill in 1878 Congressman William R. Morrison of

[31] San Francisco *Daily Exchange* quoted in New York *Sun*, August 28, 1877.

[32] Charles Bradley (ed.), *Miscellaneous Writings of Joseph P. Bradley*, 10, 223.

[33] Stephen J. Field to Tilden, December 11, 1877, Tilden Papers.

[34] New York *Sun*, September 6, 1877.

[35] Baltimore *Gazette*, Raleigh *Observer*, and Patterson *Guardian* quoted in *ibid.*, September 9, 1877.

[36] 16 Wallace, 203.

Illinois questioned the company's title to the Memphis, El Paso, and Pacific,[37] and Abram S. Hewitt interested himself in a resolution calling for an investigation of the title and the judicial procedure involved.[38] Preliminary hearings were held, but the investigation never came off.[39] The charge that the influence of Scott and his friends was decisive in determining Bradley's vote on the Electoral Commission was impossible to prove, and in all fairness it should be observed that it was the sort of charge that is impossible to disprove and difficult to deny effectively. Bradley's son was within his rights, also, in complaining that his father was expected to be freer from partisan bias than any of the other seven Republicans on the Commission.[40]

The point is that the disappointed and outraged Democrats were ready to believe the worst about the man who was wrecking their hopes — sixteen years of deferred hopes — and they *did* believe the worst. Bradley was "threatened with bodily injury . . . even to the taking of his life"; he was "inundated by a flood of vulgar and threatening communications," and the government finally placed his house under guard.[41] A sample of Democratic sentiment on the subject is provided by Senator Lewis V. Bogy of Missouri, who declared on the floor of the Senate that "the name of that man who changed his vote upon that commission . . . from Tilden to Hayes, Justice Bradley, will go down to after ages covered with equal shame and disgrace. His name will be associated with Norbury and Jeffreys, linked together by a chain of infamy, and never will it be pronounced without a hiss from all good men in this country."[42]

[37] *House of Representatives Reports*, 45 Cong., 2 Sess., No. 619, Part 2, p. 1.

[38] New York *Sun*, April 16, 18, 1878.

[39] Alfred J. Davenport, *The Title of the Texas & Pacific Railroad Co. Property Late of the Memphis El Paso & Pacific Railroad Co. Notes of Argument Before the Judiciary Committee of the House of Representatives, April 17, 1878* (New York, 1878); *Closing Argument of Douglas Campbell, Esq., in Regard to the Title of the Texas and Pacific Railway Company to the Property of the Memphis, El Paso and Pacific Railroad Company before the Judiciary Committee of the House of Representatives, April 24, 1878* (Washington, 1878).

[40] Charles Bradley (ed.), *Miscellaneous Writings of Joseph P. Bradley*, 9. His son called the justice "as staunch a Republican as any of those members of the Commission who were deliberately selected by reason of their own political predilections."

[41] *Ibid.*

[42] *Congressional Record*, 44 Cong., 2 Sess. (February 17, 1877), 1657.

If the more hotheaded Tildenites were ready to fight after the Florida decision they were probably in a worse state of mind after the Louisiana case. Democrats at that time believed their case in Louisiana was their strongest and that here they were invincible. No one could deny that the chicanery was gross, the forgery patent, the procedure irregular and illegal, and that the returning board seemed eagerly for sale. But the results were all the same. Were not two of the alleged electors Federal officeholders and ineligible according to the Constitution? The answer was eight to seven. Did not the Democratic electors receive a majority of the votes? Eight to seven. Was not the returning board composed of four persons of one party instead of five of different parties as required by the state law? Eight to seven. Would not the Commission hear readily available evidence of falsification and forgery of returns? Eight to seven. Was not Kellogg's certificate void because he was not governor at the time? Eight to seven.[43] So it remained to the bitter end. And on top of that Senator Conkling broke what Hewitt considered a definite commitment to make a rousing speech in the Senate denouncing the action of the Louisiana returning board and rallying sufficient Republican votes against Hayes to keep the state's electoral vote out of the hands of the Commission. Conkling left town on the appointed day.[44]

Rapidly the conviction grew upon the partisans of Tilden that they were the victims of some gigantic hoax. "Conspiracy!" became their cry.[45] And the suspicion did not leave untouched the minds of more moderate and judicious Democratic leaders, men of the caliber of Randall and Hewitt. It came to appear to many that the Republicans were ready to close their eyes to the most glaring corruption and wink at forgery and chicanery, that they no longer felt constrained by the plain law of the Constitution, that they were perfectly prepared to set aside the will of the people and dictate a choice of rulers.

[43] *Proceedings of the Electoral Commission in Congressional Record,* 44 Cong., 2 Sess., vol. V, Part IV, 117–118.

[44] Nevins, *Hewitt,* 375–377.

[45] For an expression of the "conspiracy" theory see Jeremiah S. Black, "The Electoral Conspiracy," *North American Review,* CXXV (1877), 1–34.

To scores of honest and excited congressmen it seemed that their opponents had abandoned the common ethical standards that made democracy workable. If this were true, and if "The Eight" had placed themselves at the head of the conspiracy, why should honest men feel obliged to abide by the decisions of the Commission and carry the work of the conspirators into law? Was it not rather their duty to expose the fraud and defeat it by every means at their disposal?

Tension of the public mind, relaxed temporarily since the adoption of the Commission plan, snapped taut again. Newspapers resumed the inflammatory tendency manifested in December and January; tempers became shorter and debates angrier in Congress. Once more there were reports of warlike preparations by Democratic governors and war veterans. Hewitt, who had reports of the gathering of forces in fifteen states, was convinced that an outbreak of violence was near at hand.[46] In Washington the administration indulged in sword-rattling by the conspicuous reviewing of troops and had a Democratic newspaperman indicted for sedition when he wrote that if Hayes could "pass in safety from the Executive Mansion to the Capitol to be inaugurated, we are fitted for the slavery that will follow the inauguration."[47] In Columbus, Ohio, a bullet crashed through a window while the Hayes family was at supper one night and buried itself in the library wall.[48] In New Orleans a Pennsylvania Democrat shot and wounded Stephen B. Packard, Republican claimant of the governorship, and confessed that he had conspired with others to assassinate Packard.[49]

On February 10, the day that the findings of the Electoral Commission on the Florida case were officially announced to Congress, the Democrats moved and carried by strict party vote a recess of the House until the following Monday. This was the first of a series of such recesses that had the effect of a filibuster, slowing down danger-

[46] Nevins, *Hewitt*, 380.

[47] New York *Times*, February 5, 1877; Washington *National Republican*, February 21, 1877.

[48] Eckenrode, *Hayes*, 235.

[49] New York *Times*, February 16, 1877.

ously the progress toward completion of the electoral count. Republicans protested vainly that these rash tactics violated the spirit of the compromise and led to disaster, but the filibusterers were not diverted. A continuation of the filibuster, in John Sherman's opinion, was "simply revolution and must be met firmly and boldly." [50]

One ominous feature of the vote on the recess of February 10 was the fact that the Southern Democrats voted with their Northern brethren — and solidly.[51] It remained to be seen whether the renewal and intensification of the electoral crisis had healed the threatening breach in the Democratic party. Only if that were true, and the Southerners could be held in line, could the filibuster be continued successfully.

[50] John Sherman to Colonel C. W. Moulton, February 17, 1877, Hayes Papers.
[51] *Congressional Record,* 44 Cong., 2 Sess. (February 10, 1877), 1486.

CHAPTER VIII

The Apostasy of the South

SO CONFIDENT was General Boynton in the effectiveness of the work that he, Kellar, Dodge, and Scott had been doing among Southern Democrats that the threat of a Democratic filibuster left him completely without apprehensions. In fact he wrote William Henry Smith on February 11 that "as a republican" he strongly hoped the Democrats would attempt a filibuster. "My wish to have it begun by the democrats," he explained, "rests upon a confidence that the plan we were at work upon before the compromise bill was passed will work beautifully & effectively in case the hotheaded democrats attempt to defeat Hayes by delay. Of course it will be a splendid thing to have the democrats submit quietly; but it would be a much better thing to have them start a filibustering themselves & have thirty-five or forty of their party refuse to carry it on — as I am now convinced they will refuse after a little, the moment it begins to appear that the real object is to defeat the working of the bill through filibustering. . . . I feel certain the Tilden men can not hold their forces long enough to make it successful."[1]

Colonel Kellar, back in Washington since January 26 and in constant touch with Boynton, was equally sure that his Southern associates in Congress could be relied upon. "Col Kellar feels confident that his friends can & will control the situation now," reported Boynton. "For them it is much simplified. They have only to say that good faith, honor, & respect for law all bind them not to impede the execution of the new law for the counting." Then, of course, there was the ace up the sleeve of the plotters. "If our purely political part

[1] Boynton to Smith, February 11, 1877, Smith Papers.

of the plan does not defeat democratic success through filibustering, I am sure the Scott help will. I shall expect to see hard & effective work there."[2] General Dodge likewise viewed the immediate future with serenity and assured Jay Gould that the situation was well in hand.[3]

Governor Hayes read the confident reports of Boynton and Kellar that Smith forwarded to him,[4] but he was not altogether convinced thereby. He was under pressure from other advisors who thought that additional assurances to the South were needed, public assurances, and he told Carl Schurz that "the South is more in my mind than anything else."[5] Hayes sought Schurz's opinion particularly on the advisability of promising the South aid "to internal improvements of a national character" in his inaugural.[6] Schurz undoubtedly realized that he was being seriously considered for a place in Hayes's cabinet by that time, and he was evidently apprized of the significance of the magical phrase, "internal improvements of a national character." As reformer par excellence he would find his position in an administration committed to a railroad deal extremely embarrassing. His reply to Hayes was therefore the most forthright piece of advice the governor had found in his heavy mailbags in a long time.

"Remember the Credit Mobilier, the Blaine letters etc.," wrote Schurz. "It looks almost as if a railroad could not come within a hundred miles of a legislative body without corrupting it. It will be difficult for you, I should think, to say anything, in your Inaugural in the sense you indicate, that will not be liable to be construed as an endorsement of that policy, which in the past has proved so injurious to our public morals and so dangerous to the Treasury, that the Republican party has been itself forced to abandon it in deference to public opinion. Neither would it be well, in my opinion,

[2] Boynton to Smith, February 11, 1877 (second letter of same date), *ibid.* As usual Boynton wrote two letters covering the same ground. A copy, also in the Smith Papers, is marked "Original sent to Gov. Hayes."

[3] Dodge to Gould, February 12, 1877, letterbook in Box 384, Dodge Papers.

[4] William Henry Smith to Hayes, February 12, 1877, Hayes Papers.

[5] Hayes to Schurz, February 4, 1877, Schurz Papers.

[6] Hayes to Schurz, January 29, 1877, *ibid.*

if you *appeared* as trying to gain the favor of the Southern people by a bid of such a nature. It would seem to me best, not to mention the matter at all." [7]

Hayes professed to be "very strongly" impressed with the force of Schurz's words. "My anxiety to *do* something to promote the pacification of the South is perhaps in danger of leading me too far," he admitted. "The more I think of it," he added, "the more I see in what you say." [8]

Tension in Washington concerning the Democratic filibuster did not ease as rapidly as General Boynton had hoped, however, and even he joined in pressing Hayes for a statement that would help with the Southern Democrats. He thought this might take the form of an assurance that Hayes would stand by the view of Southern policy expressed in his letter accepting the nomination, but suggested that something in addition would be useful. Referring to Boynton's suggestion, Hayes wrote Senator Sherman that he preferred to make no new statement. "But you may say if you deem it advisable," he added, "that you *know* that I will stand by the friendly and encouraging words of that letter, and by all that they imply. You can not express that too strongly." [9] Sherman replied: "I talked with Boynton about it and with many Southern men and have said that you undoubtedly would stand by the words of your letter of acceptance in spirit and in substance and that you would make the Southern question a specialty in your administration." Sherman added that he had not quoted Hayes directly and did not think it wise to do so.[10]

Later in the crisis, however, the *National Republican* did quote Hayes directly as saying: "Assure any of our Southern friends that I am impressed with the necessity of a complete change of men and policy. I shall stand by the ideas uttered in my letter of last summer." The *National Republican* took the liberty of spelling out the meaning for doubting Thomases: "This, more fully interpreted means, not only the entire right of self-government, but also a large and liberal

[7] Schurz to Hayes, February 1, 1877, Hayes Papers.
[8] Hayes to Schurz, February 4, 1877, Schurz Papers.
[9] Hayes to Sherman, February 15, 1877, Hayes Papers.
[10] Sherman to Hayes, February 17, 1877, *ibid.*

policy in respect to matters of internal improvement."[11] This was a Radical Republican paper speaking, but there was no doubt whatever that it meant by "self-government" the same thing the Redeemers meant.

In Hayes's mind the problem continued uppermost. "I would like to get support from good men of the South, late Rebels," he noted in his diary on February 17. "How to do it is the question. I have the best disposition towards the Southern people, Rebels and all. I could appoint a Southern Democrat in the Cabinet."[12] The governor's closest advisors were in general agreement that in view of the circumstances there should be two native Southerners in the new cabinet, one Democrat and one Republican, and that men of Whiggish antecedents were most acceptable. The question of cabinet appointments belonged more to what Boynton was pleased to describe as "the purely political part of our plan," but it was not always entirely divorced from the other part.

Both Stanley Matthews and Charles Foster, who were in close touch with the Southern Democrats of Whig and internal-improvement leanings, reported to Hayes that talks with their Southern friends on the subject revealed that John C. Brown of Tennessee was considered a desirable cabinet appointee.[13] An ex-Whig, Governor Brown was vice president of the Texas & Pacific Company, and Kellar called him "head of the movement in Washington" for the Scott bill.[14] A third advisor thought that the fact that Brown was "an active man in the lobby" would "tell against him," and that in any case, "The Texas, Pacific Railroad formation . . . will certainly come to your support in the South as they are realizing that there is nothing progressive in the Democracy."[15]

Colonel Kellar's choice of a Southern Democrat for the cabinet was Senator David M. Key of East Tennessee, whose term expired

[11] Washington *National Republican*, March 1, 1877.

[12] Williams (ed.), *Diary and Letters of Hayes*, III, 417.

[13] Charles Foster to Hayes, February 10, 1877; Stanley Matthews to Hayes, February 13, 1877, Hayes Papers.

[14] Kellar in Memphis *Avalanche*, February 11, 1877. Kellar probably meant Brown was the "front" for the lobby.

[15] A. B. Norton, Washington, D.C., to Hayes, February 27, 1877, Hayes Papers.

March 4. In his efforts to re-elect Key in January, Kellar had assisted in rallying ten Democratic members of the legislature and the solid Republican membership in support of his candidate. Although he was a Breckinridge elector in 1860, Key had not favored secession, but had commanded a Confederate regiment during the war. He was elevated to the Senate by appointment to fill the unexpired term of Andrew Johnson after the death of the ex-President in 1875. Montgomery Blair attributed the subsequent appointment of Key to Hayes's cabinet to the fact that he was "the intimate friend of Gov. Brown," and hence thought it due to Texas & Pacific influence.[16] This may have been a factor, but the evidence tends to indicate that Key's appointment belonged more to the "purely political part of the plan" — if, indeed, the two parts were really separable.[17]

"Were Key in the Cabinet," wrote Kellar to William Henry Smith, "I could take the aggressive and warmly co-operate with Gov. Hayes & help to lead the conservative national citizens of Tenn. Arkansas & Texas to a higher platform & to a better era of politics."[18] A letter from Key dated February 16 and presumably addressed to Kellar was forwarded to Hayes in which the Senator declared himself quite available for a cabinet appointment. "If I were to become a member of an administration," wrote Key, "I should not feel at liberty to place myself in opposition to its general policy, but should feel bound to build it up and strengthen it in the hearts of the people." He would enter "in an independent position," but should the administration "develop a broad and liberal policy towards the people of the South, I would not hesitate to incorporate my fortunes and self with it."[19]

Senator Key's candidacy was also endorsed by a caucus of "some Southern men," otherwise unidentified, held at the home of Senator

[16] Montgomery Blair to Charles A. Dana, May 15, 1878, Gist-Blair Papers.

[17] The distinction was usually drawn by Boynton.

[18] Kellar to Smith, February 16, 1877, Smith Papers.

[19] Key's letter of February 16, minus the addressee, was released to the press after his appointment as an answer to the complaint that Hayes had appointed a "rabid Southerner." It appeared in the New York *Tribune,* March 8, 1877. See Albert V. House, Jr., "President Hayes' Selection of David M. Key for Postmaster General," *Journal of Southern History,* IV (1938), 90.

Alcorn of Mississippi shortly after the beginning of the Democratic filibuster in the House. Alcorn was nominally a Republican, but it is clear that the caucus consisted largely of men nominally Democratic. These gentlemen specified the Postmaster General's post as the one desired for Key. They placed their request in the hands of a Major M. J. Waldron of Memphis, who took it to Joseph Medill in Chicago with a letter of introduction from Colonel Kellar.[20] Medill turned Major Waldron over to William Henry Smith, who reported to Hayes in detail on the reasons for the request of the caucus. "The reason for this is," wrote Smith, "that such action will make the political break desired in the South; that the conservative men there in the States of Tennessee, Arkansas, Miss., & Texas will follow him and support your administration."[21] But there were additional reasons.

The portfolio of the Postmaster General, traditional dispenser of patronage, was a high price for Southern Democrats to be demanding of a Republican administration. It was a demand without precedent. Yet the Southern bargainers were perfectly aware that they had much to offer. For it was within the power of this minority to deliver into the hands of the Republicans two great prizes denied them by the American electorate as expressed by majority vote in the election of 1876. Not only could they break the Democratic filibuster, facilitate the completion of the electoral count, and assure the inauguration of Hayes—actions which, as Boynton pointed out, and some Southerners no doubt genuinely felt, could be attributed to patriotic motives—but it was also in their power to give the Republicans control of the next House of Representatives.

The election of 1876 had greatly reduced the majority the Democrats enjoyed in the House and left them a margin of only six or eight votes. These were sufficient, of course, to enable them to organize the House, elect a Democratic speaker, and control the committees. Once in control it would be possible, Medill feared, for the Democrats to increase their majority "to 15 or 20 by turning [out]

[20] Joseph Medill to William Henry Smith, February 17, 1877, Hayes Papers.
[21] Smith to Hayes, February 17, 1877, *ibid.*

our fellows in the close and contested districts," of which there were several. "It is all important to the success of President Hayes's administration," Medill wrote, "that they have a Republican working majority in both Houses. How shall it be secured? Obviously it can only be done by attracting to the administration a number of Southern conservatives who feel friendly to Mr. Hayes."[22] Stanley Matthews had discussed this problem earlier with "a Southern Democrat, well posted and in communication with the leaders," and had written Hayes on February 13 that his informant "spoke about the organization of the next House of Reps. as within our control," and believed "that enough Southern democrats will keep out of their caucus to control it."[23] The group who met at Senator Alcorn's home came to an agreement on the matter, and their emissary presented the offer to Medill and William Henry Smith in Chicago as part of the inducement for meeting their request for the Postmaster General's portfolio. Smith laid this proposal also before Hayes, marking his letter "Confidential."

"Already nine Southern members of Congress are pledged to aid in giving the Republicans the organization of the new House by electing Garfield, Speaker," wrote Smith. "Enough are to be absent at the opening to permit this to be done, if not enough in the meantime do not agree to vote directly for Garfield. [Casey] Young of the Memphis district will vote for him, & has a speech already prepared in support of the new departure in the South. The plan also includes a scheme to keep Isham G. Harris out of the Senate until a Committee can inquire whether or not he took the oath of allegiance to the Maximilian Govt. in Mexico. There is hardly any doubt that this plan would revolutionize Tennessee."[24]

The entire coterie of Western Associated Press men who had launched the movement for detaching the South — Boynton, Medill, Halstead, William Henry Smith, and Richard Smith — took up the

[22] Medill to Richard Smith, February 17, 1877, *ibid.*

[23] Matthews to Hayes, February 13, 1877, *ibid.*

[24] Smith to Hayes, February 17, 1877, *ibid.* Harris had fled to Mexico after the collapse of the Confederacy.

latest elaboration of their scheme with enthusiasm. Major Waldron, the messenger of Kellar and the caucus of Southerners, continued from Chicago to Cincinnati, where he conferred with Halstead and Richard Smith.

While Medill had lost faith in the Scott plan after his first tentative endorsement, he proved one of the most enthusiastic supporters of the "purely political part of the plan." Convinced that the policy of "Negro rule in the South officered by carpet baggers" had proved a complete failure, he favored a new policy based on "the old Whig feeling." Under a new administration, "if carpet-bagging can be got rid of, and 'home rule' in state affairs be substituted a Southern white Republican party can be organized down there which, with the aid of the blacks, will give us control of half the South." Medill thought that Tennessee was "the key of the Southern situation," and that her influence would be powerful in Arkansas, Georgia, Louisiana, North Carolina, and Kentucky. Memphis was "an important citadel for us to capture and hold," and this could be achieved if Colonel Kellar would take charge of the post office in that city and Key were in the cabinet. In addition to Kellar and Key, so Medill was informed, Casey Young and William P. Caldwell, two Democratic congressmen from Tennessee, could be relied upon to co-operate with the Republicans. Medill was also satisfied that Senator-elect Garland of Arkansas could be "made a supporter of Hayes."[25]

As William Henry Smith interpreted Kellar's scheme, the appointment of Senator Key was "the one thing that would at once settle the South."[26] While Hayes apparently left no record of his views on the plan in detail, he appears to have fallen in readily with the ideas of his advisors. So congenial did the governor find the views of Joseph Medill that he thought they indicated that the Chicago editor "would make a very sensible President."[27]

[25] Medill to Richard Smith, February 17, 1877. See also William Henry Smith to Richard Smith, February 17, 1877, and Boynton to William Henry Smith, February 27, 1877, Hayes Papers.

[26] William Henry Smith to Hayes, February 21, 1877, *ibid.*

[27] Hayes to Murat Halstead, February 18, 1877, in Williams (ed.), *Diary and Letters of Hayes*, III, 418.

While General Dodge was not openly participating in the "purely political" aspects of the plan, he was evidently pretty well informed of current developments on that front. Actually, Dodge did not believe that purely political inducements were sufficient to accomplish Republican ends, either in the electoral crisis or in future policy in the South. His faith lay in economic inducements, particularly "internal improvements of a national character." With them he believed it was possible not only to inaugurate Hayes but to rebuild the Republican party in the South. "My connection with the internal improvements in the South for several years past," Dodge wrote Governor Hayes, "has brought me into contact with the people of that section, and with very many of their leading men. I feel confident that your administration can build up the Republican party to such strength in several States that they can be held firmly and surely to our party in the future." In that respect he was even more optimistic than Medill. "We ought to have and to hold," said Dodge, "North and South Carolina, Florida, Alabama, Mississippi, and Louisiana, and should be able to get a strong and firm footing in Texas. I am confident that proper action will bring to us most of the best men in these States who have been acting against us, but who do not feel at home in the present Democratic party."[28]

A summary of "the purely political part of the plan" at this point would embrace a series of agreements between the two parties. For their part the Southerners undertook to co-operate with the Republicans: (1) in completing the electoral count for Hayes, (2) in organizing the next House with Garfield as speaker, and (3) in laying the foundation for a revival of Republicanism in parts of the South under conservative native leadership. Obviously, the parties to all parts of the agreement were not the same. While the completion of the electoral count would require the co-operation of a large number of the Southern congressmen, on the other hand the Republican capture of the new House would necessitate the connivance of only a half-dozen or so members, and the revival of Republicanism in parts of the South would turn upon private arrangements regarding

[28] Dodge to Hayes, February 15, 1877, letterbook in Box 384, Dodge Papers.

patronage and other concessions. Parts 2 and 3 of Southern undertakings were confined largely to Tennesseeans and certain of their friends in adjoining states. There is little doubt that those parts of the plan would have been unacceptable to the great majority of Southern congressmen and would have been repudiated had they been generally known.

Republican commitments, apart from the appointment of Senator Key and the patronage policy that this implied, are more difficult to summarize. This is because they consisted largely of verbal assurances based on a few phrases of Hayes's letter accepting the nomination, in which he promised Southerners to "regard and cherish their truest interests" and "wipe out forever the distinction between North and South in our common country."[29] This was interpreted by Hayes's friends and understood by Southerners generally to mean the wiping out of the features of Radical Reconstruction that still remained, the abandonment of the use of troops to support Carpetbagger administrations, and the restoration of "home rule." Since Hayes instructed Senator Sherman to assure Southerners that "you *know* that I will stand by the friendly and encouraging words of that letter, and by all that they imply,"[30] it would seem that the Southerners were fully justified in interpreting the commitment the way they did.

At Washington in the meantime, after the beginning of the electoral count, the friends of the Texas & Pacific redoubled their efforts to bring Lamar's bill to a vote. Their lobby was joined by that of Gould and Huntington, who were attempting to put through Gordon's sinking-fund bill. "The Texas Pacific Railroad lobby are carrying matters with a high hand in Washington," reported the Chicago *Tribune*. "They are making a prodigious effort to rush the bill through before the end of this Congress."[31] Colonel Kellar was positive that if the Lamar bill could be brought to a vote "the opposition by Northern Democrats, such as Hewitt and Willis, of New

[29] Williams, *Life of Hayes,* I, 462.
[30] Hayes to Sherman, February 15, 1877, Hayes Papers.
[31] Chicago *Tribune,* February 3, 1877.

York, and Western Democrats, like Holman and Morrison," could be "readily overcome by the Republican vote." He attributed the delay to rulings by Speaker Randall and the construction of the law regarding the counting of the electoral votes.[32]

The difficulty with respect to the electoral law was overcome by a resolution adopted on February 12 amending the rules of the House so as to permit it to proceed with business "as though the legislative day had expired by adjournment."[33] With only 17 working days remaining before the fateful March 4, with 241 bills on the private calendar, and 50 public bills undisposed of, with the greater part of the electoral vote to count, and a persistent Democratic filibuster and dilatory measures, the House was a vast log jam. Yet in spite of this the railroad men recklessly continued their drive to force their bills through before the end of the session. "Their agents, attorneys, and lobbyists have swarmed in our corridors," complained one lawmaker from the floor; "they have blocked the way to our committee-rooms, and have set spies upon our actions."[34] The Speaker had to stop proceedings repeatedly to have lobbyists cleared from the floor.

Obstacles created by the log jam and the vigilant Northern Democrats proved too much for the most skilled lobbyists, however. General Dodge gave up hope for the Gordon bill on February 15 and wrote Jay Gould that "some of the friends of the U.P. took the matter up and told Mr. Huntington plainly that it was impossible to put this Gordon Bill through in its present shape."[35] Dodge drew hope for the future, however, from "a long talk with McCrary"—George W. McCrary of Iowa, whom he considered an excellent choice for Hayes's cabinet. "I find he is in favor of our settlement or something like it," he told Gould.[36] Dodge wrote Hayes urging McCrary for the cabinet. "He is a sound, safe, able man and brings

[32] Memphis *Avalanche,* February 11, 1877.
[33] *Congressional Record,* 44 Cong., 2 Sess. (February 12, 1877), 1506; New York *Times,* February 14, 1877.
[34] *Congressional Record,* 44 Cong., 2 Sess. (February 14, 1877), 1551.
[35] Dodge to Gould, February 15, 1877, letterbook in Box 384, Dodge Papers.
[36] Dodge to Gould, February 12, 1877, *ibid.*

to us an influence that will greatly help us to get and hold a portion of the Southern states," he told Hayes. He added that he had "no other motive in this matter, except that I believe that the safety and security of the American Republic depends upon holding it in the hands of the Republican party for some time to come."[37]

By February 17 friends of the Texas & Pacific had pretty much abandoned hope of getting action on the Lamar bill before the end of the session. The New Orleans *Times,* as other Southern spokesmen interested in the bill, took the defeat hard. "The fact that the Texas Pacific Railroad bill would, if reached, pass by a large majority, is poor consolation," lamented the paper.[38] The *Times* held the Northern and Western Democrats responsible for the loss of the Texas & Pacific cause. "Southern men are growing restive under the imputations heaped upon them by Western Democrats," it reported. "They will refuse to abide longer under the crack of the party whip." The political crisis was making friends for the South who did not take friendship for granted and who lived up to obligations better than fair-weather friends of the Democracy. "A movement is on foot to call a caucus of representatives of this section today to devise what action they should take as a body."[39]

On Saturday morning, February 17, the Democrats carried a motion in the House to take a recess until the following Monday, thereby delaying and postponing completion of the count of the electoral vote of Louisiana.[40] That evening the party met in caucus and the leaders of the filibuster movement, "hot-heads" and "fire-eaters" according to their opponents, attempted to gain official endorsement for their course. They introduced several resolutions condemning or repudiating the Electoral Commission and calling for a defeat of the count, one of which demanded resort to all possible dilatory measures "with the view of multiplying issues, and thereby

[37] Dodge to Hayes, February 15, 1877, *ibid.*
[38] New Orleans *Times,* February 19, 1877.
[39] *Ibid.*, February 24, 25, 1877.
[40] *Congressional Record,* 44 Cong., 2 Sess. (February 17, 1877), 1665.

defeating the inauguration of the usurper." Congressman Alexander G. Cochrane of Pennsylvania introduced one such motion that received enthusiastic support from Northern and Western congressmen. Among those who made speeches in behalf of Cochrane's motion were Frank H. Hurd of Ohio, William P. Lynde of Wisconsin, and Charles P. Thompson of Massachusetts. The gentleman from Massachusetts was said to have made "the most bitter and vehement speech of the evening." But while support came "almost entirely from the North and West," on the other hand "the South was almost a unit in favor of standing by the decision of the Commission." And in the "stormy scenes that followed" it was the voices of John Young Brown of Kentucky, Otho R. Singleton of Mississippi, John Reagan of Texas, and Ben Hill of Georgia that were heard denouncing Cochrane's resolution as "unwise, unpatriotic, and revolutionary."[41]

On a substitute for Cochrane's resolution introduced by Reagan calling for an end to the filibuster and completion of the electoral count in good faith the caucus divided, 68 "yeas" to 49 "nays," with a large number absent or not voting. The Southern members lined up solidly behind Reagan's motion, only one of the negative votes coming from their ranks.[42] It was a clear sectional cleavage within the Democratic party—North versus South—and it was now in the open. Northern Democrats were quoted in the Republican press as declaring that "the Southern Representatives have deserted them in a body, so as to make fair weather with the Republican Party."[43]

General Boynton could hardly contain his elation over the result. "Words are unnecessary with you," he wrote William Henry Smith, "for I know you must fully appreciate the situation & the victory. Please ask Mr. Medill if he now doubts that 36 votes can be commanded by the honorable means proposed. It is difficult to distin-

[41] New York *Times,* February 18, 19, 1877; *Nation,* XXIV (February 22, 1877), 109.

[42] This according to the Cincinnati *Enquirer,* February 19, 1877, a Democratic paper. The Republican New York *Times,* February 19, 1877, reported 56 negative votes, only one Southern. No official figures are available.

[43] New York *Times,* February 19, 1877.

guish between the comparative effect produced by the two elements—the purely political & the Scott forces—both worked earnestly, & you have the resultant of both." Colonel Kellar, with whom he tended to identify the "purely political forces," deserved much credit in the opinion of Boynton. "You never did a more important act than when with your friends you sent Col. K. here. He was just the man to reach the Southern men. . . . He merits great praise." But the "other forces" had undoubtedly "contributed much" and deserved their due. "I am sure the Scott force has performed enough of the work to entitle it to claims the execution of which appeared in the letters I received," added the general.[44]

Richard Smith had followed developments in both plans and was inclined to distribute credit equally. "That work Kellar and Boynton have been putting in has defeated Tilden's filibustering scheme," he observed to William Henry Smith. "Hayes knows all about this."[45]

In alarm and dismay Northern Democrats saw themselves betrayed by their Southern brethren. "The Southern disaffection is no longer an illusion," declared the Cincinnati *Enquirer*. "Last night's caucus settled beyond peradventure that their representatives have made terms. Two cabinet places are claimed, and the mess of pottage also includes other favors."[46] To Colonel Kellar the results of the caucus meant that "at last the conservative members from the South have openly cut loose" from their false friends, the Northern Democrats.[47]

But the fight against the filibuster was not quite over. The Northern Democratic managers were reported to be frightened and worried by the "defection of the Southern Democrats," but they did not accept the caucus action on Saturday as final. After a day of violent speeches in the House over the counting of the Louisiana vote on Monday, party leaders called another Democratic caucus

[44] Boynton to Smith, February 18, 1877, Smith Papers.
[45] Richard Smith to William Henry Smith, February 18, 1877, *ibid.*
[46] Cincinnati *Enquirer,* February 19, 1877.
[47] Memphis *Avalanche,* February 25, 1877.

that evening. This time the Northern filibusterers brought their heaviest artillery to bear on the recalcitrant Southerners. Democratic Speaker Randall, whose rulings had encouraged the filibuster by allowing repeated recesses, bluntly accused the Southern leaders of a bargain with Hayes. In a "fire-eating speech" he warned them that they were delivering their part of the bargain before they had any assurance that Hayes would deliver his promises. Randall predicted that Hayes would revive bayonet rule and that his policy would be of "such a character as to overwhelm any southern man in ruin who aided in carrying out their agreement in good faith." [48] He then proposed that the caucus agree that the House should amend the Act of 1792 so as to make the Secretary of State acting President of the United States until a new election could be held. He suggested that the Senate be coerced into agreement by a recess in the House from day to day until the Senate accepted the amendment. If that failed the House could bring the session to a close without completing the electoral count and force a new election under the law as it then stood. In spite of additional fireworks and pressure the caucus adjourned without taking action on Randall's drastic proposal and decided to take no action until after the vote of Oregon had been counted.[49]

The Southern wing held against Randall, but it was visibly shaken by the attack. Even Colonel Kellar, a man of cool nerve and sanguine disposition, was upset by the caucus. "I am greatly discouraged today," he wrote William Henry Smith. "The policy of Tammany Hall is to make matters so bad, that the South cannot co-operate with Hayes." [50] He believed the situation so desperate that Hayes would have "to say something or do something" in addition to what he had already said in order to keep the Southerners in line.[51] Boynton admitted three days later that, at the time,

[48] Foster to Hayes, February 21, 1877, Hayes Papers. Foster was reporting the caucus as Hayes's Southern Democratic friends told him the story on the evening the caucus took place.

[49] Albert V. House, Jr., "The Political Career of S. J. Randall" (Ph.D. dissertation, Wisconsin, 1934), 98–99.

[50] Kellar to Smith, February 19, 1877, Smith Papers.

[51] William Henry Smith to Hayes, February 21, 1877, Hayes Papers.

"the struggle to break the democrats on the plan to fillibuster [*sic*] seemed so desperate & so close to me that some means of *convincing* the leaders in our movement seemed almost absolutely necessary." [52]

Finally Charles Foster took the bit in his own teeth. At a late hour on the night of February 19, after the caucus had adjourned, a group of Southerners called at Foster's house and begged for immediate help in the emergency. "The Southern people who had agreed to stand by us in carrying out the Electoral law in good faith," Foster explained to Hayes, "were seized with a fright, if not a panic." Foster consulted with Matthews, Garfield, and William M. Evarts, all of whom agreed that he should at once make a strong speech denying the implications of Randall's caucus address and that he should do so without waiting to get the permission of Hayes.[53]

On the following day, February 20, Foster was recognized by Speaker Randall and spoke his piece. "Representing as I do the district in which Governor Hayes resides, and being a life-long acquaintance of his . . . I say that his administration will be wise, patriotic, and just," he promised. And it would be particularly just to the mistreated South: "The flag shall float over States, not provinces; over freemen, and not subjects." Hayes would "administer the government so patriotically and wisely as to wipe away any and all necessity or excuse for the formation of parties on a sectional basis and all traces of party color lines." [54] Foster wrote Hayes that his speech had been "very kindly received by gentlemen from the South," and harshly denounced by "the democratic malcontents of the North." [55] William Henry Smith thought that the speech might "help out" the work Kellar and Boynton were doing, but that it was the latter that would be decisive.[56]

As a matter of fact, a few minutes before Foster spoke, though not before the Southerners knew approximately what he would say,

[52] Boynton to Smith, February 22, 1877, Smith Papers.
[53] Foster to Hayes, February 21, 1877, Hayes Papers.
[54] *Congressional Record,* 44 Cong., 2 Sess. (February 20, 1877), 1708.
[55] Foster to Hayes, February 21, 1877, Hayes Papers.
[56] Smith to Hayes, February 21, 1877, *ibid.*

a division occurred in the House that revealed the way the wind blew. This occurred over a motion by an Ohio Democrat that the House take a recess until the following day. A recess would postpone completion of the count of the Louisiana vote and was clearly dilatory. Randall ruled the motion in order. On a show of hands the recess was defeated by 163 to 86, and on a call for the ayes and nays the filibuster was supported by only 57 votes. Thirty Southern Democrats voted against the dilatory motion.[57] The *National Republican* boasted that the division showed "all the prominent Southern members voting with the Republican party" and that "this was glory enough." Among them were Watterson, Lamar, Hill, John Young Brown, Roger Q. Mills, and Otho R. Singleton. The Republican paper believed that the conservative Southerners had at last learned that "their true friends are not among the hypocritical riff-raff Copperhead faction of the North, but among those who were brave enough to meet them like true heroes on the battlefield." Optimistically the editor predicted that the breach in the Democratic lines could never be healed and that through it "the Republican party will march to twenty years more of usefulness, power, and beneficence." [58]

With the filibuster scotched, the two caucuses successfully handled, and the Louisiana count completed, Hayes's advisors believed by February 22 that the crisis was over and his inauguration assured. Boynton wrote on that day that although the filibusterers had been "working hard all day to rally a sufficient force" to block the count of Oregon votes, he was sure they would fail. "Gen. Dodge has the whole of Scott's force at work, & that with the purely political force will I feel *confident* defeat the desperate men. It is still difficult for me to judge which of these two forces has been the most potent element in the long fight. Both have been of the greatest consequences, & I have grave doubts whether either could have carried the day alone." [59]

[57] *Congressional Record,* 44 Cong., 2 Sess. (February 20, 1877), 1705.
[58] Washington *National Republican,* February 21, 1877.
[59] Boynton to William Henry Smith, February 22, 1877, Smith Papers.

It would be futile to attempt to decide at this late date what so well-informed an authority as General Boynton was unable to decide in 1877 — which of the "two forces" was the more effective in winning the Southerners over and breaking the filibuster. They were complementary, sometimes closely interrelated, and occasionally indistinguishable. The views of General Dodge on the contribution of the Scott force are admittedly lacking in disinterestedness, but are nevertheless of some relevance. "Since our interview here with Boynton," the general wrote Tom Scott, "I have followed up the policy indicated then and have come to a very clear understanding with those people, and results of it have shown themselves pretty forceably here during the last few days. So much so that it has brought the attention of Hayes to the matter." Dodge assured Scott that Hayes was ready to co-operate with them in advancing the cause of the Texas & Pacific.[60]

To account for the action of the Southerners without reference to patriotism and the more statesmanlike motives would be to adopt a deplorably cynical interpretation of human conduct. On the other hand, to offer such motives as the complete explanation would be to advance a questionable theory regarding the sectional distribution of the more admirable virtues. The charitable supposition would be that while patriotism was equitably distributed between Northern and Southern Democrats, the patriotic course of resisting violence and complying with the Electoral Commission law happened to coincide more nearly with the interests of the Southern than of the Northern Democrats — as they understood their interests.

Oddly enough it remained for the Northern Republican press, normally not addicted to charitable views of ex-Rebels, to advance the theory that among Democrats, at least, probity, righteousness, and public rectitude were largely Southern monopolies. As soon as it became reasonably clear that the Southern Democrats would refuse to support the filibuster and would throw their weight on the side of completing the electoral count the Republican papers broke out in a chorus of praise. "It must be confessed," said the New York

[60] Dodge to Scott, February 20, 1877, letterbook in Box 384, Dodge Papers.

Times, "that the consistency and decency of the Democratic Party in Congress are chiefly with the Southern members thereof."[61] The Chicago *Tribune* rejoiced that revolution had been averted, that "the counsel for moderation came from the Southern Democrats, and that it was through their combined votes that the contemplated resistance was defeated."[62] Praising "the high sense of honor and immovable good faith and loyalty of the South," the New York *Herald* marveled that "the great section which has the most reason for dissatisfaction, whose wishes have been thwarted and its electoral votes nullified, is foremost in counselling patriotic submission."[63]

The Washington *National Republican,* loosely referred to at times as the administration mouthpiece, outdid them all with a series of editorials entitled "The South Declines Dishonor," "Southern Men to the Rescue," "Wise Act of Southern Men."[64] "A new political era dawned upon the Republican party yesterday," declared the editor, referring to the Southern vote against the filibuster on February 20. "The Southern statesmen, the true and patriotic, bade farewell to the tricky, scheming, filibustering, dough-faced faction composing the Northern Democracy, and boldly put themselves on record as being against any attempt to evade the decision of the Judicial Tribunal or thwart its result. *It is the bravest and wisest act that has been recorded in the annals of political history for half a century.*"[65] That took in a good deal of territory. It took in such notable Republican acts, for example, as the Emancipation Proclamation, the Reconstruction Acts, the Thirteenth, Fourteenth, and Fifteenth Amendments, and the Civil Rights Act. Perhaps the editor did not have them in mind at the moment. At any rate he thought that events had proved the Negroes incapable of self-government, the Carpetbagger regimes unworthy of Republican support, and the conservative ex-Rebels the only element in the South worthy of Republican confidence and admiration.

[61] New York *Times,* February 19, 1877.
[62] Chicago *Tribune,* February 19, 1877.
[63] New York *Herald,* February 19, 1877.
[64] Washington *National Republican,* February 19, 20, 21, 1877.
[65] *Ibid.,* February 21, 1877. Italics mine.

The *Nation* had a quiet smile over the pro-Southern effusions of the very men who in the Presidential campaign were engaged "in wickedly converting the canvass into a 'bloody-shirt' crusade against the South, and in presenting Mr. Hayes's election to the public as a continuance of the civil war." Among the converts were all "the leading Republican papers, including even the organs of the Desperadoes"—that is, the journals of the Radical Republicans and the extreme anti-Southern wing of the party.[66]

[66] *Nation,* XXIV (February 22, 1877), 110.

CHAPTER IX

The End of the Crisis

THEN at the very moment when Republican effusions over the loyalty, honor, and sterling patriotism of Southern Democrats had reached a climax, the applecart was suddenly upset by what appeared to be an embarrassing accident. It was merely the latest of a series of political gaucheries — of which Judge Davis's sudden election to the Senate was an outstanding example — that beset the election crisis from beginning to end.

This time it was an editorial that appeared in the Columbus *Ohio State Journal* of February 22. It was only a standard piece of Republican campaign hack work attacking the white people of Louisiana in the contemptuous terms of conventional bloody-shirt oratory. Appearing in any of scores of Republican sheets the country over, it would have occasioned no more excitement than a weather report. But the editor of the *Ohio State Journal* was General James Comly, the close personal friend of Governor Hayes. He was known in the Capital, and especially to Southern Democratic leaders, as the representative of Governor Hayes who came to Washington in January with honeyed words of the new Republican policy. It was immediately assumed that the article on Louisiana was inspired by Hayes and reflected his real policy.

The morning after the article appeared in Columbus some fifty marked copies of the *Journal* were industriously circulated among Democratic members of the House in Washington. They naturally created a sensation. Frantically Matthews, Foster, and Dennison wired General Comly for an explanation. The reply came that Comly was sick in bed, that Hayes knew nothing of the article, and that the publication of it was the mistake of a young man in the newspaper office. The explanation was printed in the *National Republican,* but it would take more than that to undo the damage.[1]

The article from Comly's paper placed in the hands of the Northern Democrats just what they needed. For here was apparent evidence to substantiate Speaker Randall's warning to the Southerners in caucus that Hayes was an unregenerate, bloody-shirt Republican addicted to bayonet rule and that his policy would "overwhelm in ruin" any Southern politician who attempted to carry out the bargain. The Southerners had scarcely recovered from the panic into which Randall's speech had thrown them and were still trying to believe the reassuring words that Foster spoke in reply. The Comly paper made them harder to believe than ever. What if Randall turned out to be right? What real assurance was there that after the Southerners had delivered their part of the Bargain the Radicals might not compel the repudiation of the Republican commitments? Even if Hayes delivered the cabinet place, the new patronage policy, and "internal improvements of a national character"—Texas & Pacific subsidies included—how could the politicians defend their desertion of Tilden if the Republicans refused to abandon military force in supporting Carpetbagger governments? Who then would dare face angry constituents who wanted to know why Southern Democrats helped seat a Republican usurper in the White House? It was easy enough to imagine being "overwhelmed in ruin."

Ominous rumbles from below the Potomac, from people who did not understand what was going on, were already reaching Washington. On February 17, the day of the caucus in which the Southern members made their eloquent speeches about honor and patriotism, the North Carolina Senate, with only three Democrats opposed, passed a resolution denouncing "the fraud of Electoral Boards" and "the wicked partisanship of the Electoral Commission," declaring that Hayes had "not been elected President according to law," and asserting that he could not "be lawfully installed as the Chief Magistrate of the people."[2]

[1] Washington *National Republican,* February 24, 1877.
[2] New York *Times,* February 19, 1877.

It was not a simple matter to explain to inquiring constituents the advantages of securing the portfolio of the Postmaster General, nor what railroad subsidies, levee bills, and internal improvements had to do with the completion of the electoral count. The Southeastern states had not been so deeply stirred by the movement for internal improvements as had the Southwest, and even in that part of the country there were plenty of impoverished cotton farmers who were slow to see how any railroad subsidy would help them clothe their ragged children. When the New York *Times* congratulated "the Southern Democrats" for "taking a good-natured view of the situation," it was referring to the politicians in Washington. Back home, and particularly in the Southeast, people were not so "good natured" about it.

During the crisis an intelligent South Carolinian wrote in the *Atlantic Monthly* that "the excitement in the South over the presidential contest is literally frightful. Should it be adverse to Mr. Tilden, the national House of Representatives and Mr. Tilden have it in their power to cause an explosion in the South so terrific that the outbreak of 1860–61 will be almost forgotten. The most dangerous hopes and emotions are agitating the bosom of every Southerner. At every street corner and fireside, on the steps of every store, you may hear men saying that the hour of the republicans is striking, that they have got to submit, the North is split, and 'We'll try them this time with Tilden and New York to help us.' "[3]

That leaves an exaggerated impression of tension in the South. But even Henry Watterson's paper, whose sudden conversion from fire-eating bellicosity to good-natured submission had been the marvel most frequently cited by Republican journals as proof of the South's essential "soundness" and "patriotism," took a different tone after the bloody-shirt article appeared in Comly's paper. There was no renewal of the call for a hundred thousand Southerners to march on Washington, but in place of the temperate counsel of moderation there appeared a stern note of warning. "*The Republican party*

[3] A South Carolinian, "The Political Condition of South Carolina," *Atlantic Monthly,* XXXIX (1877), 190.

must be held to its pledges made in the hour of its distress," declared the Louisville *Courier-Journal.*[4] "If that party is confirmed in its lease of power," said the editor, "the people of the South, recognizing the perfidy in the past, will be as slow of belief as the Poles would be in accepting a similar backdown on the part of Russia, until the pseudo philanthropists crystalize their words into acts." [5]

Southern Redeemers who played the leading role in the *rapprochement* with Republicans were seriously alarmed by what they were finding in their daily mail from the home district. "I have received dispatches and letters from home," John Young Brown told Charles Foster, "from cherished and trusted friends, conveying the most emphatic remonstrance against my course." [6] Brown was not the only one. Although they were safer from popular wrath for having been recently elevated to the Senate, the mighty Lamar and his friend Ben Hill were also receiving depressing news of popular reactions at home.[7] And crowding the streets and lobbies of Washington was a "vast army of office seekers, who have spent their money and had their expectations raised regarding the success of Tilden." They were said to be "in a state of furious excitement," and ready to "resort to any device to put a stop to the inauguration of a Republican President." [8]

On the morning that the fifty copies of General Comly's paper were circulated in the House the counting of the electoral vote of Oregon was up for consideration. When the joint session to hear the report of the Electoral Commission adjourned and the senators filed out, the Democrats of the House moved and promptly carried a motion to take a recess until the following day. It meant a return to the dilatory tactics of the filibusterers. This time the recess was carried by a strict party vote.[9] None of the thirty Southern Demo-

[4] Louisville *Courier-Journal,* March 1, 1877.
[5] *Ibid.,* February 27, 1877.
[6] Quoted in Raleigh *Observer,* March 31, 1877.
[7] Mayes, *Lamar,* 304.
[8] New York *Daily Graphic,* February 23, 1877.
[9] *Congressional Record,* 44 Cong., 2 Sess. (February 23, 1877), 1884.

crats who had voted with the Republicans against a recess three days earlier joined the opposition on February 23. In the party caucus called during the recess the filibuster element had the upper hand. The entire Mississippi delegation, all the congressmen from Louisiana, and all from Georgia save Ben Hill and James H. Blount swung their support to the movement. By a vote of 66 to 44, which almost exactly reversed the proportional strength of the two sides on February 17, the caucus decided upon an additional recess the following day. That would adjourn the House over the week-end and leave only six working days before the end of the session in which to break the great log jam of legislation and complete the electoral count.[10]

The filibustering motion for a recess on the 24th failed by a vote of 158 to 112. And when a motion to reconsider followed, Speaker Randall "astounded his opponents, many of his party, and all of the New York newspaper correspondents" by ruling it out of order.[11] He had turned against the filibuster. Hewitt also, after bitterly denouncing the Electoral Commission as a fraud, pleaded for an end to the filibuster and the completion of the count to keep peace in the country. The New Yorker had been deeply impressed by the flood of petitions from business interests begging relief from the political crisis that had brought business to a standstill, and had decided that four years of Hayes were better than four years of civil war.[12] Following the leadership of Randall and Hewitt, a wing of Northeastern Democratic congressmen was detached from the filibuster and joined the twenty or so Southerners who still refused to go over to the movement. The filibuster therefore received a check at the same time it gained new impetus. But in the process the extremists had more than doubled their numbers. Temporarily, at least, they had forty-two Southerners with them, and if they could hold their pres-

[10] Washington *National Republican,* February 24, 1877.

[11] House, "Political Career of Samuel J. Randall," 100; *Congressional Record,* 44 Cong., 2 Sess. (February 24, 1877), 1906. According to Nevins, *Hewitt,* 381, Randall had received a telegram from Tilden that the count must be completed.

[12] *Ibid.,* 386; *Congressional Record,* 44 Cong., 2 Sess. (February 24, 1877), 1914–1915.

ent strength together for a week they might block completion of the count.

It was now the turn of the Republicans to lose nerve and become panicky. Foster, Matthews, Dennison, Garfield, and Sherman seem to have spent their waking hours in a succession of inconclusive conferences on the crisis, and Senator Sherman appeared to be the most apprehensive of the lot. On the 24th he wrote Governor Hayes of "great anxiety felt as to filibustering movements," reported that "all sorts of rumors are current still," and warned that there was still a possibility that the extremists would resort to "revolutionary means."[13]

Not until this late phase, the final week of the crisis, does the Bargain of the history books, the result of the so-called Wormley Conference, put in an appearance. It was the only part of the long and involved story that the Southern Redeemers saw fit to release to the press during the crisis and divulge in more detail during the congressional investigation of 1878. All the history of the three months of negotiations prior to February 22 that has been unraveled so far in these pages was passed over in silence. This is all the more remarkable in view of the fact that by that date the defection of the Southern conservatives had become the most conspicuous sensation in the national crisis. It was regarded as an accomplished fact and the papers were full of it. The Democratic press of the North was bitterly accusing the South of selling the party out, and the Republican papers were seeking to outdo each other in praise of the Southern conservatives.

The inner circle of Hayes's advisors who had developed the "purely political plan" and the "Scott plan" had no part in the Wormley Conference. William Henry Smith, Boynton, Kellar, Halstead, Medill, Dodge, and Scott proceeded with their plans as before, with no heed to the new negotiations. These were the concern mainly of a group of Louisiana Democrats on the one side and Ohio Republicans on the other, and they had to do entirely with

[13] Sherman to Hayes, February 24, 1877, Hayes Papers.

arrangements for the recognition and establishment of a Democratic government in Louisiana, and incidentally in South Carolina. "Home rule" in principle was already promised by Hayes's friends as part of the "purely political plan." But the Louisianans were concerned with settlement of the practical "how" and "when" of home rule. They wanted the business pinned down.

The fully accredited representative of Francis T. Nicholls, Democratic claimant of the Louisiana governorship, was Major E. A. Burke. He worked closely with Congressmen Randall L. Gibson, William M. Levy, and E. John Ellis of Louisiana, but Burke remained the dominant figure.[14] In a period as crowded with picturesque rogues as was the Gilded Age, the major was not so conspicuous as he might have been in more commonplace times. But at the Southern end of the scene there were few who could match his splendid audacity. His talents were of the order that produces masterful poker players. He spoke of himself vaguely as "a Kentuckian," but his origins are a matter of dispute and appear to have been Northern. Burke arrived penniless in New Orleans in 1870 after unfortunate adventures in Texas and went to work as a day laborer in a stonecutter's yard. Six years later he emerged as chairman of the state Democratic committee in full charge of the campaign for redemption. With his fingers in scores of pies, Burke later became the most powerful newspaper editor of New Orleans, a dominant figure in railroads, in the Louisiana Lottery, and in civic affairs, as well as state treasurer for a dozen years. In 1889 it was discovered, during his absence in Europe, that he had defrauded the state of more than a million dollars while he was state treasurer. He did not return to Louisiana to answer the charges but operated subsequently in Central America. In 1877, however, Major Burke was Redeemer-extraordinary with the destinies of a state in his fingers and a Presidential election at stake. He played his cards masterfully.

[14] Ellis called Burke "the factotum of that whole series of conferences from beginning to end." "Presidential Election Investigation," *House Miscellaneous Documents,* 45 Cong., 3 Sess., Doc. No. 31, vol. III, 598.

Burke first opened negotiations with Grant's Secretary of War, J. Don Cameron, early in February. Cameron's price for a free hand in Louisiana state government was the two United States senatorial seats of the state filled with worthy Republicans. According to Burke, "We could always have had the State upon those terms."[15] Burke thought the price too high, however, especially in view of the fact that Grant's policy of benevolent neutrality had already permitted Nicholl's government to establish *de facto* control in Louisiana.[16]

The major returned to New Orleans to await developments. He realized that he was asking a good deal of the Republicans. For he was demanding that they abandon Packard, who received more votes for governor of Louisiana than Hayes received for President, while they were basing their claim to the Presidential election on the contention that Hayes had carried Louisiana.

On February 16, the day the Electoral Commission decided (eight to seven) that Hayes carried Louisiana, Burke returned to Washington. That evening and again on the 18th he conferred with Stanley Matthews, who expected shortly to be elected Senator from Ohio. Matthews repeated assurances regarding Hayes's policy toward Louisiana, but Burke was not interested in these. He was prepared by this time to believe in Hayes's good intentions, he said, but he feared that the opposition of "the strong Republican leaders like Sherman, Garfield, Morton and others" would prevent Hayes from delivering his promises. Burke wanted assurances from leaders of that sort. Matthews regretted that he "could not speak for those people." Whereupon Burke declared that he and his associates would advise their friends "to join the filibustering movement and swell it to such proportions as to force the Republican leaders to agree to the yielding up of Louisiana and South Carolina." He repeated his threats to Foster and Dennison and had a Republican friend from Texas wire the substance of his position to Hayes through Lieutenant Governor Thomas L. Young of Ohio.[17]

[15] *Ibid.*, vol. I, pp. 975, 1010–1011.
[16] *Ibid.*, 973.
[17] *Ibid.*, 967–970.

This was an empty bluff on Burke's part and the Republicans knew it. For the Democratic caucus of the 17th had just passed a resolution with solid Southern support in favor of ending the filibuster and completing the electoral count. During the next five days the Republican-Southern Democratic collaboration was in full swing. In effect, the Republicans called Burke's bluff, for they ignored his threats for a week.

On the 20th, after Foster's conciliatory speech, Lamar urged Ellis of Louisiana to go to Columbus immediately and get personal assurances from Hayes. Ellis was willing but Nicholls advised against the trip, and Burke pronounced it "useless."[18] Hayes's promises were good enough as promises go. It was necessary, Burke insisted, to have party leaders committed to those promises. He believed the only way to extract commitments from those gentlemen was by pressure of a filibuster—and the filibuster had collapsed. Lamar, Watterson, Hill, Reagan, Brown, Young, and all the strong Southern Democrats had taken their stand on "patriotism" and refused to give any aid.

Then on the 24th, for reasons entirely unconnected with Burke's threats and due to the editorial in Comly's paper, filibuster strength soared suddenly to 112 votes. Seizing this opportunity, Burke renewed his pressure upon the Republicans while he and his Louisiana friends did all in their power to sustain the revival of the filibuster. On the following day Foster showed Burke a letter from Hayes approving Foster's speech of the 20th and saying that it represented his policy accurately.[19] Again Burke reiterated his stand that he did not want more promises from Hayes but solid commitments from Radical Republican leaders who could prevent Hayes from fulfilling his promises. With the roar of the revived filibuster in their ears, the Republicans did not call Burke's bluff this time.

On Monday the 26th things happened fast. In the morning Burke

[18] *Ibid.*, III, 595, for Ellis's testimony. Lamar at Ellis's request later put his suggestion in writing, but omitted the suggestion of the trip to Columbus. *Ibid.*, I, 973–974.

[19] E. A. Burke to F. T. Nicholls, February 25, 1877, in *ibid.*, III, 618.

had an interview with Grant in which the President approved for public release a dispatch representing him as saying "unequivocally that he is satisfied that the Nicholls government is the government which should stand," that it was "sustained by the most influential elements in the State," that the Republican government could not stand without military force, and that public opinion was "clearly opposed to the further use of troops in upholding a State government." He promised no further interference with the Nicholls government unless there were "violent excesses."[20]

Shortly after the Grant interview Burke received word that Sherman wished to see him. In December Sherman had signed a report to Hayes that the Louisiana whites had seized the state by terror and intimidation. The Senator had just returned from a trip to Columbus where he had accepted a place in Hayes's cabinet. This was a man Burke wanted to see. They met in a Senate committee room in the presence of Matthews and Dennison of Ohio. The doors were locked. Sherman came to the point bluntly. What was the price of lifting the filibuster? Burke modestly — but not too vigorously — denied that he controlled the House. He proposed that the gentlemen go to Grant and say that the immediate withdrawal of troops would not embarrass Hayes. "My God," exclaimed Sherman, throwing up his hands, "there's no use talking about going to Grant. He is surrounded by such influences that we can do nothing with him." Whereupon the major played his ace — dramatically drawing from his pocket the dispatch Grant had just approved. When they had recovered from their astonishment the gentlemen agreed to go to see the President the following morning and, according to Burke, "they did go." The three Republicans repeated in turn to Burke, as if in preconceived formula, that they felt authorized from intimate and long acquaintance with Hayes to say that as President he would follow the policy toward Louisiana indicated by Grant. For his part, Sherman had two requests in addition to the fundamental one of lifting the filibuster. First he wanted assurances from the Democratic Nicholls government of Louisiana regarding treatment

[20] Burke to Nicholls, February 26, 1877, *ibid.*

of Negroes and other Republicans once the troops were gone. Second he proposed that the new Louisiana legislature postpone the election of a long-term Democratic senator until March 10 so as not to provoke a Republican revolt against Hayes that might defeat confirmation of his cabinet nominations by the United States Senate. It was tacitly understood that the other Louisiana senator would be a Republican. Burke thought both conditions could be met. The meeting then broke up with the understanding that a further conference would meet that evening to which additional members would be invited.[21]

The Wormley Conference on the evening of the 26th actually added nothing to the agreements reached earlier in the day, but merely went over the same ground for the benefit of new participants. Burke brought with him Ellis, Levy, and Henry Watterson. Gibson was ill at the time. It was explained vaguely that Watterson was there "to represent South Carolina," but his presence was probably more accurately attributable to his newspaperman's instinct for being in at the kill. With Sherman, Matthews, and Dennison came Garfield, the only new Republican participant. Sherman, said Ellis, was "cool as an iceberg, as usual, and silent as a sphinx." Each of the Republicans nevertheless repeated the set speech about the good intentions of Hayes. Garfield made a more guarded one. His diary reveals that he was acutely unhappy over his situation. As a member of the Electoral Commission, still sitting, he had gravely voted that Hayes had carried Louisiana. And now in a smoky hotel room he was, in effect, acknowledging that the Democrats had carried it. For a Presidential aspirant this was a complex position in which to be placed. While he declared that he "had no doubt that the new administration would deal justly and generously with the south," he solemnly added that "those Southern Democrats who are resisting filibustering are doing so on the ground of high public duty & honor; and any bargain would make their motives far lower." He thought "the whole nation would honor those Southern men who are resisting anarchy—and thus are preventing Civil War; but

[21] *Ibid.*, I, 974–975. Substantially the same account is in vol. III, 619–620.

neither they nor we could afford to do anything that would be or appear to be a political bargain."[22]

That was probably Garfield's elaborate way of informing Major Burke that he was perfectly aware that the Louisianans did not possess the power they claimed of turning the filibuster on or off at will. After all, Garfield was the man Kellar and Boynton had sought out first in Washington at the inception of their work in December. And he was the candidate for speaker whose election was arranged as part of the "purely political plan." Garfield was much better informed than Burke concerning the "ground of high public duty & honor" on which the Southern opponents of the filibuster stood.

On the following day Burke gave the story of the Wormley Conference Bargain to the Associated Press, prefaced by the statement that it was "no bargain." Of course he gave only part of the story: the assurances that Hayes would acknowledge the government of Nicholls, and the promises of the Nicholls government that it would respect the rights of Negroes and Republicans.[23] Burke also handed Matthews a formal ratification of the agreement by a caucus of the Nicholls legislature guaranteeing acceptance of political equality, civil rights, and equal education for the Negro and immunity of all from persecution for past political acts.[24] The same day, the 27th, on the floor of the House, Watterson read into the *Record* the dispatch that Grant had approved for Burke, representing the President as favoring the Democratic Nicholls government and disapproving the use of troops to support the Republican Packard in Louisiana. At the same time the House, by party vote, passed a resolution that Congress recognize the Hampton government in South Carolina as well as the Nicholls government in Louisiana.[25]

In the meantime John Young Brown, with Senator Gordon as witness and support, practically "bulldozed" Foster and Matthews into signing statements embodying the set formula that "we feel authorized, from our acquaintance and knowledge of Gov.

[22] Garfield Diary, February 26, 1877, Garfield Papers.
[23] *House Miscellaneous Documents,* 45 Cong., 3 Sess., Doc. No. 31, III, 623.
[24] *Ibid.,* 622.
[25] *Congressional Record,* 44 Cong., 2 Sess. (February 27, 1877), 1984–1985.

Hayes . . ." which all the Republican spokesmen had repeated in turn to Burke and his associates. One of these was signed by Foster on the 26th and another by Foster and Matthews on the 27th.[26] They added nothing new to the situation save that they specified South Carolina as well as Louisiana, and they were written and signed instead of verbal commitments. They contained no reference to the other terms of the Bargain.

It was now more essential than ever to maintain a bold front to the languishing Democratic filibuster delaying completion of the electoral count. For one thing Hayes was to be heard from. Burke had his Texas Republican friend wire Lieutenant Governor Young the full terms of the conversations for the governor's reaction.[27] Then there was still hope that Grant might be pushed into ordering the withdrawal of troops. And more important yet, in Burke's opinion, was the reaction of the congressional oligarchy of Radical Republicans — Morton, Conkling, Blaine, and their like. If they did not concur in the Bargain, at least by giving silent consent to the published terms, the party would not be truly committed. It was no time to relax the filibuster until these matters were clinched.

Unfortunately for Burke the strength of the filibuster fell from 112 votes on the 24th to 84 on the 26th, only 27 of which were from Southern Democrats. On another attempt the extremists could muster only 67 votes.[28] They apparently dared not risk a major attempt to hold up the count the following day and contented themselves with badgering motions providing for succession to the Presidency in case of no election.

Watching developments from hour to hour, Kellar, Boynton, and Dodge felt no cause for alarm. On the 27th Boynton wired William Henry Smith, "There are no signs of breaking among Southern men. Reverse is true." And again the same day he wired, "Col K says everything in our force is strong and solid so says Gen Dodge."[29]

[26] *House Miscellaneous Documents,* 45 Cong., 3 Sess., Doc. No. 31, III, 624. "Bulldozed" was General Dodge's expression for the action.

[27] *Ibid.,* 621.

[28] *Congressional Record,* 44 Cong., 2 Sess. (February 26, 1877), 1939–1940.

[29] Two telegrams, Boynton to Smith, February 27, 1877, Smith Papers.

Dodge kept his lobby constantly on the job. The confidence Boynton and Kellar professed in their Southern friends did not prove misplaced, for none of the important Southern leaders with whom they had dealt and few of the "Texas & Pacific force" ever broke ranks to join the filibuster. Lamar, Watterson, and John Young Brown have often been pictured as heroes of Redemption because of their peripheral connection with the Wormley Bargain. Actually, in the critical days that followed they never once voted with the group sustaining the filibuster to assist Major Burke's maneuver and help frighten the Republicans. Nor did Ben Hill, Hancock, Throckmorton, Reagan, and numerous others.[30] In the House, Henry Watterson deplored any further resistance from Southerners. "The time has passed when bold movements could avail us," he urged. "To-day, we have little impulse but our anger left. . . . In this present battle all is lost except our honor, the memory of our struggle, the glory of our triumph, the lesson of our surrender. It chokes me to think about it. I will not think about it. I will turn away from it. . . ."[31] Throughout the remaining struggle Watterson and his group steadfastly maintained their "ground of high public duty & honor"—if one prefers Garfield's phraseology.

Burke and his friends were compelled to look elsewhere for their desperately needed recruits to revive the filibuster. They succeeded in finding enough, but the new recruits were summer soldiers who carefully specified that they enlisted for a skirmish and not a campaign. "Many of them told us at the time," Burke testified later, "that they did not dare to assume the responsibility of final defeat of the count."[32] They were already thoroughly committed to the seating of Hayes. As Burke wired Nicholls, they were "independent of original opponents of the count," that is, of the fifty or so irreconcilables determined to defeat Hayes, and "cannot be held together" except briefly "for purpose [of] securing substantial guarantees [for] our state government."[33]

[30] *Congressional Record,* 44 Cong., 2 Sess. (February 28, 1877), 2007, 2008, 2009, 2025; (March 1, 1877), 2030, 2048–2049.

[31] *Ibid.* (February 24, 1877), Appendix, 189.

[32] *House Miscellaneous Documents,* 45 Cong., 3 Sess., Doc. No. 31, I, 990.

[33] Burke to Nicholls, February 28, 1877, *ibid.,* III, 624.

On the last day of February the filibuster came back with a substantial 92 votes.[34] Only 32 of them were cast by Southern Democrats, and that represented less than half of the full strength of the Southern delegation. These 32 votes constituted the maximum number Burke and his friends were able to muster from the South. Undoubtedly a generous impulse to help out South Carolina and Louisiana was the predominant motivation of those Southerners who lent a hand.

Burke received even more substantial assistance from an unexpected source by an appeal to Abram S. Hewitt, who agreed to help in spite of the public stand he had taken against the filibuster. Toward the end of the session on the 28th Hewitt amazed his friends by drawing out a sealed package purporting to contain electoral votes from Vermont and demanding that Senator Ferry, presiding over the joint session, receive them. The package was known to have been sent by a minority Democratic candidate who claimed to be elected because his Republican opponent was a postmaster. Ferry had refused to receive the package at an earlier date and in the midst of great outcry he refused again.[35] Here was the opportunity for a prolonged demonstration by the filibusterers.

The session on March 1, opening at ten o'clock in the morning and continuing for eighteen hours, is said to have been "probably the stormiest ever witnessed in any House of Representatives."[36] Reinforced by new recruits, the extremists kept up an uproarious bombardment of dilatory motions — motions for a recess, for reconsideration, for a roll call on the presence of a quorum when it was perfectly obvious there was a quorum present. In the confusion it was learned that the package from Vermont had mysteriously disappeared. Angered by what appeared more foul play and by the obstinate refusal of Speaker Randall to put their motions, members drowned out each other with yells and shrieks. Many were addressing the speaker simultaneously and one member mounted his desk. Crowded galleries joined in the demonstration wildly. In spite of

[34] *Congressional Record,* 44 Cong., 2 Sess. (February 28, 1877), 2007.
[35] *Ibid.,* 2021.
[36] Haworth, *Disputed Election of 1876,* 276.

repeated attempts of the speaker to clear out the lobbyists, they continued at their work, much to the annoyance of the filibusterers. "Look at those lobbies, Mr. Speaker," shouted one member. "I have tried to get the Speaker's ear so that I could direct attention to them. We are mobbed by the lobby!"[37]

Filibuster strength reached its highest point when 116 votes were cast for a motion that the House refuse to proceed with the count until the President of the Senate opened the package of Vermont votes and submitted the question to the Electoral Commission.[38]

By this time Major Burke and the Louisianans had satisfied themselves on several doubtful points. In an interview with Grant on the 28th the President assured Burke that he would order the withdrawal of troops just as soon as the electoral count was completed.[39] By means that he did not choose to reveal, Hewitt had access to all telegrams exchanged between Hayes and his Washington spokesman,[40] and by March 1 he was able to assure the Louisianans that these telegrams indicated a satisfactory commitment on the part of the Republicans. The Radical oligarchy in Congress had not lifted a voice in dissent. Their silence was interpreted as acquiescence.

After hours of filibuster, when the clamor was at its height, William M. Levy of Louisiana arose and announced that he had "solemn, earnest, and, I believe, truthful assurances" both from Hayes's friends and from Grant of "a policy of conciliation toward the Southern States" and the abandonment of the use of troops. He urged all "who have been influenced in their action . . . by a desire to protect Louisiana and South Carolina" to join him in helping complete the count.[41]

Very quickly after Levy took his seat the uproar subsided and the strength of the filibuster dropped from 116 to 80 and then leveled off around 57—the residue of irreconcilables. The ritual of the count proceeded to the end. At about four o'clock on the morn-

[37] *Congressional Record,* 44 Cong., 2 Sess. (March 1, 1877), 2034.

[38] *Ibid.,* 2048–2049.

[39] E. A. Burke to F. T. Nicholls, February 28, 1877, *House Miscellaneous Documents,* 45 Cong., 3 Sess., Doc. No. 31, III, 625.

[40] Nevins, *Hewitt,* 382.

[41] *Congressional Record,* 44 Cong., 2 Sess. (March 1, 1877), 2046–2047.

ing of March 2 Senator Ferry declared Hayes elected by a majorit of one vote. The crisis was ended.

On the morning of March 2, after the completion of the coun President Grant told Major Burke that he had sent a dispatch t Packard notifying him that the troops could no longer be used t uphold his claims in Louisiana. The President read and correcte with his own hands a message from Burke to Nicholls stating tha Grant intended the people of Louisiana to be "as free in thei affairs from Federal interference as the people of Connecticut." Burke released this message to the Associated Press the followin day. Grant also assured Burke that he had given instructions tha orders to remove the troops from the vicinity of the State Hous in New Orleans be sent to General Augur. For reasons that are no entirely clear these orders failed to reach General Augur through official channels before Grant's term expired. The troops were no removed and Packard remained in the possession of the State House though of little else. Final solution of the problem would be left up to Hayes.[42]

Governor Hayes and his party, which included William Henry Smith, arrived in Washington on March 2 in a private car furnished by Tom Scott of the Pennsylvania Railroad.[43] Hayes had received many warnings that attempts would be made on his life at Baltimore, but nothing happened. He was inaugurated privately at the White House on Saturday, March 3, to prevent an interregnum over Sunday, and again publicly on March 5.

On the same day that Hayes was privately sworn in the Democrats of the House relieved their pent-up feelings by passing a resolution over the Republican opposition declaring that Tilden had been "duly elected President of the United States for the term of four years, commencing on the 4th Day of March, A.D., 1877."[44] The resolution could have been the basis of a revolutionary action

[42] *House Miscellaneous Documents,* 45 Cong., 3 Sess., Doc. No. 31, I, 960–961; III, 626–630.

[43] J. Don Cameron to Hayes, February 19, 1877; L. C. Wier to Hayes, February 26, 1877, Hayes Papers.

[44] *Congressional Record,* 44 Cong., 2 Sess. (March 3, 1877), 2226–2227.

if Tilden had been of a revolutionary turn of mind. He was not.

The extremists among the Tildenites of the House were not finished with Hayes yet. As indicated earlier in this narrative, they reported an army appropriations bill containing a clause specifically forbidding that troops be used to support the claims of either of the rival governments in Louisiana, or the claims of governments in any other state "until the same shall have been duly recognized by Congress." The clause also made anyone guilty of violating the act subject to imprisonment "at hard labor for not less than five nor more than ten years." Charles Foster protested against an act that compelled the President to choose between violating his oath of office and serving a term at hard labor. The act was nevertheless passed without a roll call. The Republican majority of the Senate knocked out the objectionable clause, but the House refused to agree to the change. In the last hectic hours of the session three successive committees of conference were appointed by each house to attempt to compromise, but all of them reported failure to agree. Foster repeated his assurances that Hayes would live up to his promises, but the extremists were adamant. And even Hayes's Southern friends could see that the army appropriation clause put "teeth" and "sanctions" into their agreements with the Republicans. The Southern conservatives did not resist the movement. In the last few minutes of the expiring Congress Foster offered a bill making an army appropriation for only half the year. That also proved inadmissible. He then desperately made a final plea.

> FOSTER: I will make the suggestion that the House agree to make the appropriation for three months — a quarter of a year.
>
> MORRISON OF ILLINOIS: No, sir.
>
> BLACKBURN OF KENTUCKY: No, sir; not for three days.
>
> FOSTER: Then the responsibility must rest on you.
>
> O'BRIEN OF NEW YORK: We will take the responsibility.

These words closed the final debate of the Forty-fourth Congress and the session ended without making any appropriation for the army.[45]

[45] *Ibid.*, 2241–2252.

CHAPTER X

Interpretations of the Compromise

IN THE SUMMER of 1878 two figures of unhappy notoriety in Louisiana legend faced each other for three days before a congressional investigating committee. One was bluff Ben Butler, celebrated as the insulter of New Orleans womanhood and a pilferer of silver spoons. The other was Major E. A. Burke, more justly accused somewhat later of pilfering New Orleans silver on a grander scale. One was the man of Radicalism and Reconstruction — the old order. The other, who overturned and replaced that order, was the man of Conservatism and Redemption — the new order. Butler and Burke were cast in antagonistic roles, and yet they had a number of traits in common. As they sparred warily, Butler as interrogator, Burke as witness, there crept into the questions of the old Radical a tone of admiration. The subject of their exchange was the overthrow of Reconstruction and Burke's role in the disputed Presidential election.

"Then it was a little bluff game?" suggested Butler.

"It was a bluff game," admitted Burke.

"And in your judgment," continued Butler, "our friends, the Secretary of the Treasury [Sherman], and Mr. Garfield, and Mr. Matthews got bluffed into an agreement which, if they had only kept their fingers out a day or two, would have all gone right without it?"

"I think the count would have been terminated," said the Major, blandly.[1]

"Was there anything said there," asked Butler, referring to the

[1] "Presidential Election Investigation," *House Miscellaneous Documents,* 45 Cong., 3 Sess., Doc. No. 31, I, 990.

Wormley Conference and those preceding it, "which leads you to believe that President Hayes modified his opinion or adopted his views upon that subject in consequence of any assurances that were given by you or by your friends whether at or before the Wormley Conference?"

"I will frankly state," replied Burke, "that I believe that was the view of Mr. Hayes before these negotiations were entered into or these guarantees were given by myself and the Representatives of Louisiana."[2]

Coming from the architect of the famous Bargain, these admissions provide an important commentary upon its historical significance. For Burke's statements amounted to an admission that the Bargain had no appreciable effect upon the outcome of the Presidential election crisis. He admitted also that the concessions and solemn promises he and his friends won from the Republican leaders were not the inducements that persuaded the Southerners to resist the filibuster and "revolution." The Southerners were thoroughly committed to that course before Burke entered the picture. Their leaders—Lamar, Watterson, Hill, Hancock, Brown—could not even be diverted from their commitment for a few hours to accommodate the maneuvers of Burke and his associates. And finally Burke admitted frankly that the pressure he brought to bear did nothing toward changing the Southern policy of Governor Hayes, since he was already committed to that policy.

All of this reflects glory upon Burke's capacities as an operator at the same time that it diminishes his role in history. A man of the major's talents and associations, however, probably took more pride in his prowess at poker than in his place in history. He did venture the claim that his activities assisted in smoothing the path for the later enactment of Hayes's policy, and in that claim history will lend him some support. But the historians cannot blame Major Burke for misleading them about the importance of his Bargain. He did his best, with Ben Butler's assistance, to set them straight. They were misled in spite of him.

[2] *Ibid.*, 1015.

An illuminating corroboration of Major Burke's assessment of the Wormley Bargain is provided by General Dodge, an authority entitled to a respectful hearing on this subject. Dodge was writing to General Boynton a month after Hayes's inauguration regarding the implementation of that part of the "purely political plan" having to do with the organization of the House and the election of Garfield as speaker with the help of a few Southern Democrats.

"I am afraid of the Political Combination in this matter," said Dodge. "You saw how much political fiddling there was at the very last end of the session by Mathews [*sic*], Foster and others. *When everything was secure new men came in and made agreements that in my opinion did not make the change of a single vote.* Those things were all new to me. However, if Hayes is as smart as I think he is he will not allow this political combination to defeat his administration. The votes on organization [of the House] are to be had from the material interests of the South. There is no question about this. If you don't believe it, read the Galveston News, the New Orleans, Memphis, and other Southern papers; and I say to you, confidentially, that if you expect to capture the next House, you have got to do it in that way. You may set up as many Nichols [*sic*] and Hamptons in the south as you please in a political point of view, and after they get them they will stand back for something else."[3]

Of course, from General Dodge's rather specialized point of view the Road to Reunion was a railroad — or rather a large combination of them. And there were, in his opinion, no barriers in the way of Reconciliation that could not be smoothed out by a suitable subsidy. This was an oversimplification. But General Dodge was probably the foremost national authority on the politics of railroads, and he had no little practical experience in the arts of Reconciliation. His views commanded the respect of Hayes as well as Boynton.

What neither General Dodge nor Major Burke appeared to appreciate (though the major may have) was the practical uses to

[3] Dodge to Boynton, April 2, 1877, letterbook in Box 384, Dodge Papers. The italics are mine.

which the Wormley Bargain lent itself among Southern politicians. The fact was that the Bargain was much easier to explain to puzzled constituents than were complicated arrangements regarding the election of speakers, the organization of the House, the control of patronage, cabinet appointments, railroad finance, branch roads, and numerous "internal improvements of a national character." Unlike those complex matters the Wormley Conference could be, and was, made to appeal to the chivalrous Southern heart as a knightly deed — the rescue of a distressed sister state from the tyrannical heel of the Carpetbagger. And there was no need to labor the distress of the sister. The Louisiana Carpetbaggers were a low crowd, and no mistaking it.[4] Such a chivalrous deed would excuse much — even voting with Republicans. And so the whole complicated arrangement could be explained in terms of one of its parts. And it was so explained, and has been ever since.

But this does not make it "one of the most important events in American history." Nor can it be said of this Wormley Bargain that "it ended Reconstruction and started the South on the road to prosperity and power."[5] Reconstruction was ended, all right, and enough momentous policies were altered to mark the close of one era and the beginning of another (though "starting the South on the road to prosperity and power" was not one of the achievements), but one will not find the explanation in or about Wormley's Hotel.

The most remarkable thing about the true explanation — for which the Wormley Legend has been universally substituted — is that so much of it was public property in 1877. All the essentials appeared repeatedly in the public press during the crisis — in both Democratic and Republican papers, North as well as South. How all this was obliterated from the public memory and the Wormley story substituted for it would make one of the most intricate studies in American historiography.

[4] On this point see Roger W. Shugg, *Origins of Class Struggle in Louisiana* (Baton Rouge, 1939), 226–228. Mr. Shugg quotes Republican Governor Henry C. Warmoth as saying, "Why, damn it, everybody is demoralized down here. Corruption is the fashion." *Ibid.*, 226–227.

[5] Eckenrode, *Rutherford B. Hayes*, 227.

"The plan is this," said the Cincinnati *Enquirer* as early as February 14, and proceeded to unravel much of the Republican effort to "reward Democratic apostasy" in the South and thereby win enough votes in the House to complete the election of Hayes. "As an inducement to secure these votes," revealed the *Enquirer,* "the guarantees to the South are: First, one or two cabinet places; second, the control of their own State Governments; third, a guaranteed policy on the part of the Republicans of liberal appropriations for Southern internal improvements; fourth, the passage of the Texas Pacific Railroad Bill. The plot even extends farther and contemplates the capture of the House of Representatives after the 4th of March next. If Hayes is counted in there will be no extra session of the House. During the recess enough Southern Democrats will be favored with patronage to induce them to stand in with the conspirators and enable the Republicans to secure its organization."[6]

It is difficult to see how the *Enquirer* could have done much better had the current letter files of a dozen prominent Republican leaders been placed on the city editor's desk. Colonel Kellar evidently admired it as an achievement of journalism, for he copied the whole story in his Memphis paper—without comment.[7]

Charles Nordhoff, the able Washington correspondent of the New York *Herald,* pronounced it "an open secret" that "considerable grants for levee and other internal improvement purposes, and the passage of the Texas Pacific Railroad bill" were among the Republican commitments accepted by the South. "It is very thoroughly understood here by Southern men," wrote Nordhoff, "that Mr. Hayes means, if he should become President, to cut adrift from the carpet-baggers and make an alliance with respectable party leaders of Whig antecedents in the South." Hayes's "policy as to the South has become so well understood here by southern men that there is not the least danger of factious opposition from that section." But even if Hayes failed to become President "an alliance of the repub-

[6] Cincinnati *Enquirer,* February 14, 1877.
[7] Memphis *Avalanche,* February 16, 1877.

lican with southern men is equally certain," mainly because of the South's eagerness for internal improvements.[8]

In Washington even the *National Republican* discussed these arrangements with that candor which the public morals of the Gilded Age often permitted its journalists. Stressing the significance of the Texas & Pacific movement, the editor fixed upon it as the controlling factor in the crisis and in the sterling patriotism of the Southern conservatives he so lavishly praised. Among the leaders of the movement he mentioned Lamar, Hill, Hancock, Ellis, and Casey Young.[9]

Few editors in the South were so candid about the business as Colonel Kellar. Yet even he disdained to call a "bargain" the elaborate agreements he had done so much to promote. "There is no bargain in this movement," he declared in a signed editorial. "It is a policy. If Gov. Hayes urges the construction of great public works, and Tilden opposes them, why should the [Washington] *Union* and Tammany Hall complain if those who support the Texas and Pacific, Mississippi levees, Barataria Ship Canal and the jetties favor the election of Hayes?"[10] And perhaps the colonel was right. When political agreements involve the destinies of millions of people and areas of continental expanse, they ordinarily achieve a dignity above the bargain level and become diplomacy. The treaties arrived at by sectional diplomacy in America have been traditionally called "compromises."

For weeks Montgomery Blair had been alternately "red and white with rage," according to Colonel Kellar, as he "denounced the Texas and Pacific Railroad and other measures of relief to the South" along with the perfidy of the South's political apostasy.[11] When he learned of the unco-operative position the Southerners took in the Democratic caucuses of February 17 and 19, Blair broke out with his bit-

[8] New York *Herald,* February 15, 1877. The Galveston *News,* February 22, 1877, copied the *Herald* story in full.

[9] Washington *National Republican,* February 13, 23, 1877.

[10] Memphis *Avalanche,* February 25, 1877.

[11] *Ibid.,* February 27, 1877.

terest invective. "Thus jobbery can effect reconstruction and 'conciliation,'" he wrote, "when the military failed, and we are enabled to see that it was not Wells, Packard, Kellogg, Stearns & Co. [Carpetbaggers] who gave Southern votes to Hayes, but *Southern* Democrats — Tom Scott's Democrats!"[12] On March 3 he published the last edition of the Washington *Union* and closed its doors forever. On the same day he wrote Gideon Welles, with whom he had served in Lincoln's cabinet: "There never was any intention of inaugurating Tilden. The House was controlled from the start by Tom Scott & Jay Gould."[13] Tilden likewise attributed Hayes's election, or "counting in," to railroad influence, though he told John Bigelow that Gould, rather than Scott, was chiefly responsible.[14]

Montgomery Blair could not understand the detachment and philosophic calm with which Tilden accepted the "fraud." With Blair the experience became almost an obsession and for years thereafter he pondered and speculated on its meaning. He was prone to read into recent events a recurrence of the pattern of party politics in Jackson's time. The Southern "alliance with Hayes to defeat Tilden," wrote Blair, "finds a precedent in the alliance of Calhoun and the Nullifiers with Mr. Clay to overthrow Jackson and Van Buren after the defeat of nullification. . . . The jobbers and monopolists of the North made common cause with the Southern oligarchy."[15] And Tom Scott's railroad played the role in the seventies that Nick Biddle's bank played in the thirties.[16] The new Southern leaders reminded Blair strongly of the old. "Calhoun did not represent the people of the South then any more than Lamar does now," he thought.[17] An alliance between Southern conservatives and Northern wealth had eventually driven Blair and his family out of the Democratic party in ante-bellum days. The silent rise of old Whigs to

[12] Washington *Union,* February 19, 1877.

[13] Quoted in Smith, *Francis Preston Blair Family,* II, 484.

[14] Bigelow Diary, February 13, 1877, Bigelow Papers.

[15] New York *Sun,* December 5, 1877. The letter is unsigned, but Blair's authorship is established not only by internal evidence but by correspondence with Charles A. Dana, the editor.

[16] Washington *Union,* February 19, 1877.

[17] Montgomery Blair to Charles A. Dana, May 15, 1878, Blair Papers.

capture leadership of the Democratic party in the South and the revival of the Whiggish affinity under the leadership of Hayes were once more undermining Democratic unity. Blair urged Tilden "to speak out on this matter" as General Jackson would have done, but he could not stir the New Yorker to action.[18] Tilden was not cut from the block from which Old Hickory was hewn.

If the Compromise of 1877 revealed deep cleavages within the old party of Jackson, it also revealed profound changes in the party of Thad Stevens and Charles Sumner. It revealed the party of Radical Reconstruction in alliance with ex-Rebels and ex-slaveholders. It revealed the party of Carpetbaggery repudiating the Carpetbaggers, the party of emancipation and freedmen's rights abandoning the Negro to his former master. The compromise did not mean that the Republicans had given up hope of controlling the voting strength of the freedmen for party advantage. It only meant that the Carpetbagger had proved an ineffective means of controlling those votes and that it was hoped that the old masters might be more resourceful in accomplishing the same end.

Nowhere was the revolution in Republican policy and thought more clearly revealed than in the columns of the *National Republican,* spokesman of the Radical, bloody-shirt, bitterly anti-South wing of the party — not the reformist, liberal wing of which Hayes was presumed to be a mild representative. The mincing euphemisms of the writer do not disguise the complete recantation his words represent. "When hostilities ceased," he wrote, "some of the Southern States were found to be under the control of an alien element [Carpetbaggers], sustained by the votes of the native menial classes [Negroes], and the former governing classes were excluded from all participation in public affairs. . . . This was an abnormal condition of the body politic which could not long continue." Happily, "the ever-springing impulse of nature has done its perfect work." The Negro contrived to "divert himself for a time with the bauble of suffrage"

[18] Blair to Tilden, November 25, 1877; November 13, 1879, Tilden Papers; also Blair to editor of Baltimore *Telegraph,* November 21, 1878, quoted in New York *Sun,* November 24, 1878.

but had been persuaded "to relinquish the artificial right to vote for the natural right to live, and to make his peace with his old master as the highest right to be subserved." The latter had realized from the first that the freedman was "as yet incapable of the intelligent exercise of the privileges of citizenship" and stood in need of friendly guidance. "There is a persuasive power in hunger and cold," added the editor philosophically, "that will conquer stronger wills and firmer moral convictions than could be expected to actuate those simple-minded dependents in choosing between an empty privilege and daily bread." As for the oft-repeated stories of the bloody-shirt orators concerning intimidation and coercion, the *National Republican* was now inclined to discount them. "We are persuaded that instances of this kind bear the same proportion to the mass that cruel masters bore to the multitude of good ones in the days of slavery." The Negro seemed contented with his lot. "Satisfied with his personal liberty, he appears now, as a rule, willing to vote with his former master." This was especially fortunate in view of the statesmanship and sterling patriotism his former master was demonstrating in the electoral crisis.[19]

The changes within the South were complacently regarded as the inevitable consequence of economic forces that somehow worked toward beneficent, if unforeseen ends. "The landed proprietors in agricultural districts, and the capitalists in cities," observed the organ of Radicalism, "have it in their power to control the laboring classes to a very large extent, and this has been done in the South to such a degree that the alien element [Carpetbaggers], which made common cause with the colored people, finds itself abandoned by its allies and unable to maintain its position without the aid of the general government." The old policy of maintaining "the alien element" in power with Federal troops was clearly discredited and should be discontinued. The estrangement of the Southern landed proprietors and city capitalists from the Northern Democrats was only to be expected, since "the Northern dough-faces have always been the riff-raff element in the Democratic organization." And

[19] Washington *National Republican*, February 21, 1877.

on the other hand, what could be more natural and proper than a realignment of the "governing classes" of the South with classes of like mind in the North. "There is no longer anything to hold the North and South apart, but everything to counsel union and harmony."[20]

A writer in New Orleans placed a narrower construction upon the North's change of heart toward the South. He thought it represented a shift from political to economic exploitation, induced by economic necessities. "In Pittsburgh, the most intensely Republican city on the continent," he wrote, "resolutions favoring a speedy solution of impending difficulties were most emphatic. If these manifestations mean anything, they mean that any further attempt to kill the goose that laid the golden egg has been abandoned. . . . They require other fields for their surplus labor and capital, and more and better customers for their surplus manufactures. . . . Home-rule in the South is considered essential to their prosperity."[21]

Numerous corresponding interpretations are found in the North. "Philadelphia," declared the *Times* of that city, "wedded as her people are to the Republican faith, would lead in determined resistance to a revival of sectional discord. Already her trade has suffered most unjustly because of the violence of her partisan journals in the desperation of our political campaigns. They are presumed to speak for the business men of Philadelphia when they pervert and denounce indiscriminately, every effort of the South to rescue its States from the rule of the most desperate adventurers of modern history." As a matter of fact, said the *Times,* "no business community could be more just to the South than the community that is thus libeled by its political journals." The Philadelphia paper believed "the business interests of the nation would crush out any party or any administration" that attempted to revive Reconstruction and its issues.[22] Likewise the New York *Commercial and Financial Chronicle* agreed that abandonment of Reconstruction policies

[20] *Ibid.*
[21] New Orleans *Times,* January 28, 1877.
[22] Philadelphia *Times* quoted in Raleigh *Observer,* November 19, 1878.

was the first condition of a return of prosperity, not only for the South, but for the North as well.[23]

The reactions of the mass of the people to the solution of the crisis — what they knew of it — were much more spontaneous than the calculating assessments that have been reviewed. "The heart of the nation gave a great leap for joy" when Hayes was finally inaugurated without violence. "The mists which hung over the political affairs of the nation at once disappeared, the depression gave way to cheerful confidence, and dangerous excitement was supplanted by general content, without even a momentary stage of uncertainty and doubt."[24] The spontaneity of popular reaction was a measure of the degree of tension in the public mind over the fear of an outbreak of violence or a return to war. The people were not generally informed of the price paid, of course, nor of the bargains struck.

In the mood of reconciliation there were few who mourned the cause of the Negro or gave much thought to the revolution in Northern sentiment on this, the original center of the whole storm now passing. This was true of many of the Negro's champions. The *Nation* observed philosophically that "the negro will disappear from the field of national politics. Henceforth the nation, as a nation, will have nothing more to do with him."[25] And the New York *Tribune* declared that "after ample opportunity to develop their own latent capacities" the Negroes had only proved that "as a race they are idle, ignorant, and vicious."[26]

As for the feelings of the mass of Negroes themselves, there was undoubtedly widespread fear and apprehension among them over the withdrawal of Federal protection and disillusionment over their abandonment by the Republican party. When they looked to their own leaders for guidance, however, they found them eagerly taking favors and appointments from Hayes. With alacrity and gratitude Frederick Douglass accepted from Hayes an appointment as Marshal of the District of Columbia and settled down in a twenty-

[23] New York *Commercial and Financial Chronicle,* XXIV (March 17, 1877), 236–237.

[24] Anon., "The New Federal Administration," *International Review,* IV (1877), 297.

[25] *Nation,* XXIV (April 5, 1877), 202.

[26] New York *Tribune,* April 7, 1877.

one room house in the suburbs of Washington. The appointment was taken as evidence of "Mr. Hayes's desire to satisfy the colored people that his plan of conciliation does not involve forgetfulness of them."[27] With Douglass, the foremost Negro spokesman, and Schurz, foremost reformer, taken into camp, both Negroes and Reformers might consider themselves parties to the compromise.

There were a few discordant voices that spoke out of the revolutionary past. The two aging abolitionists, Wendell Phillips and William Lloyd Garrison, found the new mood of reconciliation uncongenial to their souls. The South, declared Wendell Phillips with the voice of a Cromwell, should be "crushed." What it needed was "the heavy hand and fearless grasp which holds disorderly and struggling forces quiet."[28] Garrison warned that "the South is still rebellious at heart," and as for the Compromise of 1877, it was but a renewal of the old "covenant with death"—the old abolitionist's favorite description of the Constitution of the United States.[29]

But the year 1877 was not attuned to the revolutionary fervors of the years 1861 or 1866. The Men of 1877 were rather like the Men of 1787. They were of smaller stature than the great Federalists, to be sure, and their work was less celebrated and certainly less known. But if the Men of 1787 made the *Thermidor* of the First American Revolution, the Men of 1877 fulfilled a corresponding part in the Second American Revolution. They were the men who come at the end of periods of revolutionary upheaval, when the great hopes and soaring ideals have lagged and failed, and the fervors have burned themselves out. They come to say that disorder has gone too far and the extremists must be got in hand, that order and peace must be established at any price. And in their deliberations they generally have been more concerned with preserving the pragmatic and practical gains and ends of revolutions than the more idealistic aims. In this respect the Men of 1877 were not unlike those who had been cast in the same historical role before them.

[27] *Nation,* XXIV (March 22, 1877), 169.

[28] Quoted in New York *Tribune,* March 28, 1877.

[29] *Letters of Mr. William E. Chandler Relative to the So-called Southern Policy of President Hayes, Together with a Letter to Mr. Chandler of Mr. William Lloyd Garrison* (Concord, 1878), 46–48.

CHAPTER XI

The Politics of Reconciliation

APART FROM the long-range and larger consequences of the compromise, many of which would not be apparent for generations to come, there remains a whole set of short-range and immediate consequences to be explored. These included the fulfillment of the "purely political plan" and the "other plan."

In spite of opposition within his own party and some awkwardness and embarrassment, Hayes managed to initiate his Southern policy with a fair degree of success. The first step was the nomination of the ex-Confederate General David M. Key as Postmaster General. Hayes sent his name to the Senate for confirmation on March 7 along with his other cabinet nominations. Immediately the old Radical Republican oligarchy of the Senate, led by Blaine, Conkling, and Cameron, opened a fierce attack not only upon Key but also upon the reformers Schurz and Evarts. Their strategy was to combine with Democrats to defeat confirmation of the cabinet. But in this they were countered by Southern Conservatives under the leadership of Lamar and Hill, who had just entered the Senate. Hayes gave the Southerners credit for securing confirmation of his cabinet and defeating the strategy of the Republican opponents. The opposition of the latter, wrote the President, "only failed to be formidable by [reason of] the resolute support of the Southern Senators like Gordon, Lamar, and Hill."[1]

So far the coalition between Southern Conservatives and Northern Republicans was working famously. Colonel Kellar was delighted. He and General Boynton spent a most gratifying hour and a half

[1] Williams (ed.), *Diary and Letters of Hayes,* III, 427.

with the President shortly after Key was confirmed, and the colonel "left full of hope in the future success of his administration."[2] Kellar informed Joseph Medill that he had just had "a satisfactory talk with Senator Hill" on the subject of the Republican coalition. Garland, the newly arrived senator from Arkansas, had been "exceedingly frank in his opinions with me & you may expect him to lead with Ben Hill the Administration party from the South." On the other hand, "The Secession leaders & Senators will not stick. Lamar will not do in an emergency. Gordon is unstable & is no thinker, he will follow Lamar." The colonel expected Tennessee, Arkansas, Virginia, and North Carolina to be "the first States that will be for the Administration."[3]

Kellar believed that if an extra session of Congress could be avoided or postponed for four months in order to give Hayes's policy of conciliation and patronage distribution time to have its effect in the South, the new House of Representatives could be captured by the Republican party. "To do this," he told Medill, "Judge Key should be sustained by the Presidents' friends, and a wise discretion should be given to him outside of his own department relating to Southern appointments. It is utterly impossible for a member of the Cabinet from the North to understand our political troubles. The distrust on both sides must be removed. I am not too bold or confident in saying that such a course will enable Key to make the House in favor of the administration by a good working majority without endangering the Senate. In other words, the Southern policy will not offend the Republican North—the controlling power in it—and will dismember the democratic party in the South."[4] Adopting the same point of view, William Henry Smith advised the President that "a wide and wise discretion given to Gen. Key now [will] enable him to organize things in the South as to give you control of the House."[5]

But before any progress whatever could be made in that direction

[2] Kellar to William Henry Smith, March 25, 1877, Smith Papers.
[3] Kellar to Medill, March 20, 1877, *ibid.*
[4] *Ibid.*
[5] Smith to Hayes, March 22, 1877, Hayes Papers.

Hayes would have to remove the troops from Louisiana and South Carolina and recognize the governments of Nicholls and Hampton. This step was hedged about with serious embarrassments. Apart from the fact that Packard received a larger number of votes than some of the Hayes electors and therefore had stronger claim to the governorship of Louisiana than Hayes had to the Presidency of the United States, there were new difficulties. Republican congressmen from the South were threatening a rebellion against Hayes's desertion of the Carpetbaggers. Twelve Republicans were returned to the new Congress from the South, and they were reported to be prepared to bolt the party caucus in protest: "They have declared their unalterable purpose of joining the Northern Democrats in the organization of the House if Packard and Chamberlain are abandoned."[6]

Here was the basic dilemma of Hayes's Southern policy. In his effort to split the Democrats he ran the risk of splitting his own party. If he abandoned the Carpetbaggers he would lose Republican supporters. If he did not abandon them he would lose his Southern conservative support. In either case, apparently, he would lose control of the House. For he stood to alienate at least as many Republicans as he gained Democrats. Caught in the dilemma, Hayes marked time, procrastinated, did nothing. Two weeks went by, three weeks, and nothing happened.

The patience of the Southern conservative collaborationists, already under strain, began to break. Hayes was not delivering his promises. One of Lamar's Mississippi constituents wrote: "Our people are very much depressed here, cursing everybody, you with the balance. They talk like you, Gordon, and Hill could have had the thing your own way if you had tried."[7] The only way to quiet such criticism of Southern policy in the electoral crisis was to produce the withdrawal of troops. Upon hearing that Hayes was thinking of appointing a commission to report on the Louisiana situation,

[6] New York *Sun,* March 27, 1877; also Hayes Diary, March 16, 1877, in Williams (ed.), *Diary and Letters of Hayes,* III, 427.

[7] Mayes, *Lamar,* 304.

Lamar wrote the President a stinging letter of rebuke. Reminding him that certain Southerners had given his administration "that cordial support which extreme partisans in your own political following seemed unwilling to give," Lamar then declared, "But the support, to be honorable to us and useful to you, must have a sure foundation. . . . It was understood that you meant to withdraw the troops from South Carolina and Louisiana. . . . Upon that subject we thought you had made up your mind; and indeed, Mr. President, you told me that you had. . . . We cannot willingly acquiesce in the delay which is to be prolonged at the expense of so much suffering and in the face of so much danger." As for the opposition of certain Republicans, "nothing will reconcile them," and the President should accept that fact.[8]

In a passage that he struck out before sending the letter to the President, Lamar complained that "men who have loved me are beginning to grow cold in their affections," and that "men who have trusted me have begun to falter in their confidence."[9] It is quite probable that Southern congressmen of less strength and security than Lamar found themselves under the same difficulties. At any rate toward the end of March some of those who had sat in on Major Burke's "little bluff game" filled the press with numerous versions and a few of the documents of the negotiations, all calculated to embarrass the President and compel action.[10] Southern hospitality toward Hayes was plainly beginning to freeze around the edges.

The day after he received Lamar's letter, whether influenced by it or not, the President invited both Hampton and Chamberlain of South Carolina to come to Washington for an interview. And a few days later he dispatched a commission to Louisiana. There was obviously nothing Hayes could learn by these means about the situation in either state that he did not already know. In each state the

[8] Lamar to Hayes, March 22, 1877, Hayes Papers.

[9] Quoted in Mayes, *Lamar,* 308.

[10] New York *Sun,* March 26, 27, 29, 1877; Louisville *Courier-Journal,* March 29, 1877; Raleigh *Observer,* March 31, 1877; New York *Tribune,* March 30, 1877.

Democrats had already established a *de facto* government and the authority of the rival Republican governments did not extend much beyond the state houses and the plots of ground on which they stood. In this limited tenure the Carpetbaggers were secure only so long as protected by Federal troops. The only thing Hayes apparently hoped to find by his interviews and the commission was some means of easing the Carpetbaggers out more gracefully. Stanley Matthews had unofficially written both Chamberlain and Packard on March 4 suggesting that they solve the problem by voluntarily abdicating, but he had received no encouragement.[11] Hayes finally accomplished the desired result in South Carolina by having the troops withdrawn from the State House in Columbia to their barracks on April 10. Chamberlain promptly surrendered his office to Hampton.

The bipartisan commission that Hayes sent to Louisiana consisted of five dignified public figures. While Colonel Kellar was not one of them, he accompanied them and assisted in their work. "You thoroughly understand," he wrote William Henry Smith, "that many things necessary to be done, but which the commission cannot do, must be accomplished in order to reach results that will be accepted by public opinion."[12] The most important of these things was to induce enough of the Negro members of the Packard Republican legislature to desert and join the Nicholls legislature in order to give the latter a quorum of members whose election was conceded by both sides. In this delicate work, accomplished largely by the use of money, Kellar found the gentlemen of the New Orleans Cotton Exchange quite co-operative. Also of great aid in the same work was the Louisiana State Lottery Company. Owned by Northern men, chartered by the Carpetbaggers, and a mainstay of their regime until 1877, the powerful Lottery Company now identified itself with the Redeemer regime in a substantial way by generous contributions, one of which amounted to $34,000.[13] De-

[11] Williams, *Life of Hayes,* II, 41–44.

[12] Kellar to Smith, April 12, 1877, Smith Papers.

[13] A bill abolishing the Lottery Company had passed the House of the Nicholls legislature on March 20, but was subsequently defeated in the Senate. Two years later the Louisiana Redeemers wrote the Lottery charter into the new constitution of

serted by his own legislature, Packard capitulated when the troops were withdrawn to their barracks on April 24. Louisiana had at last joined the ranks of the "redeemed" states.

To millions the Redemption of Louisiana was the last act in the fulfillment of a long-cherished dream — as to others it was the sordid death of a cherished dream. It was fitting that Colonel Kellar, chief Southern architect of the Compromise of 1877, should have played a role in that last act, though as usual it was performed behind the scene. "The part I took upon myself in the long battle for the Presidency," he wrote Smith, "was not so pleasant as that which I engaged in, as a humble factor, in New Orleans. It was worth much to see, in advance, the close of the night of the Reconstruction Period — and to turn almost instantly to see the dawn of the Restoration Era." But the colonel did not mean by using the term "Restoration" that an old regime was restored. Quite the contrary. For him it was the birth of an entirely new era, and he thrilled with anticipation upon its threshold. "Am I an enthusiast?" he exclaimed. "Am I a transcendentalist? You have not heard nor read the half which is yet to come from the South West. Before two years shall have passed there will be a new earth & a new heaven, and the carpetbagger and the old secession leader will have passed away."[14]

The President's advisors on Southern policy assured him that the leaders of both the newly redeemed states were completely in sympathy with the administration plan of breaking down Democratic solidarity in the South and winning over old-line Whigs and conservatives to a coalition with the Republicans. "Mr. Nichols [*sic*] is thoroughly in accord with this national policy," Kellar wrote Hayes from New Orleans, "and the party lines heretofore existing and which now remain, will not only be obliterated but the party names themselves will be abolished . . . the business interests are

---

the state upon the demand of the Lottery Company. Garnie W. McGinty, *Louisiana Redeemed: The Overthrow of Carpetbag Rule, 1876–1880* (New Orleans, 1941), 185–192.

[14] Kellar to William Henry Smith, April 26, 1877, Smith Papers.

with your administration and hold in check the Bourbons."[15] To Smith the colonel confided that "Gov. Nichols is no democrat, unless I am one, or you, or the President."[16] After Hampton's visit to Washington on the President's invitation General Boynton told Garfield "that Wade Hampton will aid in organizing a Republican House and that the conferences which have lately taken place between him and the President have included that subject."[17] There was no corroboration of the report from Hayes, however, and Garfield remained somewhat skeptical.

With the cabinet appointment and the troop removal satisfactorily settled, there remained a third important commitment to be disposed of — "internal improvements" and the Scott Plan. Regarding the latter General Dodge expected the prompt and personal assistance of the President. "When he gets here you and I want to see him," he had written Scott from Washington before the inauguration, "but more especially do we want our Southern friends to submit to him something that he can put into his inaugural that will give us standing. He is ready to do it unless somebody coaxes him out of it. He has a clear understanding that he shall do so. I think probably such men as Hancock, Lamar and a few of that class of men would have great weight with him if they call and see him on the measure."[18]

William Henry Smith, who accompanied Hayes to Washington, discovered to his dismay that the expected paragraph on "internal improvements of a national character" was missing from the copy of the Inaugural Address that the President-elect was taking with him to the Capital. On arrival in the city, Smith got in touch with Boynton and the two made a "strategical visit to Wormley's," where they talked to Stanley Matthews. Smith recorded later that the appropriate paragraph was "added to the Inaugural after our visit to and consultation with, Stanley Matthews." Other visits and consulta-

[15] Kellar to Hayes, April 16, 1877, Hayes Papers.
[16] Kellar to Smith, April 26, 1877, Smith Papers.
[17] Garfield Diary, April 4, 1877, Garfield Papers.
[18] Dodge to Scott, February 20, 1877, letterbook in Box 384, Dodge Papers.

tions may have played a part, of course. As a matter of fact, Smith believed that "The omission from the original draft must have been fairly accidental," probably due to the demands of office-seekers on Hayes's time during his last week in Columbus.[19]

The inaugural address did contain a passage in favor of internal improvements, but in view of the high expectations of Dodge it may be doubted that he was entirely satisfied with the pronouncement. "In the important work of restoring the South," said Hayes, "it is not the political situation alone that merits attention. The material development of that section of the country has been arrested by the social and political revolution through which it has passed, and now needs and deserves the considerate care of the National Government, within the just limits prescribed by the Constitution and wise public economy." He also hinted at subsidies for public schools.

Dodge and Scott undoubtedly derived greater comfort out of subsequent assurances of the President on the subject nearest their hearts. On April 3 Garfield and Stanley Matthews had "a long interview" with Hayes on this and related subjects. Matthews, an attorney of the Texas & Pacific and kinsman of the President, had won the nomination of Ohio Republicans assuring him election to the place Sherman had vacated in the Senate. Hayes considered Matthews's victory "an endorsement of the policy of peace and home rule—of local self-government."[20] The seat that Matthews won had been within the grasp of Garfield, who desired it strongly but gave it up because of the request of Hayes that he remain Republican leader of the House and become candidate for speaker. The success of the contest for speakership depended upon Southern support, and Hayes discussed this problem at the interview. "The President believes we can organize the next House," Garfield recorded of the conversation, "and is willing to favor internal improvements in the South, including the Southern Pacific

[19] Smith to Boynton, April 7, 1877, in Smith letterbook, William Henry Smith Papers, Ohio State Museum, Columbus, Ohio.

[20] Williams (ed.), *Diary and Letters of Hayes*, III, 427.

Railroad if that will bring Southern support to the Administration to make it worth while."[21]

Word of the President's attitude was soon broadcast below the Potomac. "The President, in conversation lately," reported Watterson's *Courier-Journal,* "has expressed himself in very decided terms in favor of a system of internal improvement calculated to benefit and develop the South, and especially of such government aid as may be appropriate to secure the completion of the Texas and Pacific Railway. He stated that the Northern States had received very large benefits from this line of policy and that the South, though impoverished by the results of the war, had got nothing." It was emphasized that these reports came "from concurrent and direct sources" and that the President's opinions had been "carefully formed, and will be carried into his executive policy."[22] Returning after a two-week visit at the White House in April, Hayes's Texas friend, Guy M. Bryan, told the press of his state that an appropriately framed bill for the Pacific railroad "would receive hearty support" from the administration, which had "a good disposition" toward Southern internal improvements generally.[23]

Their truce ended, Huntington and Scott went to war again as bitterly as ever. This time the Californian admitted that Scott had the upper hand. No sooner had Huntington been able to "fix up the Railroad Committee of the Senate" than "Scott went to Washington in special train, and got one of our men put off the committee. Gordon of Georgia was taken off, and Bogy of Missouri put on."[24] Later Stanley Matthews was appointed to the committee and Huntington lost two more of his men. "There has been quite a number of senators and members of Congress in the office in the last few

[21] Garfield Diary, April 3, 1877, Garfield Papers. The name "Southern Pacific" was used interchangeably with "Texas & Pacific" in that time. Garfield doubtless meant the latter. See also Theodore C. Smith, *The Life and Letters of James Abram Garfield* (New Haven, 1925), I, 647–649.

[22] Louisville *Courier-Journal,* April 26, 1877.

[23] Galveston *News,* May 27, 1877, quoted in Winkler (ed.), "The Bryan-Hayes Correspondence," *Southwestern Historical Quarterly,* XXVII (1923–1924), 70.

[24] Huntington to Colton, March 7. 14, 1877, in Chicago *Tribune,* December 27, 1883.

days," he wrote Colton in June. "They all say Scott is making the greatest effort on the Texas Pacific . . . and most of them think he will pass it. This man Hayes, most people say, is for it to conciliate the South."[25]

Hayes postponed the calling of an extra session of Congress not four months, as Kellar proposed, but seven months. And this in spite of the fact that the Democratic House of the previous Congress had left him without a cent of appropriations for the army, a deficiency that was expected to compel the immediate calling of an extra session. Hayes muddled through the military suppression of the labor riots of the summer with unpaid and dissatisfied troops. The new Southern policy was to have until fall to demonstrate what it could do. And it would have to do more than "conciliate" the South in a sentimental way in order to placate the hard-boiled critics of the policy among Republican politicians. Blaine and his Carpetbagger friends were among this element. It would have to produce tangible partisan support to compensate the party for the losses sustained by the abandonment of the Carpetbaggers. Hayes was quite aware of that.

Postmaster General Key appears to have encountered no serious difficulty in finding respectable Southern Democrats who were willing to accept office under a Republican President. The father of thirteen children himself, he doubtless knew what appeal a regular salary carried among impoverished gentry of the region. Ex-Confederates and stanch Democrats, along with old-line Whigs and Douglas Democrats, became Hayes appointees. The post offices of Louisville, Memphis, Petersburg and numerous lesser cities and towns were turned over to Democratic postmasters, while Republican applicants for the same jobs were coolly rejected. Overriding the protests and pleas of Republican congressmen and bosses of Arkansas, Texas, South Carolina, Georgia, Alabama, Hayes appointed Democrats to office in those and all the Southern states. Upon the recommendation of Senator Gordon and Alexander

[25] Huntington to Colton, June 1, 1877, *ibid.*, December 28, 1883.

Stephens he appointed a Democratic United States marshal in Georgia, and in Tennessee he placed two of Colonel Kellar's quasi-Democratic friends in the office of Federal marshal, one of them in East Tennessee, a stronghold of native white Republicans. According to a Republican paper of Kentucky that was friendly to Hayes, one third of all the Southern appointments during the first five months of the President's administration went to Democrats.[26]

On the other hand Hayes by no means entirely abandoned his Republican friends in the South. "I shall not forget my duty to the staunch Republicans," he promised William Henry Smith.[27] He was especially careful to reward the Republican election and returning board officials in the disputed states to whom he owed his own election. They included some of the most notorious elements of Carpetbaggery. Among those for whom offices were found were sixteen officials connected with the Louisiana returning board, thirteen state officials, seven electors, twenty-seven election supervisors or persons connected with the election, and ten "visiting statesmen" to Louisiana. Hayes also appointed to office twenty election officials of Florida, including the members of the returning board, and three visiting statesmen.[28] The disappointed Republican claimant for the governor's office in Louisiana and numerous friends of his also received offices from Hayes. Apart from these, however, Key and the President appear to have courted Southern favor by appointing the best available Republican applicants when they did not actually appoint Democrats.

From Southern businessmen, industrialists, and conservatives came many letters of praise for the administration's Southern policy, letters that must have been most gratifying to Hayes. One of these was from the president of the Louisville and Nashville Railroad, "a life long Democrat,"[29] another from Senator John T. Morgan of

[26] Louisville *Commercial,* August 21, 1877.

[27] Hayes to Smith, April 22, 1877, in Williams (ed.), *Diary and Letters of Hayes,* III, 432.

[28] *House Reports,* 45 Cong., 3 Sess., No. 140, pp. 15–16, 33–34.

[29] E. D. Standiford to Hayes, October 13, 1877, Hayes Papers.

Alabama,[30] another Democrat, and many came from the old Whigs, who warmed as enthusiastically to the policy as Hayes and his advisors had hoped. Hayes was reported to be gaining strength daily in West Tennessee, and "the best evidence of this change is to be seen in the increased circulation of the Daily Avalanche," Colonel Kellar's paper, which bounced up 25 per cent during the first month of the new administration. A large mass meeting of Negroes in Memphis adopted resolutions endorsing Hayes's policy with only two dissenting votes.[31]

The most successful of several experiments in substituting Southern patricians for Carpetbaggers as leaders of the Negro masses — a part of Hayes's Whig revival — was that conducted by Wade Hampton in South Carolina. The policy was called "breaking down the political color line." Promising the Negroes justice, better schools, protection from the white race fanatics, and minor offices, Hampton made a strong and, for a time, remarkably successful appeal for their support. The Carpetbagger ex-Governor Robert K. Scott admitted in August that Hampton was "honestly carrying out the promises he made," and had "already appointed more colored men to office than were appointed during the first two years that I was Governor." And a Radical Negro leader, once an associate justice of the State Supreme Court, predicted that Hampton would "get nine-tenths of the colored vote" in the next election. In his political and race policy Hampton received the hearty support of President Hayes and the bitter opposition of the upcountry whites and race extremists who eventually overthrew him under the leadership of Ben Tillman.[32]

Southern champions of the compromise strengthened Hayes's hand by carrying assurances of good will and reconciliation to the North. Senator Gordon buried the bloody shirt before the Commer-

[30] Morgan to Hayes, December 4, 1877, *ibid.*

[31] Michael J. Waldron to David M. Key, April 26, 1877, *ibid.* Waldron of Memphis, emissary of the Democratic caucus at Alcorn's home in February to Medill and Smith, was appointed United States Marshal by Hayes.

[32] Hampton M. Jarrell, *Wade Hampton and the Negro, The Road Not Taken* (Columbia, S.C., 1949), 121–139.

cial Club of Boston, and Wade Hampton in Auburn. Senators Hill and Lamar and Alexander Stephens assisted with their oratory in the rituals of reconciliation in various parts. Effusive Blue-and-Gray speeches and tearful reunions of old troopers were the order of the day. Hardened South-haters melted and repented of their ways. Robert Ingersoll, chief of bloody-shirt spellbinders, went about in sackcloth confessing that his orations on Andersonville Prison had been made for political purposes and pleading for conciliation. John Greenleaf Whittier and a few of the old Abolitionists reversed themselves and plumped for the new Southern policy. Even *Harper's Weekly,* incorrigible organ of Radicalism, did an about-face and lined up with the others. Viewing the course taken by the new Southern leaders, the Redeemers, *Harper's* exclaimed, "If this is Southern Democracy, it is wonderfully like the best Northern Republicanism." [33] The *Nation* joined in the chorus, but was prone to scoff at all the talk of the pacificatory effect of the revival of Whiggery. It reminded its readers "that Whig principles mean the Texas-Pacific job, and that the leading 'Old Whig' is no other than 'Tom Scott.'" [34] On the whole, however, the genuineness of the national response to the policy of conciliation and peace was evident. It was probably an indication of relief over the passing of the election crisis and the release that the compromise brought from terror of renewed war.

Hayes was delighted with the progress of his program and anticipated political successes in the South as a consequence. "The pacification policy still gains," he wrote a friend in May. "I am confident it will secure North Carolina, with a fair chance in Maryland, Virginia, Tennessee, and Arkansas, and am not without hopes of Louisiana, South Carolina, and Florida." [35] On Memorial Day he went south to Tennessee to assist in decorating the graves of Confederate and Federal dead. Then in September, taking members of his family and

[33] *Harper's Weekly,* May 5, 1877. For a discussion of the mood of reconciliation see Paul H. Buck, *The Road to Reunion* (Boston, 1937), 100–106.

[34] *Nation,* XXIV (May 3, 1877), 257.

[35] Hayes to W. D. Bickham, May 3, 1877, in Williams (ed.), *Diary and Letters of Hayes,* III, 432.

several cabinet members, including the obliging Mr. Key, the President made a grand tour through Kentucky, Tennessee, Georgia, and Virginia. Beginning at Louisville he was joined by Governor Wade Hampton, who accompanied him and made speeches of reconciliation and co-operation throughout the tour. Watterson's paper outdid itself in welcome for "the first visit of a President to the South since the war closed—for the war was not really over when Mr. Lincoln went to Richmond." The President's "escort is of Confederate veterans; his greeting is the Rebel yell"; while "the eagerness with which the people respond to friendly sentiments, the warmth of their pledges . . . are fairly pathetic." It was admitted that the Negroes were somewhat "less enthusiastic" over the policy "for which their old masters cheer so lustily."[36] In Atlanta the President told the Negroes in his audience that their "rights and interests would be safer if this great mass of intelligent white men were let alone by the general Government," after which there was "immense enthusiasm and cheering for several minutes."[37]

After his return to Washington Hayes noted that he had been "received everywhere heartily. The country is again one and united! I am very happy to be able to feel that the course taken has turned out so well."[38] He returned from a third trip south to Richmond the following month with the conviction that there were "thousands of intelligent people" in the South "who would like to unite with the conservative Republicans of the North."[39] To Colonel Kellar the South's reception of the President seemed a vindication of the furtive and anxious course he and Boynton had pursued the previous winter; but the Southern response "does not exceed my anticipation," he wrote William Henry Smith, "in the dark hours at Washington."[40]

The first important test of Hayes's Southern policy in practical politics came on October 15 when the Republicans sought to organ-

[36] New York *Tribune*, September 18, 1877.
[37] Williams, *Life of Hayes*, II, 252.
[38] Williams (ed.), *Diary and Letters of Hayes*, III, 443.
[39] *Ibid.*, 450.
[40] Kellar to Smith, September 25, 1877, Smith Papers.

ize the House and elect Garfield speaker with the aid of Southern Conservatives. Although he had agreed to go along with Hayes in the scheme, Garfield was doubtful of its success from the start. "It will however be a test of the sincerity of the Southern Democratic supporters of Hayes' policy," he wrote in his Diary, "to know whether they will give him an administration House. If they do, he may succeed. If not, his friends north will not tolerate a continuance of his southern scheme." [41]

In the opinion of General Dodge, Hayes was relying too heavily upon purely political inducements in his appeal to the South. Not only would such a course "cause the South to lose sight of the T & P," he wrote Tom Scott, but it would bring the South back into the orbit of the Northern Democrats and make it lose sight of the Republican plan for internal improvements. In view of "the promises we have for the future," he believed "that we should keep our eyes upon one thing only, and that our Southern policy should be based upon material improvement." [42] Dodge thought the Southern response to the settlement of the Louisiana question bore out his views. "I do not get as much encouragement from the Southern men as before the settlement," he wrote Boynton. "They seem to think that they can better help the President with a Democratic House than with a Republican one, but I have no faith in that kind of help. They ought to give the organization of the House to the President. This idea of theirs of selecting what measures of his they will support, and what they will not, I am afraid will all come to naught, when they get to Washington and go into caucus and are under party discipline of Northern party men." [43]

In the spring one of the Louisiana congressmen had announced publicly with regard to the organization of the next House that "most of the congressmen from Louisiana, Mississippi, Arkansas, and Tennessee" had agreed to make "a formal demand" upon the Democratic caucus that it commit the party to support of the Texas

[41] Garfield Diary, April 6, 1877, Garfield Papers.
[42] Dodge to Scott, March 28, 1877, letterbook in Box 346, Dodge Papers.
[43] Dodge to Boynton, April 27, 1877, letterbook in Box 384, *ibid.*

& Pacific and Mississippi levee improvements "as a condition of receiving the support of their delegations in the contest for the Speakership." Should they fail to get satisfaction on these matters, "these delegations and many single members from other States will withdraw and seek to make a combination elsewhere," he announced.[44]

By September it looked as if the old cleavage on internal improvements that had divided the Democrats along sectional lines in the previous Congress were still at work. The convention of Pennsylvania Democrats in that month took a strong stand against all subsidies. This meant that if Randall, a Pennsylvania Democrat and a candidate for re-election as speaker, was true to the expressed wishes of his party he would turn his back on the Texas & Pacific and lose the votes of a large part of the Southern delegation. Randall was aware that he was receiving the support of Tom Scott in his race for the speakership, a fact that embarrassed him greatly. "If everybody in Texas & Pacific are for me — then they are so without promises of any sort," he told Chauncey Black. He denied that he had "ever authorized any one to communicate to Col. S. a ray of hope that I would give the least support or countenance to his subsidy." He admitted that "Throckmorton, Lamar, Atkins, Gibson & others of like opinion are for me . . . as is Casey Young & Randolph Tucker, & others who support this scheme."[45] But he insisted that he had no commitments.

As it turned out, however, a majority of the Pacific Railway committee that Randall appointed consisted of Scott men. He showed signs of balking over the elevation of James W. Throckmorton, a long-term employee of Scott's and an inveterate subsidy man, to the chairmanship of the committee. However, when Alexander Stephens "warned Randall that if he had any aspirations for the future, he had better not meddle in the matter," he yielded and Throckmorton became chairman.[46] These events led the suspicious Mont-

[44] New York *Tribune,* March 30, 1877.

[45] Randall to Chauncey F. Black, May 13 and August 14, 1877, quoted in House, "Political Career of Samuel J. Randall," *loc. cit.,* 111–113.

[46] *Ibid.,* 122–123.

gomery Blair to believe that Randall "appointed Tom Scott's committee to be made speaker."[47] Whether or not this suspicion was justified, the Southern delegations rallied solidly on October 15 to the support of the Pennsylvanian. Randall was elected and Garfield defeated.[48]

It would have required a change of but nine votes to elect Garfield and organize the House for the Republicans, but the Southern revolt failed to materialize. This marked the first breach in the Compromise of 1877. Hayes had faithfully delivered the cabinet seat, withdrawn the troops, repudiated Reconstruction, distributed Federal patronage liberally among Southern Democrats, and given public encouragement to internal improvements and the Texas & Pacific subsidy. The Southerners had fulfilled their major commitments in advance and had been reasonably faithful at first to promises regarding treatment of the freedmen and observance of the recent amendments of the Constitution. The understanding about the organization of the House could hardly have been more than contingent in nature and necessarily involved few Southerners directly. It is probably more accurate, even though Casey Young of Tennessee had a speech written by February in defense of the departure, to describe it as an earnest hope of the Republicans and a tentative agreement on the part of a few Southerners rather than as a positive understanding. Nevertheless, a deterioration of the alliance between Republicans and Southerners dates from the breach of October 15.

Garfield proved correct in his prediction that if the South did not deliver the House organization Northern Republicans would reject the President's Southern policy. Optimist though he was, Hayes admitted there had appeared "a very decided opposition to the Administration, in both houses of Congress, among the Republican members."[49] Garfield observed a strong tendency in his own party "to assail Hayes and denounce him as a traitor and a man who was going to Johnsonize the party." As for defenders of Hayes—his

[47] Montgomery Blair to Charles A. Dana, May 15, 1878, Gist-Blair Papers.

[48] *Congressional Record,* 45 Cong., 1 Sess. (October 15, 1877), 53.

[49] Hayes Diary, October 24, 1877, in Williams (ed.), *Diary and Letters of Hayes,* III, 449.

Southern policy, his civil service measures, and his other reforms — they were "comparatively few." So serious was the disaffection that the only way Garfield could prevent his party from splitting openly was to keep it from holding a caucus for a period of six months.[50]

Critics of Hayes and his Southern friends and of the compromise found another vulnerable point of attack in the great flood of internal improvement bills that descended upon the new Congress from the South. The Redeemers evidently took Hayes's encouraging words seriously and concluded that he was about to usher in a millennium of subsidies. Every Southern congressman appeared to arrive in Washington with his bags packed full of internal improvement bills for old Buncombe. In three months they introduced 267 internal improvement bills in the House and 40 in the Senate. Not a few of them were of a large and expensive character. Virginia wanted a tunnel seven miles long run through the Allegheny Mountains as well as the completion of the James River and Kanawha Canal. The Carolinas were eager for an inland waterway from Pamlico Sound to the channels behind the Sea Islands of South Carolina. Georgia, Alabama, and Tennessee desired a canal through their states along the Tennessee River, and Florida sought to have one cut across the peninsula from the Atlantic to the Gulf. Then there was the heroic project, sponsored by Senator Matt W. Ransom of North Carolina, for "The Great Southern Railway Company" (assets exclusively political) that sought government aid to lay rails from the village of Millen, Georgia, to Turtle Harbor and Key West across uninhabitable swamp and open sea. And of course the Southwesterners were back again with louder demands than ever for their levees, and their Texas & Pacific and its politically strategic branches.[51]

"We must conciliate the Solid South, undoubtedly," remarked the New York *Tribune*. "But what will it cost?" Initially friendly to

[50] Smith, *James A. Garfield,* II, 659.

[51] New York *Tribune,* March 14, 1878, prints a long list of such bills introduced between October and the Christmas recess. Also see *ibid.,* December 19, 1877. It is interesting that Louisiana received more for public works than any other state of the Union in the year, June 30, 1877–June 30, 1878. See Treasury Department Report in *Senate Executive Documents,* 45 Cong., 3 Sess., No. 9.

Hayes's plan of generous aid for the Southerners, the *Tribune* admitted "Their plea is strong." Undoubtedly the North and West had benefited disproportionately from public funds. "That they are poor while the North is rich, they clearly see, and they desire conciliation in a pecuniary form." But what the editor was wondering was "how many hundred millions it is going to cost to make the South happy." The *Tribune* noted shrewdly too that the policies of reconciliation blended beautifully with certain business interests, especially when the Texas & Pacific was concerned. "Stanley Matthews was quite successful as a conciliator," the editor observed after Matthews was appointed to the Senate Railway Committee. "He drew the memorial for the building of a Southern Pacific railway. Conciliation from Mr. Matthews 'meant business.'"[52]

A few days before Christmas the Southern subsidy seekers were brought up sharply by news of an interview Hayes had given Horace White in which he expressed unfriendly views toward the Texas & Pacific. The President was reported to be "in grave doubt, first whether it would be wise to grant aid to the Texas & Pacific road at all or not; and secondly, if aid was granted, as to the amount of it." He thought that to "make possible any more Crédit Mobilier operations would be a serious mistake," that Scott was asking too much, and that the Southern transcontinental line would be constructed without government aid within a few years anyway.[53]

General Boynton, who reported the interview for his paper, said that the news of Hayes's reversal of his position came as a complete surprise to promoters of the bill, none of whom "seemed to dream that the President would have any objection . . . but appear rather to have taken it for granted that he would sign anything that Congress might pass."[54] He wrote Benjamin Bristow that he was "both surprised & disgusted" at the President's change of heart and that he had published the story "so that those who know what I do would be surprised & disgusted too."[55] Boynton had already become alien-

[52] New York *Tribune,* December 19, 1877.
[53] Cincinnati *Daily Gazette,* December 22, 1877.
[54] *Ibid.*
[55] Boynton to Bristow, December 24, 1877, Bristow Papers.

ated by the President's refusal to recognize the reformers, and particularly his friend Bristow.[56] Both Kellar and William Henry Smith had done what they could to make peace between Hayes and Boynton, Smith urging Hayes to "fasten him with hooks of steel to you personally."[57] The President had sought a reconciliation earnestly but vainly.[58] After Hayes repudiated commitments on the Scott Plan, in which Boynton had such an important share, the general thought of publishing all his letters regarding those negotiations. "If they ever get into print," he wrote Bristow, "there will be mourning at the White House."[59] But Boynton did not publish his letters and there was no mourning.

Hayes's criticism of the Scott bill constituted the second breach of the compromise. The President may have been influenced by the South's failing him in the organization of the House, and he may have yielded to the current outcry of reformers against subsidy jobs and the corrupt influence of the Texas & Pacific. But there was more to the story than that.

Finding himself outmaneuvered on the field of politics by Tom Scott, Huntington resorted to a flank attack on the field of engineering and construction. Without government aid he extended the Southern Pacific rails southward and eastward to the United States Indian reservation at Fort Yuma, and with permission of authorities began construction of a line through the reservation and a bridge across the Colorado River into Arizona. Seeing the strategic importance of the Fort Yuma bottleneck, the Texas & Pacific also got permission to break ground in the reservation, although the end of its trunk line lay 1200 miles to the east. Then on September 1, 1877, General Dodge's friend, George W. McCrary, now Secretary of War, ordered both companies to suspend operations in the reservation. This order was obviously of more practical consequence to Hunting-

[56] Boynton to William Henry Smith, May 30, September 24, 1877, Smith Papers; Boynton to Bristow, May 30, July 4, 1877, Bristow Papers.

[57] Kellar to William Henry Smith, November 3, 1877, Smith Papers; Smith to Hayes, October 3, 1877, in Williams (ed.), *Diary and Letters of Hayes,* III, 446–447.

[58] Hayes thought he had made peace with Boynton, but was mistaken. Hayes to Smith, November 10, 1877, *ibid.,* 452.

[59] Boynton to Bristow, December 24, 1877, Bristow Papers.

ton than to Scott. Taking the bull by the horns, Huntington completed his bridge and finished construction of his road across the reservation in spite of War Department orders.[60]

The Californian then went to Washington with a *fait accompli* to make peace with the government. "I found it harder to do than I expected," he told Colton. He talked to four members of the cabinet and then went to the President. "He was a little cross at first; said we had defied the Government, etc.," wrote Huntington. But he explained to the President that he was "very much in earnest about building the S.P." and told him how the construction gang had worked at night while the soldiers slept. "The President laughed heartily at that and said he guessed we meant business. He then said, 'What do you propose to do if we let you run over the bridge?' I said, 'Push the road right on through Arizona.' He said, 'Will you do that? If you will, that will suit me first-rate.' "[61] Hayes obligingly issued an executive order authorizing the Southern Pacific to run trains over the Fort Yuma bridge, and Huntington went to work laying rails across Arizona.

Tom Scott continued to win brilliant political victories in Washington, for a time. Alexander H. Stephens introduced a new Texas & Pacific subsidy bill. His bill found favor in the eyes of a majority of the House committee, which reported it with some alterations. The Senate committee also reported a bill to accomplish the same objects. Lamar, Matthews, Stephens, and many other men of ability and prestige defended the measure eloquently before the country. Once more General Dodge and his assistants mobilized the press and public opinion. According to Huntington, "They offered one member of Congress $1,000 cash down, $5,000 when the bill passed, and $10,000 of the bonds when they got them if he would vote for the bill."[62] But while Scott was piling up political gains in Washington,

[60] C. P. Huntington to George W. McCrary, October 8, 1877; McCrary to Speaker of the House, Samuel J. Randall, January 18, 1878; in *House Executive Documents,* 45 Cong., 2 Sess., No. 33, pp. 1–2, 29–30.

[61] Huntington to Colton, October 10, 1877, in Chicago *Tribune,* December 28, 1883.

[62] Huntington to Colton, May 3, 1878, *ibid.*

Huntington was laying rails eastward through Arizona—without asking a subsidy. The outcome of such a contest, if continued on those terms, was easily foreseeable.

General Dodge with the aid of Jay Gould sought to revive the truce with Huntington so that "both companies could pass their bills," but he was unsuccessful. Dodge was alarmed because Huntington's propaganda was gaining ground "in some quarters of the South"—the stronghold of Texas & Pacific support.[63] In the meantime Scott's strength was failing in other departments. The great labor riots of 1877 had cost the Pennsylvania Railroad millions, and the strain of that crisis had brought on a temporary breakdown in Scott's health. Deserted by Hayes, weakened in the South, and faced with the implacable opposition of Huntington, Scott was never able to get his bill through Congress. He gave up in 1880 and sold his Texas & Pacific holdings to Jay Gould. Huntington and Gould came to terms in November 1881, and the following year their lines made junction a short distance east of El Paso. The South got her road to the Pacific at last, but not by the means that Scott and Dodge and their numerous friends had planned.

The Whiggish coalition on which Hayes based his Southern policy was undoubtedly shaken by breaches of agreements on both sides. It might have flourished in spite of these, however, had it not been for deeper and more powerful forces that were undermining the foundations of the conservative alliance. In less than a year after the Compromise of 1877 an irresistible tide of agrarian radicalism was sweeping the South out of control of conservative leaders and into alliance with the agrarian West.

So long as unity was imposed by the struggle to overthrow the Carpetbaggers, Southern white men of upper and lower classes closed ranks in spite of antagonistic economic interests and submerged their differences in the cause of Redemption. Leadership generally went to conservatives, many of Whig background. Once Redemption was achieved and the need for conformity was relaxed,

[63] Dodge to Scott, January 15, 1878, letterbook in Box 346, Dodge Papers.

however, deeply felt cleavages in the white South asserted themselves strongly. Almost as soon as the Redeemers seized power their leadership was challenged by impoverished farmers of the upcountry. These men, debtors for the most part, reacted to depression, currency contraction, and falling prices in the same manner as did the Western farmers who were becoming Greenbackers, Silverites, Antimonopolists. Since a large part of the Southern agrarians lived in the "white counties" of the hills, they resented the way in which the black-belt Conservatives were courting the Negro vote and using it to curb the power of the white uplanders. White Supremacy seemed to be turning out to be the supremacy of some whites over others. Nor did the agrarians like the deals and alliances the Redeemers were making with big railroad interests, monopolists, and bondholders of the Northeast.

The Conservatives did not seem to be able to deliver on their promises of bountiful subsidies for internal improvements; their failure to do so weakened their case for a continued alliance with Northern conservatives. In vain did Alexander Stephens plead that monetary reform and free silver would be "a mere drop in the bucket as a means of rehabilitating the South, the Southwest, and the Southeast, when compared with the building of the Texas and Pacific Railroad."[64] The farmers could not wait for the millennium. They now demanded railroad regulation instead of railroad subsidies, free silver instead of "sound" money, and they wished to crush the monopolies instead of foster them. They called for an alliance with the agrarian West instead of the industrial East.

When they found the conservative leaders of the one-party system slow to welcome their Radical ideas, the agrarians began organizing local third parties. They called themselves Readjusters, Independents, Greenbackers, Laborites, and they popped out like a pox all over the Southern upcountry. Sometimes they carried whole districts, and in 1879 the whole state of Virginia.

To absorb and contain the agrarian rebels, to maintain "white

[64] Stephens quoted by Lamar in *Congressional Record,* 45 Cong., 2 Sess. (May 22, 1878), 3658.

solidarity," the one-party system developed an early flexibility on matters of principle. It shifted leftward temporarily to accommodate itself to the agrarian upheaval. The ante-bellum arguments for the Jacksonian system were dusted off and put to use—the old case for unity between agrarian sections, the geographic and ethnic ties between South and West, the "natural" transportation system of rivers, the common cause of farming economies against industrial economies. "A community and intimate dependence of interests," declared Senator Morgan of Alabama in 1878, would "draw the South and West together in social, commercial, and political unity, on questions of policy, beyond the power of resistance or of future disseverance."[65] Bob Toombs reminded his old friend Stephens that "the West . . . is, always has been, and always [will] be the most valuable ally" of the South.[66]

By November 1877, the West-South alliance came out in the open in Congress. The two sections joined up solidly in the House against Eastern opposition to pass Richard P. Bland's bill providing for the free coinage of the silver dollar and making the coin legal tender without restrictions.[67] West and South linked hands also to pass the Bland-Allison silver purchase bill,[68] again to pass the bill over the indignant veto of President Hayes,[69] and again to repeal the law for the resumption of specie payments.[70]

Lamar, Hill, and a few other Conservatives tried vainly to keep the South in line with the Whiggish alliance of 1877. Lamar went so far as to violate the explicit instructions of the Mississippi legislature and vote against the silver bill. "I get a great many complimentary letters from the North, very few from Mississippi," he wrote his wife. The lower house of the Mississippi legislature, elected on

[65] John T. Morgan, "The Political Alliance of the South with the West," *North American Review*, CXXVI (1878), 318.

[66] Robert Toombs to Alexander H. Stephens, March 25, 1880, in Ulrich B. Phillips, *Correspondence of Robert Toombs, Alexander Stephens and Howell Cobb* (Washington, 1913), 740.

[67] *Congressional Record,* 45 Cong., 1 Sess. (November 5, 1877), 241.

[68] *Ibid.*, 2 Sess. (February 15, 1878), 1112.

[69] *Ibid.*, 2 Sess. (February 28, 1878), 1410–1411, 1420.

[70] *Ibid.*, 1 Sess. (November 23, 1877), 632–633.

the issue of white man's rule, passed a resolution of thanks to Lamar's Negro colleague, Blanche K. Bruce, for his vote in favor of silver, because it "reflected the sentiment and will of his constituents." [71] The implied rebuke to Lamar was about the most stinging conceivable for a champion of white supremacy, and it revealed as nothing else the intensity of regional sentiment on economic issues.

The agrarian groundswell continued through 1878. A bill for drastic Federal regulation of railroads received stronger support from the South than from any other region, including the West.[72] In a majority of the Southern states strong movements were growing, some of them already successful, to scale down, readjust, or repudiate the state debts that had been augmented by Carpetbagger extravagance. The bonds that the Readjusters were seeking to repudiate were held mainly in the Northeast. Democratic state platforms of 1878 all over the South were aflame with defiance of Eastern capitalism. That of Louisiana, for example, demanded the abolition of the national banking system, the retirement of the banknotes and the substitution of greenbacks, repeal of the Resumption Act, and redemption of United States bonds with greenbacks only.

The turn of events in the South in 1878 bore out precisely the fears of the Republican faction who had defeated Lincoln's and Johnson's plan of restoring the South to the Union and placed the region under military rule and Reconstruction. Those fears were that an impoverished, agrarian South, if readmitted under Democratic control, would join hands with discontented elements in the West and North and pull down the elaborate structure of capitalist legislation that was erected during the South's absence from the Union — the tariff acts, currency laws, banking acts, subsidies, and privileges upon which the new industrial system of the East rested. The South, moreover, might detach the West from her wartime ally and leave the East isolated as she had often been before the war.[73] It had been

[71] Mayes, *Lamar,* 331, 340–342.

[72] *Congressional Record,* 45 Cong.

[73] Howard K. Beale, *The Critical Year: A Study of Andrew Johnson and Reconstruction* (New York, 1930), *passim.*

Hayes's theory that the South could be won or appeased by giving her some of the fruits of the new system, but that did not seem to work. When this became apparent the fires of sectional animosity flamed up all over the East.

"Today the rebellion, revived and rehabilitated, is encamped in both Houses of Congress" and strengthened by "Western communists," declared the New York *Tribune*. "Because the North resists, there is a radical, irrepressible conflict."[74] In view of the menace of the South, "What is to become of the public credit, upon which rests the solvency of savings banks, trust companies, insurance companies, and other banks throughout the Union?" asked the *Tribune*.[75] "The South will still stand in need of reconstruction, in one very important sense, so long as it continues to be the home of debt-scalers, readjusters and repudiators," believed the editor.[76]

Whitelaw Reid undertook to teach the Southern agrarians the historical meaning of the revolutionary upheaval called Reconstruction. His exposition of the pragmatic purposes of Northern policy was candid and explicit. "The statesmen of the South forget history," he declared. "The North has constantly feared Southern power—why? Because it meant hostility to National credit. The Southern statesman puts the cart before the horse. Because the whole South and part of the West were on fire with repudiating schemes, the North put down [Andrew] Johnson and reconciliation, Seward and Welles . . . and elected Grant in 1868. Because the purpose of the Southern people was in this respect profoundly distrusted, Northern capital and industry roused with resistless power to turn the scale in 1872. Because there was no faith in a Democratic South, with respect to public honor, Mr. Tilden went down in 1876." Reid neglected to include the more idealistic purposes of Reconstruction so conspicuous in the Republican campaigns he mentioned. But he was writing long after those purposes had been abandoned.[77]

[74] New York *Tribune,* March 27, 1879; on the "Western communist" allies of the South see *ibid.,* March 20, 1878.

[75] *Ibid.,* February 26, 1879.

[76] *Ibid.,* February 4, 1879.

[77] *Ibid.,* December 7, 1877.

The old Abolitionists, however, joined in the outcry against the Southern menace. They too adjusted their approach to accommodate changed conditions. Wendell Phillips pointed out that the true basis of alliance between the West and the East was "moral issues." Sectional conflict, not class conflict, was the real danger, he thought, for "the interests of capital and labor were one" and "There need be no fear of communism." The rise of the silver issue and other economic issues on which "the South and West are naturally allies and closely wedded" was entirely due to the fact that the Republicans "allowed the Southern issue to fall into abeyance." "The Southern question . . . properly treated, might have delayed this material question for some years." But when it was allowed to drop in 1877, "the mass naturally sank to the care of their material interests."[78] William Lloyd Garrison agreed that the revival of moral issues was the only hope of Republicanism. "The South is still rebellious at heart though wearing the mask of submission," he declared and promised "Heaven's righteous retribution for her long-continued cruelty and oppression!"[79] And the *National Republican,* which had praised the South as the very home of patriotism in February 1877, announced the next year that "the South is in arms today, preparing and waiting for the signal to strike another blow when the hour of trial shall have come in the judgment of their leaders."[80]

Repudiating the conciliatory policy of Hayes, William E. Chandler, Conkling, Blaine, and the Radicals raised the bloody shirt again as their standard in the campaign of 1878. Western Republicans adopted belligerent platforms denouncing the South for reenslaving the Negro, defying the Constitution, and enthroning treason. The "irrepressible conflict" again. Results of the election were gratifying to exponents of "sound money," for the agrarian

[78] Wendell Phillips, "The Outlook," *North American Review,* CXXVII (1878), 102, 110.

[79] *Letters of Mr. William E. Chandler Relative to the So-Called Southern Policy of President Hayes, Together with a Letter to Mr. Chandler of Mr. William Lloyd Garrison* (Concord, 1878), 46–48.

[80] Washington *National Republican,* June 13, 1878.

tide was temporarily turned. It was the strategy of 1866 again, and as Whitelaw Reid suggested, of 1868, 1872, and 1876. The lesson of the campaign of 1878, according to William Lloyd Garrison, was plain: "'The bloody shirt!' *In hoc signo vinces!*"[81]

The lessons of the election of 1878 were more numerous than that. For one thing, Hayes's hopes for reviving his party in the South under conservative leadership were pretty well shattered. His party lost instead of gained strength, and the election produced for the first time what might be called a "Solid South." Republican strategy for years to come would stress the politics of the "bloody shirt." This, alone, would have been enough to prevent Southern conservatives from collaborating with Hayes. But there were other deterrents as well. Grossly violating the spirit of the Compromise of 1877, Southerners joined with Northern Democrats to vote a congressional investigation of fraud in Hayes's election. Republicans retaliated with an investigation of Southern elections of 1878, which revealed that the Redeemers' pledge to protect Negro rights and liberties after Hayes withdrew the troops had been badly violated in the Lower South. As a consequence Hayes refused stubbornly to approve the repeal of Reconstruction acts that he was pledged not to enforce. Each exchange of blows deepened the breach between the partners to the compromise.

On the other side the South's experiment with a Western alliance in 1878 proved a disappointment to its leaders. The West still appeared more responsive to the "bloody shirt" than to appeals for agrarian unity. Southern agrarians who led the movement for a Western combination were discredited by its outcome. Lamar and the conservatives, "who persistently resisted this movement," maintained that they had been "justified by events" and that "a further Western alliance is now out of the question." A general stocktaking on sectional diplomacy occured at Southern council tables. It was plain that the road to reunion was a forked road, that the right fork led to the East and the left fork to the West. Debate between advo-

[81] Quoted in New York *Tribune,* January 4, 1879.

cates of the left fork and the right fork raged back and forth.[82] In the end the counsel of the right-fork conservatives prevailed—as it had in the crisis of 1876–1877. There is no better statement of the conclusion than the one made by the voice of tidewater South Carolina, the Charleston *News and Courier:*

> We see no hope that a platform will be framed that is acceptable to both East and West. . . . With one section or the other the South must go, and our fixed opinion is that the *permanent interests of the South lie with the East rather than with the West.* The aim of the South being to . . . avoid whatever is revolutionary in politics, sociology or finance, the South must go with the East, despite its aggrevating self-assertion, rather than join hands with the West, which is learning the A, B, C, of statesmanship.[83]

And the South did "go with the East." By dint of much hallooing and heading-off the Conservatives succeeded in herding the mass of Southerners up the right fork. The leaders met with numerous difficulties and sometimes resorted to repressive or demagogic devices to keep the people in line. Agrarian mavericks were eternally taking off up the left fork. With the aid of the New South propagandists, however, the Redeemers managed to keep the South fairly faithful to the Eastern alignment—until the nineties.

While it is obvious that the letter as well as the spirit of the Compromise of 1877 was repeatedly violated by both sides, there is a deeper sense in which it remained unimpaired and inviolate and endured as the new foundation of sectional peace and national politics. The partisan advantages that Hayes and his Republican advisors hoped to reap failed to materialize, of course, except in so far as the more immediate ends of the election crisis were concerned. The Southern Conservatives and Redeemers of Whig antecedents, though attracted at first to the new Republicanism that Hayes promised,

[82] Charles Nordhoff wrote an illuminating analysis of the Southern debate over sectional diplomacy in the New York *Herald,* November 19, 1878.

[83] Charleston *News and Courier,* December 13, 1878. For a similar conclusion see Richmond *Dispatch,* October 22, 1878.

made their peace with the Democrats and remained in that party. They aligned themselves with the Conservative, Eastern wing of the party, however, a wing that was as devoted to the defense of the new economic order as the Republicans. A way was therefore found for Conservatives to co-operate across sectional barriers as they had in Federalist and Whig days.

So far as the historical Negro question was concerned, the Compromise of 1877 proved to be a more lasting settlement than had the Compromise of 1850 and those that preceded it. The earlier settlements had been superseded or repudiated in relatively short order. There were no serious infringements of the basic agreements of 1877 — those regarding intervention by force, respect for state rights, and the renunciation of Federal responsibility for the protection of the Negro. In 1883 the Supreme Court pronounced the Civil Rights Act unconstitutional. The decision constituted a sort of validation of the Compromise of 1877, and it was appropriate that it should have been written by Justice Joseph P. Bradley, the "Fifth Judge" of the Electoral Commission. "The calm with which the country receives the news shows how completely the extravagant expectations . . . of the war have died out," observed the New York *Evening Post*.[84]

Senator Lamar liked to point out to his colleagues from the Eastern industrial states the vital interest they shared with the Southern states in the principle of *laissez faire* and nonintervention in state affairs. He thought the East should be especially zealous in defense of those principles. "I regard that section of this Union as being now in a sense the especial representative of the most precious principle of our American Constitution at this time," he said, "the most conservative part of our government, that which alone will protect us from democratic despotism" — the principle of state rights.[85]

Under the new dispensation national political life settled back into the pattern of compromise, abandoned since 1861. There were a few noteworthy differences. The ante-bellum compromises had been made between two sides of roughly comparable strength. The pur-

[84] New York *Evening Post,* October 16, 1883.
[85] Quoted in Mayes, *Lamar,* 350–351.

pose was to keep the peace, maintain the balance of power, and preserve the essential integrity of each of the rival systems. Between the era of the old compromises and that of the new there had intervened a war that turned into a revolution and destroyed the integrity of the Southern system but failed to determine the New South's relation to the Union. The Compromise of 1877 did not restore the old order in the South, nor did it restore the South to parity with other sections. It did assure the dominant whites political autonomy and nonintervention in matters of race policy and promised them a share in the blessings of the new economic order. In return the South became, in effect, a satellite of the dominant region. So long as the Conservative Redeemers held control they scotched any tendency of the South to combine forces with the internal enemies of the new economy — laborites, Western agrarians, reformers. Under the regime of the Redeemers the South became a bulwark instead of a menace to the new order.

Notes on Sources

THE MATERIALS for this book were accumulated gradually over a period of years while the author was at work on a study of larger scope. The Compromise of 1877 and its ramifications were recognized as an unsolved puzzle in the early stages of that period of research. It is quite doubtful, however, that the puzzle would have yielded to a direct attack. The pieces were scattered in such diverse and improbable places that the task of assembling them would have put a severe strain on luck and patience. Many of the important clues turned up by chance while the author was looking for something else, or materials collected for other purposes, became suddenly relevant to the puzzle by chance discoveries. It was in that way that the picture slowly took shape. The following account of sources is confined to the more important materials quoted and omits reference to tangential sources—such as histories of defunct railroads or a casual letter buried in a collection having no apparent bearing on this subject. These would have to be classified as clues rather than sources, but they are of vital importance in the game of puzzle solving.

One basic manuscript collection is the Rutherford B. Hayes Papers in the Hayes Memorial Library, Fremont, Ohio. Hayes was circumspect in what he wrote and what he kept that others wrote him, and few of his outgoing letters of this period remain. It is nevertheless a large collection, well preserved, and intelligently administered.

William Henry Smith, Hayes's closest political advisor in this period, was somewhat less circumspect about his correspondence. His papers are in the William Henry Smith Memorial Library of the Indiana Historical Society, Indianapolis. They contain numerous letters from his Western Associated Press friends, Henry V. Boynton,

Andrew J. Kellar, Joseph Medill, Murat Halstead, and Richard Smith. The same library has the manuscript "Memoirs of Thomas C. Donaldson," a personal friend of the Hayes family. The Hayes Memorial Library has both the Donaldson Memoir in a typed copy and the Smith Papers of this period on microfilm, in which form the author used them. The Ohio State Archaeological and Historical Society, Columbus, Ohio, has a William Henry Smith Collection and a James M. Comly Collection. Among the most interesting here is a letterbook that Smith kept during the election crisis.

The Iowa Historical and Memorial Building in Des Moines houses the huge collection of Grenville M. Dodge Papers. Dodge's incoming correspondence is thin, but his voluminous letterbooks of the period are packed with revealing material from his own hand, much of it difficult to decipher. There are letters to Thomas A. Scott, Jay Gould, George W. McCrary, Hayes, and Boynton, among others. The original copies of the Collis P. Huntington letters quoted have long been presumed lost and the validity of the copies cited is open to question. The copies were introduced as evidence in the case of *Ellen M. Colton* v. *Leland Stanford et al.*, in the Superior Court of California, Sonoma County, in 1883, and later printed by several newspapers, of which the Chicago *Tribune* edition (December 26–28, 1883) has been cited in this book. Ten years after the date of the letters many of them, with certain important names deleted, were read into the record of the United States Pacific Railway Commission (*Senate Executive Documents,* 50 Cong., 1 Sess., No. 51, Part 8). Huntington at that time admitted writing them and said he had "no personal objection" to their being printed, but declared that his "impression" was that some of them were "very much garbled." (*Ibid.,* p. 3707.) What internal evidence they contain, however, tends to support their validity. Stuart Daggett, historian of the Southern Pacific, quotes the letters extensively.

The Samuel J. Tilden Papers and the John Bigelow Papers are in the New York Public Library. The Bigelow Diary is of especial interest, and Tilden's incoming mail, though thoroughly sifted by trustees of his estate to remove items derogatory to Tilden, has some rewarding items. Among them are several letters in the microscopic script of Montgomery Blair. Many original drafts of Blair's letters are also found in the Gist-Blair Papers in the Manuscript Division of the Library of Congress. In the same library are the Benjamin H. Bristow Papers, containing scores of letters from Boynton; the Jeremiah S. Black Papers, containing letters of Samuel J. Randall to Chauncey F. Black; the James A. Garfield Papers, including the indispensable Garfield Diary; the Carl Schurz Papers, with many letters to and from Hayes; as well as the William E. Chandler Papers, which contain numbers of letters about Major E. A. Burke; and the John Sherman Papers. The Henry Watterson Papers, the Manton Marble Papers, and the Alexander H. Stephens Papers are also at the Library of Congress.

Letters from Thomas A. Scott and Collis P. Huntington are found among the correspondence of L. Q. C. Lamar in the Lamar-Mayes Papers at Mississippi State Department of Archives and History, Jackson; and in the Matt W. Ransom Papers at the University of North Carolina.

Because so many figures prominent in this narrative were editors, newspapers form an important part of the materials. Andrew J. Kellar of the Memphis *Avalanche* and Henry Watterson of the Louisville *Courier-Journal* often signed their editorials. And the personal views of editors are suggested in Joseph Medill's Chicago *Tribune,* Montgomery Blair's Washington *Union,* Charles A. Dana's New York *Sun,* Richard Smith's Cincinnati *Gazette* (in which it is possible to identify Boynton's Washington dispatches), James M. Comly's Columbus *Ohio State Journal,* and Murat Halstead's Cincinnati *Commercial.* The New Orleans *Times* is of particular interest because of the part its editor, W. H. Roberts, played in opening the negotiations between Hayes and the Southern Conservatives. The Galveston *News* and the Dallas *News* reflects support for the schemes of Scott and Dodge, as do many other Southern newspapers cited. Of the important Republican papers the most helpful were the New York *Times,* the New York *Tribune,* the Chicago *Tribune,* and the Washington *National Republican.* Two Southern Republican papers surviving in this period were the Louisville *Commercial* and the New Orleans *Republican.* The Democratic Cincinnati *Enquirer* had a Washington correspondent who called the shots of the Republican manipulators with a high percentage of accuracy. Charles Nordhoff, Washington correspondent of the New York *Herald,* was a shrewd analyst of political news, and so was A. M. Gibson of the New York *Sun.* Among the weekly journals, the New York *Nation* had the most informing articles and editorials.

Of the many government documents bearing on the subject, the most important is the *Report of the Investigation of the Presidential Election of 1876* in *House Miscellaneous Documents,* 45 Cong., 3 Sess., No. 31. Majority and minority reports of the House Pacific Railway Committee on the Texas & Pacific bill are in *House Reports,* 44 Cong., 2 Sess., No. 139; and in *ibid.,* 45 Cong., 2 Sess., No. 619. The *Proceedings of the Electoral Commission* are in *Congressional Record,* 44 Cong., 2 Sess., vol. V, pt. IV. Light on the lobby activities of Huntington is provided in *Testimony Taken by the United States Pacific Railway Commission* in *Senate Executive Documents,* 50 Cong., 1 Sess., No. 51. The background of economic conditions is illuminated by the *Investigation Relative to the General Depression, 1878–1879,* in *House Miscellaneous Documents,* 45 Cong., 3 Sess., No. 29. For figures on expenditures for internal improvements in the various states, the Treasury Department report on "Public Works in States and Territories," in *Senate Executive Documents,* 43 Cong., 1 Sess., No. 12, is indispensable.

The large collections of railroad pamphlets and publications in the Library of the Bureau of Railway Economics, Washington, D. C., the John Crerar Library, Chicago, and in the Hayes Memorial Library, Fremont, Ohio, provide much material essential to the understanding of the political activities of railroad companies. There is a complete file of the *Annual Reports* of the Texas & Pacific for the early years of the company's history in the Bureau of Railway Economics. Other Texas & Pacific material is contained in *Resolutions of the Legislatures, Boards of Trade, State Granges, Etc., Favoring Government Aid to the Texas & Pacific Railway* (Philadelphia,

1874); *The Press and the People on the Importance of a Southern Line Railway to the Pacific and in Favor of Government Aid to the Texas and Pacific Railway Co.* (Philadelphia, 1875); *Southwestern Pacific Railroad: Address to the People of the United States Calling a National Convention in Saint Louis on the 23d of November, 1875, to take Action in Favor of a Southwestern Pacific Railroad . . .* (St. Louis, 1875); *Proceedings of the National Railroad Convention at St. Louis, November 23 and 24, 1875, in Regard to the Construction of a Southern Transcontinental Railway Line from the Mississippi Valley to the Pacific Ocean* (St. Louis, 1875); *By-Laws and Organization for Conducting the Business of the Texas and Pacific Railway Co. Approved by the Board of Directors* (Philadelphia, 1875); L. U. Reavis, *The Texas & Pacific Railway or a National Highway along the Path of Empire* (New York, 1878); J. Alfred Davenport, *The Title of the Texas & Pacific Railroad Co. to Property Late of the Memphis El Paso & Pacific Railroad Co. Notes of Argument Before the Judiciary Committee of the House of Representatives, April 17, 1878* (New York, 1878); L. Q. C. Lamar, *The Texas Pacific Railroad Speech in the United States Senate, May 22, 1878* (Washington, 1878). Samples of counterpropaganda by Huntington are Thomas M. Norwood, *The Texas Pacific Railway (A Dependency of the Great Pennsylvania Monopoly) Contrasted with a Real Southern Pacific R.R. A Letter to the People of the South* (n.p. 1878); and the *Closing Argument of Douglas Campbell, Esq., in Regard to the Title of the Texas and Pacific Railway Company to the Property of the Memphis, El Paso and Pacific Railroad Company before the Judiciary Committee of the House of Representatives, April 24, 1878* (Washington, 1878).

Apart from listing a few biographies and special studies, no attempt will be made to include in these notes the numerous secondary works used and cited. Biographical works most frequently consulted are Charles R. Williams, *The Life of Rutherford Birchard Hayes, Nineteenth President of the United States,* 2 vols. (Boston, 1914), and the work edited by the same author, *Diary and Letters of Rutherford Birchard Hayes,* 5 vols. (Columbus, 1922–1926); Allan

Nevins, *Abram S. Hewitt, with Some Account of Peter Cooper* (New York, 1935); and, edited by the same author, *Selected Writings of Abram S. Hewitt* (New York, 1937). Other biographies that proved helpful are Alexander C. Flick, *Samuel J. Tilden, A Study in Political Sagacity* (New York, 1939); Leon B. Richardson, *William E. Chandler, Republican* (New York, 1940); Theodore C. Smith, *The Life and Letters of James Abram Garfield,* 2 vols. (New Haven, 1925); Charles C. Tansill, *The Congressional Career of Thomas Francis Bayard, 1868–1885* (Washington, 1946); William E. Smith, *The Francis Preston Blair Family,* 2 vols. (New York, 1933); Israel G. Blake, *The Holmans of Veraestau* (Oxford, Ohio, 1943); Jacob R. Perkins, *Trails, Rails and War, The Life of General G. M. Dodge* (Indianapolis, 1929); Claude Elliott, *Leathercoat, The Life History of a Texas Patriot* (San Antonio, 1939), and Hampton M. Jarrell, *Wade Hampton and the Negro, The Road Not Taken* (Columbia, S.C., 1949). Edward Mayes, *Lucius Q. C. Lamar: His Life, Times, and Speeches, 1823–1893* (Nashville, 1896), though an old work, is still extremely useful. A broad perspective on sectional reconciliation is provided in Paul H. Buck, *The Road to Reunion, 1865–1900* (Boston, 1937).

Among the monographs, the old study of Paul L. Haworth, *The Hayes-Tilden Disputed Presidential Election of 1876* (Cleveland, 1906), is blind to certain large aspects of the subject. Two studies are of especial importance in illuminating the history of the period preceding the one under survey. They are Robert R. Russel, *Improvement of Communication with the Pacific Coast as an Issue in American Politics, 1783–1864* (Cedar Rapids, 1948); and Howard K. Beale, *The Critical Year: A Study of Andrew Johnson and Reconstruction* (New York, 1930).

INDEX

Index

C. Vann Woodward was born in Vanndale, Arkansas. He received his Bachelor of Philosophy degree from Emory University in 1930 and went on to take his M.A. at Columbia University in 1932 and his Ph.D. at the University of North Carolina in 1937.

He has been a lecturer and professor of history at numerous colleges and universities. From 1948 to 1961 he was Professor of History at Johns Hopkins University, and since then has been Sterling Professor of History at Yale University.

Professor Woodward is the author of **Tom Watson:** Agrarian Rebel; **The Battle for Leyte Gulf; Origins of the New South; The Strange Career of Jim Crow** and **The Burden of Southern History.**

He now resides in Hamden, Connecticut, with his wife. They have one son.